FLIGHTS

Senior Author
William K. Durr

Senior Coordinating Author
John J. Pikulski

Coordinating Authors
Rita M. Bean
J. David Cooper
Nicholas A. Glaser
M. Jean Greenlaw
Hugh Schoephoerster

Authors
Mary Lou Alsin
Kathryn Au
Rosalinda B. Barrera
Joseph E. Brzeinski
Ruth P. Bunyan
Jacqueline C. Comas
Frank X. Estrada
Robert L. Hillerich
Timothy G. Johnson
Pamela A. Mason

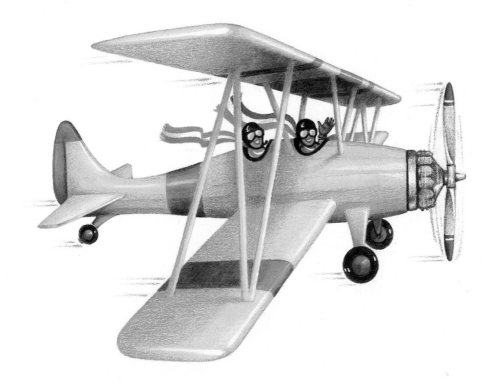

HOUGHTON MIFFLIN COMPANY   BOSTON

Atlanta   Dallas   Geneva, Illinois   Lawrenceville, New Jersey   Palo Alto   Toronto

Acknowledgments

For each of the selections listed below, grateful acknowledgment is made for permission to adapt and/or reprint original or copyrighted material, as follows:

"About Elephants," an adaptation of *Seven True Elephant Stories*, by Barbara Williams. Copyright © 1978. Reprinted by permission of Hastings House Publishers, Inc.

"The Ants at the Olympics," by Richard Digance. Reprinted by permission of Michael Joseph Ltd.

"Are Your Arms a Hundred Years Old?" from *The Hundred Penny Box*, by Sharon Bell Mathis. Copyright © 1975 by Sharon Bell Mathis. Reprinted by permission of Viking Penguin, Inc. and Curtis Brown, Ltd.

"The Arrival of Paddington," from *Paddington On Stage*, by Alfred Bradley and Michael Bond. Adapted and reprinted by permission of Houghton Mifflin Company and Harvey Unna & Stephen Durbridge, Ltd.

"The Bicycle," from *Cinnamon Seed*, by John Travers Moore. Copyright © 1967 by John Travers Moore. Published by Houghton Mifflin Company. Reprinted by permission of the author.

"Bicycle Rider," slightly abridged from text of *Bicycle Rider*, by Mary Scioscia. Text copyright © 1983 by Mary Hershey Scioscia. Reprinted by permission of Harper & Row, Publishers, Inc.

Continued on page 535.

Printed in the U.S.A.

ISBN: 0-395-37609-2

CDEFGHIJ-KR-943210/89876

Contents

Magazine Two

Magazine Three

Magazine Four

Flights
Magazine One

Contents

The Third Avenue Elevated

by Carla Stevens

A ride on the elevated train in the Great Blizzard of 1888 turned into an exciting adventure for Anna and her grandfather. How did Anna help the other people on the train?

Anna's grandfather Jensen was visiting her in New York City in 1888. He was bored with city life and said he didn't like the city too much. For something to do, he offered to take Anna to school, as it had started to snow very hard. Anna was eager to get to school because she was doing well in spelling and hoped to win that day's spelling bee. So they set out.

Anna followed Grandpa up the long flight of steps to the Fourteenth Street El station. No one was at the ticket booth, so they ducked under the turnstile to the platform. They stood out of the wind at the head of the stairs. Anna could see only one other person waiting for a train on the uptown side.

Anna looked at her rosy-cheeked grandfather. Snow clung to his mustache and eyebrows and froze. They looked like tiny icebergs.

"Here comes the train!" Grandpa shouted. A steam engine, pulling two green cars, puffed toward them. When the train stopped, Anna and Grandpa hurried across the platform and stepped inside. There were lots of empty seats. They sat down behind a large woman. She took up most of the seat in front of them.

Anna pulled off her hat. Her pompom looked like a big white snowball. She shook it, spraying the floor with wet snow. The conductor came up the aisle and stopped at their seat.

Grandpa said, "No one was at the station to sell us a ticket."

"That will be five cents," the conductor said. "Each."

"You mean I have to pay for her too?" Grandpa's eyes twinkled.

Grandpa and the conductor laughed. Anna didn't like to be teased. She turned away and tried to look out, but snow covered the windows.

Grandpa leaned forward. "Quite a storm," he said to the woman in the seat in front of them. "Nothing like the Blizzard of '72, though. Why it was so cold, the smoke froze as it came out of the chimney!"

A woman holding a basket sat across from them. She leaned over. "In Poland, when I was a little girl, it snowed like this all winter long."

The woman in the seat ahead turned around. "This storm can't last. First day of spring is less than two weeks away."

"That's just what I was telling my daughter this morning!" Grandpa said.

Anna could see that Grandpa was growing more cheerful by the minute.

Suddenly the train stopped.

"What's the trouble?" the woman from Poland asked. "Conductor, why has the train stopped?"

The conductor didn't reply. He opened the car door and stepped out onto the platform. No one inside said a word.

Then Grandpa stood up. "I'll find out what's the matter."

Anna tugged at his coat sleeve. "Oh, please sit down, Grandpa." He didn't seem to understand how scared she felt. How she wished she had stayed home!

The door opened again, and the conductor entered the car. He was covered with snow. "We're stuck," he said. "The engine can't move. Too much snow has drifted onto the tracks ahead. We'll have to stay here until help comes."

"Did you hear that, Anna?" Grandpa almost bounced up and down in his seat. "We're stuck! Stuck and stranded on the Third Avenue El! What do you think about that!"

When Anna heard the news, she grew even more frightened. "Mama will be so worried. She doesn't know where we are."

"She knows you are with me," Grandpa said cheerfully. "That's all she needs to know." He leaned forward again. "We might as well get acquainted," he said. "My name is Erik Jensen, and this is my granddaughter, Anna."

The woman in the seat ahead turned around. "Josie Sweeney," she said. "Pleased to meet you."

"How-dee-do," said the woman across the aisle. "I'm Mrs. Esther Polanski. And this is my friend, Miss Ruth Cohen."

Someone tapped Anna on her shoulder. She turned around. Two young men smiled. One man said, "John King and my brother, Bruce."

A young woman with a high fur collar and a big hat sat by herself at the rear of the car. Anna looked in her direction. "My name is Anna Romano," she said shyly.

"I'm Addie Weaver," said the young woman. She smiled and wrapped her coat more tightly around her.

It was growing colder and colder inside the car. When the conductor shook the snow off his clothes, it no longer melted into puddles on the floor.

"We'll all freeze to death if we stay here," moaned Mrs. Sweeney.

"Oooooo, my feet are so cold," Addie Weaver said.

Anna looked at her high-button shoes and felt sorry for Addie Weaver. Even though Anna had on her warm boots, her toes began to grow cold too. She stood in the aisle and stamped her feet up and down.

Suddenly Anna had an idea. "Grandpa!" she said. "I know a game we can play that might help keep us warm."

"Why Anna, what a good idea," Grandpa replied.

"It's called 'Simon Says.'"

"Listen, everybody!" Grandpa shouted. "My grand-daughter, Anna, knows a game that will help us stay warm."

"How do we play, Anna?" asked Mrs. Polanski. "Tell us."

"Everybody has to stand up," said Anna.

"Come on, everybody," Grandpa said. "We must keep moving if we don't want to freeze to death."

Miss Weaver was the first to stand. Then John and Bruce King stood up. Grandpa bowed first to Mrs. Sweeney, then to Mrs. Polanski and Miss Cohen. "May I help you, ladies?" he asked. They giggled and stood up. Now everybody was looking at Anna.

"All right," she said. "You must do only what Simon tells you to do. If *I* tell you to do something, you mustn't do it."

"I don't understand," Mrs. Sweeney said.

"Maybe we'll catch on if we start playing," Grandpa said.

"All right," Anna said. "I'll begin. Simon says, 'Clap your hands.'"

Everybody began to clap hands.

"Simon says, 'Stop!'"

Everybody stopped.

"Good!" Anna said. "Simon says, 'Follow me!'" Anna marched down the aisle of the car, then around one of the poles, then back again. Everybody followed her.

"Simon says, 'Stop!'"

Everyone stopped.

Anna patted her head and rubbed her stomach at the same time.

"Simon says, 'Pat your head and rub your stomach.' Like this."

Everyone began to laugh at one another.

"Simon says, 'Swing your arms around and around.'"

"Ooof! This is hard work!" puffed Mrs. Sweeney.

"Now. Touch your toes!"

Mrs. Sweeney bent down and tried to touch her toes. "Oh! oh! You're out, Mrs. Sweeney!" Anna said.

"Why am I out?" she asked indignantly.

Anna giggled. "Because Simon didn't say to touch your toes. *I* did!"

Mrs. Sweeney sat down. "It's just as well," she panted. "I was getting all tired out."

"Is everyone warming up?" Grandpa asked.

"Yes! yes!" they all shouted.

Snow was sifting like flour through the cracks around the windows. Just then, the door opened. A blast of icy cold air blew into the car. Everyone shivered. It was the conductor coming back in again.

"Get ready to leave," he said. "The firefighters are coming!"

Everyone rushed to the door and tried to look out. The snow stung Anna's eyes. The wind almost took her breath away.

The conductor closed the door again quickly. "The wind is so fierce, it's going to be hard to get a ladder up this high. We're at least thirty feet above Third Avenue."

"Ladder! Thirty feet!" Anna shivered.

"Oh, help me," groaned Mrs. Sweeney. "I'll never be able to climb down a ladder." She gave Grandpa a pleading look.

"Oh, yes, you will, Mrs. Sweeney," he said. "Once you get the hang of it, it's easy."

"In all that wind?" Mrs. Sweeney said. "Never!"

"Don't worry, Mrs. Sweeney. You won't blow away," said Grandpa.

Anna looked at Grandpa. "I'm scared too," she said.

"And what about me?" asked Mrs. Polanski. "I can't stand heights."

The door opened and a firefighter appeared. He shook the snow off his clothes. "We'll take you down one at a time. Who wants to go first?"

No one spoke.

"Anna," said Grandpa. "You're a brave girl. You go first."

"I'm afraid to climb down the ladder, Grandpa."

"Why, Anna, I'm surprised at you. Don't you remember how you climbed down from the hayloft last summer? It was easy."

"You can do it, Anna," said Miss Cohen.

"Pretend we're still playing that game. Simon says, 'Go down the ladder,'" said Mrs. Sweeney.

"So go now," Miss Cohen said. "We'll see you below."

"I'll be right below you to shield you from the wind. You won't fall," said the firefighter.

Anna shook with fear. She didn't want to be first to go down the ladder. But how could she disappoint the others?

Grandpa opened the door. The conductor held her hand. Anna put first one foot, then the other, on the ladder. The fierce wind pulled her and pushed her. Icy snow stuck to her clothes, weighing her down.

The firefighter was below her on the ladder. His strong arms were around her, holding her steady. With her left foot, Anna felt for the rung below.

Step by step by step, she cautiously went down the ladder — thirty steps. Would she never reach bottom?

One foot plunged into snow and then the other. Oh, so much snow! It covered her legs and reached almost to her waist.

"Stay close to the engine until the rest are down," the firefighter said.

Anna struggled through the deep snow to the fire engine. The horses, whipped by the icy wind and snow, stood still, their heads low. Anna huddled against the side of the engine. The roar of the storm was growing louder.

First came Mrs. Polanski, then Ruth Cohen — then Bruce and John King — then Addie Weaver. One at a time, the firefighter helped each person down the ladder. Now only Grandpa and Mrs. Sweeney remained to be rescued.

Anna could see two shapes on the ladder, one behind the other. The firefighter was bringing down someone else.

"Oh, I hope it's Grandpa," Anna said to Addie Weaver.

Suddenly she gasped. She could hardly believe her eyes. One minute the two shapes were there. The next minute they weren't!

Everyone struggled through the deep snow to find out who had fallen off the ladder.

Anna was the first to reach the firefighter who was brushing snow off his clothes. "What happened?" she asked.

"Mrs. Sweeney missed a step on the ladder. Down she went, taking me with her," the firefighter replied.

Mrs. Sweeney lay sprawled in the snow nearby. Her arms and legs were spread out, as if she were going to make a snow angel.

"Are you all right, Mrs. Sweeney?" Grandpa asked. Anna had not seen Grandpa come down the ladder by himself. Now he stood beside her.

"I'm just fine, Mr. Jensen. I think I'm going to lie right here until the storm is over."

"Oh, no, you're not!" Grandpa said. He and a firefighter each took one of Mrs. Sweeney's arms and pulled her to her feet.

Anna couldn't help giggling. Now Mrs. Sweeney looked like a giant snow lady!

"Climb onto the engine," said a firefighter. "We must get the horses back to the firehouse. The temperature is dropping fast."

"We live only two blocks from here," Mrs. Polanski and Miss Cohen said. "We're going to try to get home."

"We'll see that you get there," John King said. "We live on Lafayette Street." The young men and the two ladies linked arms and trudged off through the snow.

"What about you, Miss Weaver?" Grandpa asked. She looked confused.

"Hey, everybody, this is no tea party! Let's go!" said the firefighter.

"You come with us then, Miss Weaver," Grandpa said. "You too, Mrs. Sweeney."

Anna's fingers were numb with cold. She could hardly hold onto the railing of the engine. Often she had seen the horses racing down the street to a fire. Now they plodded along very, very slowly through the deep snow.

No one spoke. The wind roared and shrieked. The snow blinded them. One firefighter jumped off the engine and tried to lead the horses forward.

Anna huddled against the side of the engine, hiding her face in her arms. It was taking them forever to reach the firehouse.

Just then, the horses turned abruptly to the left. The next moment they were inside the stable, snorting and stamping their hooves.

Several men ran forward to unhitch the engine. Everyone began brushing the icy snow off their clothes.

Suddenly Grandpa became very serious. "The thermometer says five degrees above zero, and the temperature is still dropping. We must get home as fast as possible. Mrs. Sweeney, you and Miss Weaver had better come with us."

"Here, miss," a firefighter said. "Put these boots on. You can return them when the storm is over."

"Oh, thank you," Addie Weaver said.

Anna had forgotten about Addie's high-button shoes.

"Whatever you do, Anna, you are not to let go of my hand," Grandpa said firmly.

"Mr. Jensen, would you mind if I held your other hand?" asked Mrs. Sweeney.

"Not a bit," said Grandpa. "Anna, you take hold of Miss Weaver's hand. No one is to let go under any circumstances. Do you all understand?"

Anna had never heard Grandpa talk like that before. Was he frightened too?

They plunged into the deep snow, moving slowly along the south side of Fifteenth Street. The wind had piled the snow into huge drifts on the north side of the street.

When they reached Broadway, the wind was blowing up the avenue with the force of a hurricane. Telephone and telegraph wires were down. Thousands of them cut through the air like whips. If only they could reach the other side, Anna thought. Then they would be on their very own block.

No one spoke. They clung to one another as they blindly made their way across the avenue. Mrs. Sweeney lost her balance and fell forward in the snow. For a moment Anna thought she was there to stay, but Grandpa tugged at her arm and helped her get to her feet.

They continued on until they reached the other side. Now to find their house. How lucky they were to live on the south side of the block! The snow had reached as high as the first-floor windows of the houses on the north side. At last they came to number 44. Up the seven steps they climbed. Then through the front door and up more stairs. A moment later, Mr. Romano opened their apartment door. "Papa, you're home," Anna cried, and fell into her father's arms.

Several hours later, Anna sat in the kitchen watching a checkers game. Mrs. Sweeney, wearing Grandpa's bathrobe, was playing checkers with Grandpa, while Miss

Weaver, in Mama's clothes, chatted with Mama. Outside, the storm whistled and roared. Tomorrow would be time enough to study her spelling, Anna decided. Now she just wanted to enjoy the company.

Suddenly Grandpa pushed his chair back. "You win, Mrs. Sweeney. Where did you learn to play checkers?"

"I belong to a club," Mrs. Sweeney replied. "I'm the champ. We meet every Tuesday. Maybe you will come with me next Tuesday, Mr. Jensen?"

"Why, I'd like that," answered Grandpa.

Anna said, "I think Grandpa likes the city better now."

Mrs. Romano smiled. "It took a snowstorm to change his mind."

"You call this a snowstorm?" said Grandpa. He winked at Anna. "When you are an old lady, Anna, as old as I am now, you will be telling your grandchildren all about our adventure in the great blizzard of 1888!"

The Great Blizzard of 1888

There really was a great blizzard in 1888. It began to snow early Monday morning, March 12th. Before the snow stopped on Tuesday, four to five feet had fallen in New York City. Seventy inches fell in Boston and in other parts of the East.

The winds blew at 75 miles an hour and piled the snow in huge drifts. Everywhere, people were stranded. In New York City, about 15,000 people were trapped in elevated trains. Like Anna and Grandpa, they had to be rescued by firefighters with ladders.

By Thursday of that same week, the sun was out again. The snow began to melt. Anna went to school and won the spelling bee. And Grandpa walked down to Sullivan Street to play checkers again with Josie Sweeney.

New York City, 1888.

Author

Carla Stevens grew up in New York City, where she rode the Third Avenue Elevated as a child. Riding on the El was always a great adventure for her. Mrs. Stevens has been a teacher as well as a writer. Another of her books that is set in the past is *Trouble for Lucy*.

Comprehension Questions

1. How did Anna help the other people on the train when they were all stuck in the car?
2. Why did the train stop?
3. How were Grandpa's feelings different from the other passengers' feelings?
4. Do you think that the passengers enjoyed Anna's game? Why?
5. How did Grandpa help the others when they got off the train?

Vocabulary

The words in the box below are homophones. They have the same pronunciation but different spellings and meanings. Match each word with its homophone. Be sure you know the meaning and spelling of each word.

bored	fare	I'll	board
waist	aisle	waste	fair

Writing a News Report

Pretend that you were a news reporter on the elevated with Anna and Grandpa. Write a paragraph that describes what you saw and felt during the blizzard.

Parts of a Book

How do you look for facts in a science or history book? Do you open the book and flip through the pages until you find what you need to know? If so, you may be wasting your time. There is a better way to look for things: Learn to use the parts of a book.

What Is a Title Page?

A title page is one of the first pages in the book. Look at the title page below.

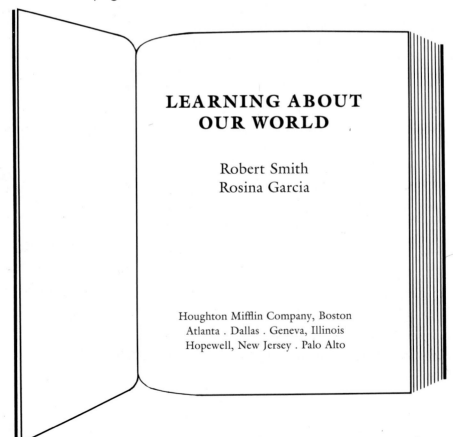

LEARNING ABOUT OUR WORLD

Robert Smith
Rosina Garcia

Houghton Mifflin Company, Boston
Atlanta . Dallas . Geneva, Illinois
Hopewell, New Jersey . Palo Alto

The title of the book is listed first. Then the names of the authors are given. The name of the book company and the places of its offices also are listed. The title page can give you an idea of what the book is about.

What Is a Copyright Notice?

The copyright notice often is found on the back of the title page. Look at the one below:

Copyright © 1985 by Houghton Mifflin Company.

It shows the year in which the book was published. What year is given in this notice? You can see that 1985 is the copyright date.

This date is important because it can tell you if the book is up-to-date. When you look for books about certain subjects, you need the most recent facts that you can find. It may be important to have up-to-date facts for a science report. You also might want a recent book if you are studying present-day governments. However, an older book can be useful if you are studying history.

What Is a Table of Contents?

The table of contents is also in the front of the book. It lists the titles of sections and chapters in the book. They are listed in order and may be numbered. After each chapter title is the number of the page on which it begins. Look at the table of contents below.

The three sections are numbered with the Roman numerals I, II, and III. What is the title of section I? It is called "What Is Earth?" What is the title of the first chapter in section I? On what page does it begin? "Wondering About Earth" begins on page 20. On what page does it end? It ends on page 25 because the next chapter "What Shape Is Earth?" begins on page 26. So you know that "Wondering About Earth" is between pages 20 and 25.

By looking over the titles of the sections and the chapters, you can get an idea of what is covered in the book. Read the other titles in the table of contents on page 34. Does this book describe how people use energy? Yes, because section III is about the way people live. Look at the chapter titles in section I. Does this tell about planets other than Earth? No, it's not likely, because no other planets are named in the titles.

Two other parts of the book are listed at the end of the table of contents. Certain maps and charts are in one part. The last part in this book is the glossary.

Using a table of contents will save you time because you can tell what is covered in the book. The page numbers can help you find quickly where to start reading. Always use the table of contents before you begin looking for the pages you need.

What Is a Glossary?

Sometimes a glossary is added at the end of a book. It is an alphabetical list of some words in the book with their meanings. This can be very useful to you.

When you look up the meaning of a word here, you will find that the meaning is often much shorter than the one given in a dictionary. A dictionary may give several meanings for a word. A glossary may give just the meaning that is used in the book. Sometimes the pronunciation for a word is given. If the word you need is not in the glossary or if there is none, then use a dictionary.

In the book *Learning About Our World,* each glossary meaning is followed by a page number. This number tells you which page in the book to look at to find out more about the word. Here are two glossary meanings:

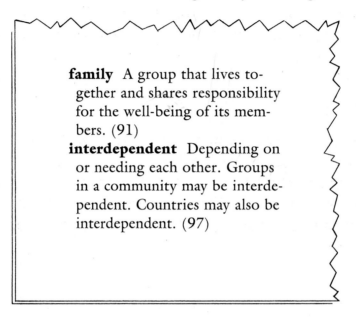

family A group that lives together and shares responsibility for the well-being of its members. (91)

interdependent Depending on or needing each other. Groups in a community may be interdependent. Countries may also be interdependent. (97)

Read the meaning for the word *family.* This word also can mean "a group of related plants or animals." Why isn't that meaning listed in the glossary? You know that meaning is not used in the book.

Using the Parts of a Book

Use the parts of the book shown in this lesson to answer these questions.

1. Who are the authors of *Learning About Our World?*
2. What tells you when a book was published?
3. What is the title of section II?

4. On what pages does the chapter "What Is Today's Culture?" begin and end?
5. Which chapter of this book probably tells about how cities get bigger?
6. On which page does the glossary begin?
7. On which page can you learn more about the glossary word *family*?

Skill Summary

If you know how to find and use the parts of a book, it will be easier for you to find information. You can use the title page and table of contents to decide if a book might answer your questions. Then you can use the table of contents and other parts, such as the glossary, to find those answers.

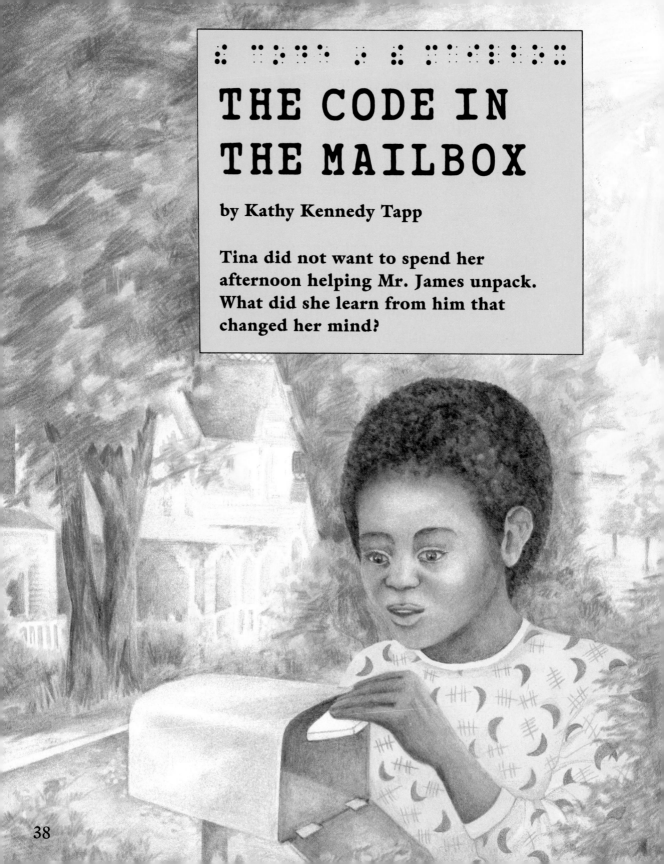

THE CODE IN THE MAILBOX

by Kathy Kennedy Tapp

Tina did not want to spend her afternoon helping Mr. James unpack. What did she learn from him that changed her mind?

"I don't want to go," Tina said for the third time.

Her mother faced her, hands on hips. "Tina Nelson, I'm ashamed of you. Mr. James is blind and needs help getting settled. I told him you'd be over."

"Mom, it's vacation. I was going to meet Penny. We made plans."

"More dumb detective stuff, I'll bet." Mike looked up from the T-shirt he was stretching out on the kitchen counter. He made his voice low. "Fingerprints . . . secret codes ——"

Tina glared at Mike. "Mind your own business."

"Codes are fine," Mom said, "but don't let me catch you using the mailbox across the street for your messages. The place is rented, so it's Mr. James's mailbox. For *his* mail, Tina."

"I know, I know," Tina muttered.

"I understand Mr. James needs help putting his things away." Mom opened the door and gave Tina a little push. "Now get going." Then she added, "We won't start dyeing the T-shirts until you get back."

Tina slammed the door. So much for her plans to go through the new book of codes with Penny.

She kicked a rock across the street, hard. It skipped right past the beautiful silver mailbox with the little door and the flag she and Penny always raised when they left secret messages for each other. Now it was Mr. James's mailbox. They'd have to find a new place to exchange coded notes and detective reports.

A deep voice answered Tina's knock. "Are you the Nelson girl?"

"Yes."

"Come on in. Careful of the boxes."

The room was dim with the curtains closed. Boxes lined the walls. "We'll start over here," Mr. James said, walking toward the wall, one arm out in front. His foot hit a box, and he reached down inside it, frowning. "Pans. They go in the kitchen. Next box should be plates ——"

Dishes in the cupboard, shoes in the closet, tapes in the bedroom. He went through box after box, his face set in a frown. He didn't talk except to tell Tina what to do.

Tina made fifty trips down the dark hall, looking eagerly at the front door each time. The whole afternoon was slipping away. One more box. Just one more ——

"Where do these white pages go?" she asked.

"Books. Leave them for now. Shelves aren't up yet."

"Books?" Tina stared. She'd never seen books like these before. Big pads of thick pages all covered with bumps.

Braille. Of course. She pulled one out, feeling the dots. Did those bumps really make words? How could anyone read them?

"Hey, Mr. James, did you learn Braille in school?"

"No need then. I learned the alphabet, just like you."

Tina put down the book. "You mean . . . you could see when you were a kid?" she asked.

"I could throw and catch with the best of them. I became blind much later." He turned to Tina. "What about you? You play ball?" His voice didn't sound unfriendly, really, just low-pitched.

"I play basketball in the winter. Now I'm busy with other stuff — detective stuff." Tina tried to make her voice sound casual.

"Oh, a detective?" The corners of Mr. James's mouth turned up just a little. "Fingerprints, secret messages — that sort of thing?"

"Well, it's codes. I like codes the best." Tina was still fingering the Braille bumps. "Can anyone learn Braille?"

"Anyone willing to spend enough time. Don't know why you'd want to learn it, though, when you don't need to. Wait a minute — " Mr. James started to feel around in the book box, frowning again. That frown almost seemed connected to his fingers — a thinking frown, not a mad one.

"Here it is." Mr. James held up a little card. "A Braille alphabet card."

"Hey, may I borrow it?"

"I don't need it any more," Mr. James said, shaking his head and smiling a little. "Detectives. That's a new one. Spring was baseball time when I was a kid. I was team captain. 'Babe' they called me."

"Babe?" Tina smiled, too, at the thought of Mr. James standing at the plate with a bat in his hands. "What was your average?"

"Well ——" Mr. James chewed his lip a second. The frown smoothed out into a thoughtful, remembering look. Then he shook his head. "It was too long ago. Let's just say it was a lot better than I could do now." He reached over to a tiny clock on the table and pushed a button.

"Four thirty-two P.M.," said a flat voice.

"A talking clock!" Tina burst out.

"Keeps me company." Mr. James got up with a little grunt. "That's enough work for today. It's getting late." He pulled out his money, and Tina noticed that some bills were folded the long way and others the short way. Mr. James fingered them, then held one out to Tina. "Thanks for your help."

A five! Tina stood there, turning the bill in her hand. A five — just for emptying some boxes. "Thanks. Oh . . . have a good evening." That sounded dumb. She tried again. "You, uh, have family coming or anything?"

"My son will be calling from Texas. If the phone is hooked up in time."

Tomorrow was Saturday. Crossing the street, Tina wondered if Mr. James's phone would be working tomorrow. Somehow she didn't think so.

"You're back just in time," Mom greeted her. We're ready to start. Mike has done one already."

"Isn't it great looking?" Mike boasted, pointing to a purple and white T-shirt on the line outside.

Batik dyeing was something Tina's family had done for a long time. First pictures were drawn on the cloth lightly in pencil. Then they were painted with hot wax. When the cloth was dyed, the waxed parts stayed white.

"Of course *you* wouldn't like it. It's not *code* or anything," Mike said.

Code. Tina fingered the hard little drops of wax spilled on the counter, remembering the Braille card in her pocket.

"Be back in a minute." Tina grabbed a stiff card from her mother's desk on her way to her bedroom and shut the door. She'd pencil it in here, by herself, then do the wax part in the kitchen. Dots were easy. Just dip a nail in hot wax and dab it on the card. If she was very careful and made perfect dots in just the right places . . . if the card showed her how . . .

She studied the alphabet. The card said that six dots made up a Braille cell, like this ⠃ and that each letter of the Braille alphabet was formed by placing the dots differently. What a code!

B ⠃ **A** ⠁ **B** ⠃ **E** ⠑   ⠃⠁⠃⠑

There! She did it on newspaper first, then on the card, frowning hard, concentrating.

"What are you doing?" Mike cried when she set the finished card carefully on the counter, each letter dotted in wax.

"You're supposed to be making designs on T-shirts, not freckles on a card."

"A lot you know," Tina answered, pleased with herself. Old smart-aleck Mike was staring right at a *real cipher*, and he didn't even know it! Tina put the card carefully into a small box and thought about someone who *would* know the code.

At quarter past ten the next morning, right after the mail had come, Tina hid behind the pine tree in Mr. James's yard, waiting.

Fifteen minutes later the cane tip-tapped down the walk. Tina hardly dared breathe as Mr. James pulled the mail out of the mailbox and opened the little box.

Did it make sense? Were the wax dots close enough? Were they in the right places for B-A-B-E? She felt ready to burst watching, waiting.

Mr. James's face wrinkled into that thinking frown as his fingers felt the bumps on the card. Suddenly he smiled, and over his face came that thoughtful, remembering look. He leaned back against the mailbox, still fingering the card.

Finally Mr. James put it carefully into his shirt pocket and picked up his cane — not like a cane, but like a baseball bat! With both hands tight on the stick, he pulled back in a fake swing.

Tina crept away, feeling a bit embarrassed, but proud too.

Case of the code in the mailbox — closed.

Author

Kathy Kennedy Tapp has written several magazine stories about Braille and codes. Mrs. Tapp's three children are critics for the stories she writes.

Thinking It Over

Comprehension Questions

1. What did Tina learn from Mr. James?
2. How had Tina planned to spend her afternoon?
3. Why was Tina proud when she saw Mr. James swinging his stick like a baseball bat?

Vocabulary

These words all have more than one meaning: *rock, bat, wax, well, box, pine*. Look the words up in a dictionary. Then use each word in two sentences, with two different meanings.

Writing About a Book

Find a nonfiction book about baseball. Use it to answer these questions: How many chapters are there? What is the copyright date? Does the book give facts about the World Series? How do you know?

Multiple Meanings

Mary is learning how to use a computer. She has to press a key to get started, but she wonders which meaning for *press* makes sense.

The word *press* has more than one meaning. Which of these meanings should Mary use?

press   1. To make smooth; to push down. **2.** A machine for printing books and newspapers.

When you read, you will come across many words that have more than one meaning. How can you tell which meaning is being used? Use the words and sentences near the word to find out.

Try to figure out the meaning of the boldface word in this sentence:

There seems to be a **bug** in this machine!

You know that the usual meaning of *bug* is "insect." However, that meaning probably is not right in this sentence.

Read the sentences below to find out more.

There seems to be a **bug** in this machine! When I push the enter key, the computer stops.

The second sentence tells you that the machine is not working right. Now you can figure out that the word **bug** can also mean "something wrong with a machine."

Read each sentence below and tell which meaning of the boldface word is used.

1. Terry sat at the computer and waited for the numbers to come up on the **screen.**
   a. a frame covered with wire mesh, used in windows to keep out bugs
   b. a surface on which pictures appear
2. The *m* **key** on this computer does not work.
   a. a tool for opening a lock
   b. an answer to a problem
   c. one of a set of buttons or levers moved by the fingers, on a typewriter, piano, or other instrument

3. Donna wrote a new **program.** It tells the computer to find out the average age of students in each grade.
   a. a list of events
   b. a set of directions fed into a computer
   c. a show; something put on for an audience

Something Extra

The words below all have more than one meaning. Choose one and write a sentence using it. Then draw two pictures. In one, show how the word is used in your sentence. In the other, show a different meaning. Ask a classmate to read your sentence and choose which picture goes with it.

trunk   **plant**
fall   **watch**

Sports

Sports have always played an important part in people's lives. This is especially true today, when we have TV shows and magazines about sports and special clothing just for sports. Modern inventions, like the computer, are changing the way many sports are played. The value of sports, however, still lies in our enjoyment of them and in what we can learn from them.

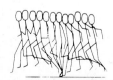

COMPUTER COACHING
by Brett M. Goodman

How much do today's athletes and their coaches depend on computers?

Many athletes today have two coaches to help them play better in sports. The first coach is a person who watches the players and shows them how to perform better.

The second coach isn't a person at all. It can't run or yell or cheer. It is made of wiring and plastic and metal and glass. The second coach is a computer.

Who Uses Computers in Sports?

More and more athletes and their coaches are using computers to help in training for sports. In fact, almost every major league baseball and football team uses computers. So do many well-known golf and tennis players. Olympic athletes and coaches use computers too.

Computers will never take the place of people as coaches, but they can help in many different ways.

What Are a Computer's Special Skills?

The computer is a machine, but it can do several things better than a person can. It can work with facts very quickly. You can set up a problem for a computer and tell it what to do. Then you must put in the facts needed to figure out the answer. It will quickly process the facts to get the answer.

Suppose you want to plan the right foods to eat before a big swimming, running, or bicycling race. A computer can help you know how much food you should eat. It can even help you decide which foods to eat to give you both quick and long-lasting energy. That way, you can get a quick start and also feel good all the way through a long race.

A second important skill that a computer has uses its memory. You can put thousands of words and numbers into the machine's brain. Then you can ask it to bring back any part of what you asked it to remember. Suppose you entered the name and birthday of everyone in your school into the machine. Then you asked it to tell you whose birthdays were between April

15 and April 20. It could print out the list faster than you could write down your own name and birthday.

The computer can't help you all by itself, however. First of all, a *computer programmer* must tell the machine what to do. Then someone must fill in the facts the machine needs to do its work. It needs to be told what a calorie is and how many there are in different foods. The machine must also be told how long the race is. Computers may seem to be very smart, but they really aren't. They can't do anything unless people help them!

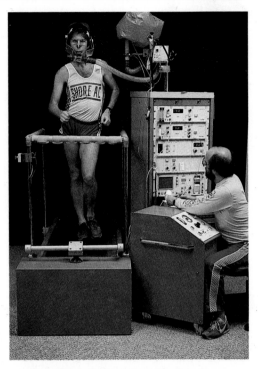

At the Olympic Training Center in Colorado Springs, a computer analyzes this race walker's performance.

How Do Coaches Use Computers?

Coaches often use computers to keep track of numbers. With these numbers, computers can help coaches make important decisions. Suppose you are a baseball manager. You are trying to decide who to send up to bat against the other team's pitcher in today's game. For a long time, you have put lots of facts about your team into the computer.

You have told the machine how each of your players has done against every pitcher on the other teams and how well each player has hit in every ball park. You ask the computer to show which of your players have hit well in this park and against this pitcher. The computer works with the facts and prints out a list. You use the list to help you set up your batting order for the game. You may still lose the game, but the machine has been a big help. It has helped you prepare for what will happen by using facts from the past.

A person just couldn't do all this work. People can't remember as much as machines can. People also can't pick out the right facts as quickly. How long do you think it would take you to read thousands of facts about baseball players? A machine could do this in just a few minutes.

Believe it or not, some baseball managers use computers in just this way. When their teams win, the managers think they have done a great job of coaching. When their teams lose, the managers sometimes blame the computers.

Computers can also keep track of measurements that are used to plan how to do things during a race.

Before the 1984 Summer Olympics, coaches on the United States Olympic bicycling team built a special training bicycle. The pedals of the bicycle measured how hard the rider was pushing on each pedal. A computer kept track of this. It also recorded just how each rider held his or her feet while riding. Next, the machine was used to print out a picture. The picture showed how the rider should push with his or her feet to get the most power with the least work. The picture showed the rider how to hold his or her feet a little differently. These changes made a big difference in how well the rider did.

How Do Athletes Use Computers?

Athletes use computers in lots of other sports too. They are the most helpful in sports that call for certain ways of holding your legs or arms. Some of these sports are golf, tennis, running, and swimming. A small change in how you stand or move can mean the difference between coming in first and being third or fourth best.

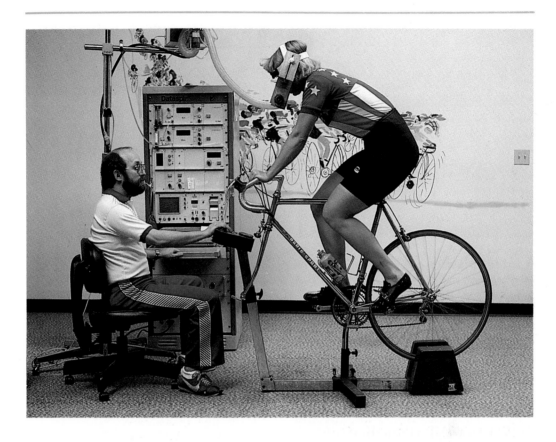

A computer can record how you hold a tennis racquet or golf club when you swing it. It can compare your way with a picture it has made of the best way to swing. The way shown by the computer may not always be the best for you. Everyone does things a little bit differently, and everyone's muscles are a little bit different. However, the computer may help you figure out a way

As this bicyclist pedals away at the Olympic Training Center, the computer measures the oxygen capacity of her lungs.

to get better results from the work you put in.

People have been playing sports for thousands of years before computers were thought of. Yet computers are making a big change in the way sports are played today. With

 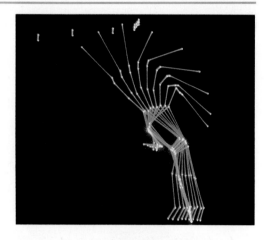

A tennis player's serve is broken into parts and displayed on a com- puter screen (right) where it is an- alyzed by his trainer (left).

coaches and computers helping them, today's athletes are racing faster, jumping higher, and eating better. And they are doing all of these things with less work than they ever did before.

There is a well-known saying that two heads are better than one. This means that two ways of thinking about an idea are better than just one way. In sports, two coaches are truly better than one!

Comprehension Questions

1. How do computers help coaches?
2. What makes a computer so useful?
3. What helpful information can computers give athletes?

Vocabulary

Some special computer words, or computer jargon, are listed below. Match each boldface word with its meaning.

print-out	**memory**
process	**programmer**
terminal	

"the unit of a computer where information is stored"

"someone who prepares programs for computers"

"to put through a series of steps"

"paper with printed words or pictures"

"something through which information is put in or taken out of the computer"

Writing a Descriptive Paragraph

Pretend that you are watching an Olympic bicycle race. Write a paragraph describing the sights, sounds, smells, and feelings of being in the crowd.

HURDLES

by Mary Blocksma with Esther Romero

How did Vicente, the class computer whiz, learn that brains and muscles could go together?

Until I invented Try-Athlon, the most popular video game ever to hit our school, nobody took much notice of me. I didn't mind much. I worked at not being noticed. The truth was, I spent most of fourth grade trying to be invisible.

To do that, I stayed away from all sports. Sports had always made me look silly. Not only did I have legs like sticks, but I ducked any ball that came to me. I hated to jump over things. Put all this together and you don't get Mr. Sports.

The Mr. Sports in our class was Ramos Alonzo. He was so good at everything that no one cared if he acted like king of the class. So I was really surprised when being a computer whiz put me right up there with King Ramos. Suddenly I was *enjoying* attention. I enjoyed it so much that I couldn't risk losing to Ramos at Try-Athlon.

I had one problem though. Ramos was very good at computer games. He could beat anyone at Try-Athlon except me, and the only reason he couldn't beat me was that I tricked him.

It wasn't hard. My game was named after the sports event triathlon. Like it, Try-Athlon was a three-part race. The first part of my game was skating. Then came swimming, and the last part was track and field. Every time Ramos came close to winning, I would program a surprise into the hurdles at the end, and the next time he would lose again.

My trick worked for a long time. Then one day it stopped working.

It was lunch hour, and both fourth-grade classes, 4-A and 4-B, were in the computer room. Ramos was playing my game, and his man was already at the hurdles.

"I'm going to beat you this time, Vicente!" he cried.

I smiled. I knew what was coming. Without warning, the hurdles began squeezing together. *KA-BAM!* His man crashed!

"Vicente!" yelled Ramos. "How can I win if you keep changing things? It's not fair!"

"You just have to keep trying, Ramos," I said coolly.

"We ought to play this game for real, Vicente," Ramos said boldly. "Then you wouldn't be smiling."

I kept smiling, though, until I heard a voice say, "I think that's a very good idea!" I turned to see Mrs. Keller, the gym teacher, march into the room.

"You can't do it for real," I told her confidently. "You've got to have a place for roller-skating and a swimming pool. Our school doesn't have them."

"I've heard about your game, Vicente," said Mrs. Keller as she turned off the machine. "I think we *can* do

it." Mrs. Keller raised her voice. "People!" she called. "Listen to me. Try-Athlon has kept you inside long enough. Let's do a real triathlon for Sports Day! Room 4-A can try to beat 4-B. You'll have four weeks to get ready. What do you say?"

They loved it. I seemed to be the only person in the room frozen to the chair. "What about the skates?" I shouted. "What about the pool?"

Mrs. Keller picked up some chalk and drew a map on the board. "You can skate from our school to City Pool on the bicycle paths," she said. "If we thank the owner in public, Sam's Skate Rental will lend us skates. Then you can swim two laps and run back to the school."

"Put hurdles at the end," said Ramos, giving me a wicked smile. "A whole *lot* of them."

"Ten hurdles!" said Mrs. Keller. "All in favor, yell *YES*."

The room filled with cheers, and when Mrs. Keller left, she had a pleased look on her face.

While Ramos laughed at what had just happened, I nearly fainted. Playing my own game for real was going to be the most embarrassing time of my life. I couldn't skate, I hated to jump, and I swam like a sick camel. My hero status had hit "game over."

Just then a classmate, Linda Robner, went over to Ramos with a group of other kids from our class. "Ramos!" she said, pointing her finger in his face, "you just lost the Sports Day Triathlon for your own class!"

"What?" said Ramos in surprise.

"You *know* Vicente can't jump," said Linda. "Even without the hurdles, he will lower our score. But now it's certain we will lose."

"So?" said Ramos. "Can I help it if he's only strong enough to push buttons?"

"You have got to help our class, Ramos," said Linda, while the others agreed. "We have decided that what you must do now is train Vicente. You two can make or break us. Unless you go along with us, our class hasn't got a chance."

Ramos shrugged. "A guy like me would never let his own class down," he said. Then he glared at me. "You better not let them down, either, Vicente. I'll train you all right, but you just better show up."

The next morning I showed up. Ramos made me work out before school. He made me run at recess. He took me to the pool after school. That night we went skating. At the end of the day, Ramos shook his head. "You may be smart, Vicente," he said, "but you've got the strength of a rabbit."

Still Ramos did not give up on me even when I looked silly. By the end of the first week, my body was in so much pain that I didn't think much about kids laughing at me any more. Embarrassment was becoming a way of life.

By the end of the second week, I felt better. I felt good enough, in fact, to look around me. What I saw surprised me. I was not the worst athlete in the class. There were kids who still had to wear a life preserver in the pool. And some kids couldn't stand up on roller skates yet. I could!

I was still the only one, however, who came to a dead stop in front of a hurdle. There was something about those hurdles that got to me. I guess I thought that they might start to jump around, the way they did in my computer game.

By the third week, I began feeling a spring in my step. I smiled a lot and I felt good. My family had happy looks on their faces. I had never felt so powerful, but I still couldn't face the hurdles.

The week before Sports Day I felt really great. By then I was pretty fair on skates — even Ramos said so. "At

least you've got strong ankles," he said, not saying anything about my arms and legs.

When the day arrived and every person in my family turned up to watch me, I felt lucky that skating came first in the Sports Day Triathlon.

That Saturday morning Ramos had picked me up at the house, and he did not leave my side for one moment. Perhaps he was afraid that I would chicken out; I certainly wanted to do that. When I pointed out my family to Ramos, he said, "Well, now you can't be last, Vicente! Not in front of all of THEM!"

"My very thought," I said, as my voice shook.

"Don't worry," said Ramos. We were crouched down near the starting line. The crowd moved around us. Mrs. Keller was testing the megaphone.

Ramos wanted to talk about our plan for winning. "At the park, you have to make a sharp turn off the street to go down the path, remember," said Ramos. "You skate fast now, Vicente, so you should make good time on this part. The swimming part ought to go well too."

He didn't say anything about all the time I would lose climbing over the hurdles; I was still afraid of them. We put on our skates and took our places in the line-ups, just as Mrs. Keller lifted up the megaphone.

"Ladies and gentlemen!" her voice boomed. "Welcome to the first Sports Day Triathlon!"

A great cheer went up from the crowd that lined the street. Then Mrs. Keller explained that we would skate to the pool, swim two laps, and then run back to the playing field. Each athlete would be timed. Then all our times would be added up and averaged for each class. "The class with the lowest average time wins!" cried Mrs. Keller, and the crowd cheered again.

Every five minutes a new line of ten athletes would start the course. "First row! Line up!" called Mrs. Keller.

The first row of ten kids moved to the starting line. At a sharp blast from Mrs. Keller's whistle, they were off. There were five rows of us left. Ramos and I were in the last one.

As each row took off, we rolled closer to the starting line. Then just as the row ahead of us took off, I remembered that Ramos was weakest in skating. I was my strongest in skating! Maybe I could get ahead of everybody before we all turned into the park.

I thought of all my family watching. As we moved up to the starting line, I even heard them. "Vicente! Go! Show them what you can do!"

"Maybe I'll just do that!" I said under my breath. I'd make them proud of me, I really would. I wasn't going to be last. No, sir, I was going to be first!

The whistle shrieked and I lunged forward. I made those little wheels whine so fast my ears hurt. I glanced back and saw with joy that I was ahead of everyone, even Ramos! I could hear the roar of the roller skates behind me, thundering toward the turn at the path ——

The sharp turn! I had misjudged the sharp turn! I came up on it too fast to slow down. I tried crossing my right foot over my left foot for one of those smooth turns, but my legs twisted like pretzels. Still in full view of the crowd, I bounced into the bushes.

I heard the skates spin by me, but I couldn't move. I couldn't face it. I was going to stay there forever when I felt a tug on my skates. "Come on, Vicente!"

It was Ramos. Painfully I got up.

"Move!" shouted Ramos.

"I'll be last!" I could barely whisper.

"Try!" begged Ramos. "Please!" Then he was gone.

Trying to feel grateful, I wobbled off behind him. In a fog, I made it to the pool and swam my two laps.

When I got out of the pool, everyone had gone. With fear squeezing my stomach, I started running toward the field.

The sound from the megaphone carried so far that I could hear it blocks away. "Ramos Alonzo, 13 minutes, 10 seconds!" boomed Mrs. Keller. I could hear the crowd's cheers. Ramos had made good time even after stopping to help me.

As I neared the field, I got my first look at the course ahead. No one was on it! Everyone had already finished. I really was going to be last, I thought. Worse, my whole family was going to watch me climb over those awful hurdles.

I couldn't do it. It didn't matter how hard I'd trained. Forget about Ramos. I had already made a fool of myself.

While my head was busy with all those awful thoughts, my feet just kept going. I couldn't seem to stop them. As I padded onto the field, the crowd began to roar. I figured they were all cheering the other class's victory.

Then I wasn't so sure. I thought I heard my name. At first, it sounded like my family. Then it sounded as if my whole class had joined in. By the time I was halfway down the field, the whole crowd was screaming it. "VICENTE! VICENTE! VICENTE! VICENTE!"

They were cheering for me! I couldn't believe it! Me! The cry got louder and louder, and soon I heard clapping and stamping feet. The whole world seem to scream and clap and stamp, and all I could hear was "VICENTE! VICENTE!"

I climbed aboard that cry and rode it like a horse. I galloped toward the first hurdle and didn't even slow down. I flew over it as if it were a tiny stick. My body was an oiled machine and running smoothly. Over the second hurdle I sailed, and the third and the fourth. Hurdles flew under me like chalk lines on a sidewalk.

Then, suddenly, the sound broke into screaming and whistling. I had crossed the finish line. I must have collapsed, because now the megaphone seemed very far away. I could still hear my time though: 16 minutes and 2 seconds.

I covered my ears and buried my face in the grass. It was a terrible time. I could never face my family or my classmates again.

Then somebody grabbed my legs. Someone else grabbed my arms. I started to fight them until I felt that I

was being moved through the air. My classmates were carrying me across the field!

"What's going on?" I yelled to Ramos.

Ramos's face was one big smile. "WE DID IT!" he yelled back. "WE WON! You didn't give up!"

We won? I couldn't believe it. I had been last, but our average time was better than Room 4-B's average time. Ramos and I had not let our own class down after all!

I grinned at Ramos. I grinned at my family, who were standing up and cheering. I grinned at everybody in the whole world.

I'd played my own game for real — even the hurdles. Right then and there, I made myself a promise not to program Try-Athlon so that Ramos would lose every time. He might beat me once in a while, but then I'd jump that hurdle when I got there.

Authors

Mary Blocksma has been writing books and stories for years. She is familiar with the computer world she writes about in "Hurdles"—she does her writing with a computer. Esther Romero lives in Colorado where she and her family are active in all kinds of sports.

Thinking It Over

Comprehension Questions

1. How did Vicente become athletic enough to finish the Triathlon?
2. Why did Vicente feel he had to beat Ramos at his computer game?
3. What events were planned for the Triathlon?
4. Why is "Hurdles" a good name for this story?

Vocabulary

Vicente tried to be *invisible*. He *misjudged* the fast turn. He was *unsteady* on his skates. Write sentences using the boldface words. What do the prefixes mean?

Writing a Paragraph

Write a paragraph about something difficult you have learned how to do, such as riding a two-wheeled bicycle.

The Ants at the Olympics
by Richard Digance

At last year's Jungle Olympics,
the Ants were completely outclassed.
In fact, from an entry of sixty-two teams,
the Ants came their usual last.

They didn't win a single medal.
Not that that's a surprise.
The reason was not lack of trying,
but more their unfortunate size.

While the cheetahs won most of the sprinting
and the hippos won putting the shot,
the Ants tried sprinting but couldn't,
and tried to put but could not.

It was sad for the Ants 'cause they're sloggers.
They turn out for every event.
With their shorts and their bright orange tee shirts,
their athletes are proud they are sent.

They came last at the high jump and hurdles,
which they say they'd have won, but they fell.
They came last in the four hundred meters
and last in the swimming as well.

They came last in the long-distance running,
though they say they might have come first.
And they might if the other sixty-one teams
hadn't put in a finishing burst.

But each year they turn up regardless.
They're popular in the parade.
The other teams whistle and cheer them,
aware of the journey they've made.

For the Jungle Olympics in August,
they have to set off New Year's Day.
They didn't arrive the year before last.
They set off but went the wrong way.

So long as they try there's a reason.
After all, it's only a sport.
They'll be back next year to bring up the rear,
and that's an encouraging thought.

Science

What Is Important in Reading Science?

When you read a science lesson, it is important to understand and remember the information that you learn. You should use what you have learned as you read your science lesson.

Before you begin to read your lesson, notice how it is organized into parts with headings above the paragraphs. You have already learned about one way to read a lesson. That is SQR.

Why Is a Survey Important?

When you first look through a lesson and read the title and headings, you are doing the first step of SQR, Survey. Also be sure to look at the pictures and the words below them. By going through the lesson, you have a good idea of what it is about before you read it. Then think about what you already know about the subject before you begin to read.

Why Are Headings Important?

Next, read the first heading. If it isn't a question, turn it into one. The question gives you a purpose for reading. It tells you what to look for in the material below. Then read below the heading to find out the answer to the question.

How Should You Read a Science Lesson?

When you read a science lesson, you should read it more carefully and slowly than when you read a story for fun. You want to be sure to understand the important details that tell how and why certain things happen. Sometimes you may have to read a sentence or paragraph again to fully understand it. You should reread, too, when you can't answer the question in the heading.

How Can You Learn Special Science Words?

You will notice as you read that some words are in boldface. These are often important science words. You should know the meaning of each of these words so you can understand what you are reading. Often the meaning for a boldface word is given in the sentences that you are reading. However, if you need help, look up the word in the glossary at the back of the book or in a dictionary. It may help to build your science vocabulary if you keep a list of these words and their meanings.

How Are Pictures Important?

As you read, take time to look closely at the diagrams and other pictures. They often show things that help you to understand better what the lesson is about because a picture can tell you something that is not easy to say in words. Often below a picture, there are words, called a caption, that give you more information.

Summary

When you read a science lesson, remember these points:
- Think about the organization and purpose of the lesson before reading.
- Use SQR to study the lesson.
- Learn the meanings of new science words and keep a list of them.
- Look at the pictures and read the captions.

Preview

The next selection, "Weather," is written like a science lesson. When you read "Weather," practice what you learned here. After reading, be able to tell how the selection was organized and what steps you followed as you read it.

WEATHER

Where Does Weather Come From?

When you think of Earth, you think of the land on which you walk. But Earth is really made up of three parts: land, water, and air. About three quarters of Earth is covered by water, and all of Earth is covered by a blanket of air called the **atmosphere.**

This blanket of air is made up of layers. The lowest is where our weather happens. It is here that winds blow, clouds form, and storms start. The air protects Earth from the sun's full power but allows some of its rays to pass through. The sun heats and lights Earth. It also makes the weather.

What Causes Weather?

For scientists to be able to tell what kind of weather is coming, they must know about these four things:

1. the amount of water, or **humidity,** in the air
2. the **temperature,** or how warm the air is
3. the **air pressure,** or how hard the air pushes down on Earth
4. the direction and speed of the wind

All four of these — together with the sun — cause sunny days or storms.

What Is Water in the Air?

If you go out early on a summer morning, the grass is wet. On a very cold day, you can see your breath. This is because the air has water in it, but it is often in a form you cannot see.

Water comes in three forms. When it is in its liquid form,

you can see it coming out of a hose. When water freezes, it is in its solid form as ice or snow. The third form of water cannot be seen. It is a gas called **water vapor.**

Warm air can hold more water vapor than cool air. As warm air rises, it becomes cooler. Some of the vapor gathers around dust in the air and changes back to liquid water. Then a great many of these very small drops of water come together to form clouds. When the drops become larger and heavier, they fall as rain. If the air is cold enough, it snows.

Above: This iceberg is water in its solid form. Below: This diagram of the *water cycle* shows how water is constantly changing form.

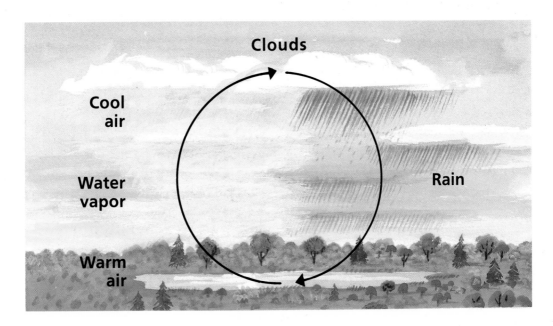

Clouds

Cool air

Water vapor

Warm air

Rain

How Does the Air Change Temperature?

The atmosphere gets some heat from the sun, but the air is mostly either warmed or cooled by the land beneath it. Air over the Poles is cold. Air over the tropics is warm. Look at the picture. Which part of Earth receives the most sunlight? Which rays have to go the farthest? Where is it the coldest?

The sun heats Earth, which then warms the atmosphere. Direct rays give more heat than slanted ones.

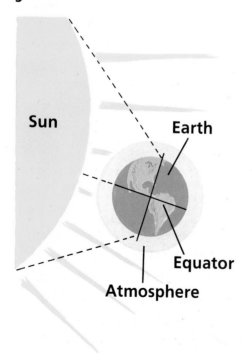

Sun

Earth

Equator

Atmosphere

What Causes Wind?

When air is warm, it expands. The **particles,** or tiny parts that make up air, are farther apart. This makes it weigh less than cold air so it can't push as hard on Earth as cold air can. Therefore warm air has less pressure. Changes in air pressure can warn of a weather change.

When cooler air pushes down on Earth, the warmer air rises. Then cooler air is heated in turn by the land below it and rises up. This moving air is called wind.

What Causes Stormy Weather?

When large amounts of warm and cool air meet, they do not mix. The place where they come together is a **front.** Most storms happen along fronts.

How Is Weather Reported?

The National Weather Service keeps track of the weather. People who study weather, or

meteorologists, measure the air pressure, temperature, humidity, and wind speed and direction. They also write down what they see.

Meteorologists are trying to find ways to change weather. Some day they may be able to move the paths of storms, bring needed rain, and clear fog.

The wind has forced these limber pine trees to grow in one direction.

Comprehension Questions

1. What must meteorologists know in order to predict the weather?
2. How is water vapor in the air changed to liquid water?
3. How does air become warm or cool?
4. Why is it helpful to know where warm and cold fronts are?

Activity

Record the outdoor temperature where you live, at the same time each day. Note the date and the temperature. After ten days start a line graph of the temperatures you have written down. Unless you live near the equator, you will see a slow change in the temperatures during the year.

If you continue your records for a whole school year, you will see a pattern of falling and rising temperatures.

Unfamiliar Words

Can you figure out what **delicious** means? Read the words and sentences near the unknown word. The words and sentences will help you discover the meaning of *delicious*. The words *tastes great* and *a great treat on a hot day* tell us that **delicious** means "very good to eat."

Now use the other words in the sentence below to figure out what the boldface word means.

Whenever I went into the gift shop, I looked first at my favorite **figurine** on its glass shelf.

You know from the sentence that a figurine can be sold in a

gift shop and that it is small enough to go on a shelf. What does it look like? Read on to find out.

Mother would never let me pick it up because it was made of china. I loved the tiny lady in the pink dress, but Mother's favorite was the little balloon man.

You can tell that a figurine is easy to break because Mother would not let it be picked up. In the next sentence, the words *tiny lady* and *little balloon man* tell that a figurine can look like people. Now you know that a figurine is a little statue, just by using the words and sentences around it.

Use words and sentences as clues to figure out what the boldface words mean in the sentences below. Choose the correct meaning for each word.

1. I wish my little sister wouldn't **harass** me. Every single day she asks me to take her to the park. Her constant whining is really irritating.
   a. bother   b. watch   c. kick

2. Mark wondered who would move into the **vacant** apartment next door. His father had said that it would be filled quickly because of the low rent. Mark was hoping for another boy.
   a. large   b. nice   c. empty

3. The winning team was **boisterous** on the bus after the game. "Let them make noise," the coach said. "They need to relax."
   a. happy   b. mean   c. loud

When you read the next story, you will find some hard words like **auditorium.** Remember to look at the words and sentences around these words to help you figure out their meaning.

Two Piano Tuners

by M. B. Goffstein

Debbie's grandfather hoped she would become a concert pianist. How could Debbie show him she wanted to be a piano tuner like him?

Reuben Weinstock lived with his granddaughter, Debbie. He was a piano tuner and had often tuned the pianos that great pianists used in their concerts. One day he went down to the auditorium to tune the piano that would be used in a concert that evening. Debbie went with him to watch. She wanted more than anything to be a piano tuner, but her grandfather wanted her to become a great concert pianist. When they arrived at the auditorium, they discovered that the famous pianist performing that evening was Reuben Weinstock's old friend, Isaac Lipman.

Mr. Weinstock began to tune the concert grand piano. Suddenly he remembered he'd promised Mrs. Perlman he'd tune her piano that afternoon. He sent Debbie to tell her why he couldn't make it that day. Debbie left for the Perlmans', but on the way, she decided that maybe this was her chance to show her grandfather that she could be a piano tuner. So she went home first to get some tuning instruments.

Their house was painted yellow, with a dark red roof. It was at the end of the block, behind a grassy, empty lot. Debbie cut through the lot and went in the back door and through the kitchen.

In the living room, next to the piano, was a bureau with a lot of old tuning instruments in its bottom drawer. Debbie sat down on the carpet and pulled the drawer out. She took out the tuning hammer that Reuben Weinstock never used because its handle was too long. It was a little bit rusty, but so was the only tuning fork Debbie could find that said *C* on it. She found one gray felt wedge and one black rubber one.

Debbie brought them upstairs to her room and put them on the bed while she took off her coat, got out of her jumper, stepped into her pants, and put the coat back on. Her pants had an elasticized waistband that was perfect for holding the tuning hammer up inside them, and she put the tuning fork and wedges into her back pocket. She buttoned her coat on the way downstairs and went out the door, back through the vacant lot, and down the block to Mrs. Perlman's house.

She climbed the front steps and pressed the doorbell and waited for a long time. Finally she pressed the bell again.

"Why, Debbie," said Mrs. Perlman opening the door. "I looked out the window before, but I couldn't see anyone!"

"That's all right," said Debbie.

"Won't you come in?"

"My grandpa says he hopes you don't mind if I tune your piano."

"What?"

"Well, his friend Isaac Lipman came to give a concert. Grandpa Reuben says you should come."

"Isaac Lipman came here?"

"He's at the auditorium, and Grandpa Reuben is tuning the piano for him," Debbie explained.

"Do you mean to say that Isaac Lipman is giving a concert here, this afternoon?"

"Yes, and I have to help my grandpa. He asked me to come to tune your piano."

"Oh, how thrilling!" exclaimed Mrs. Perlman.

"I'll do a good job," said Debbie, taking off her coat on her way over to Mrs. Perlman's little upright piano in the living room.

"But ——" said Mrs. Perlman. "Oh, what does it matter?" she thought. "She's too little to hurt anything, and Mr. Weinstock will certainly do it over again, anyway." So she followed Debbie into the living room and began to take the little round lace doilies and candy dishes and china figurines away from the top of the piano.

Debbie put her coat and hat down on a slippery satin chair, and took off her overshoes and put them in the hall. Then, when Mrs. Perlman had finished clearing the piano top, she helped Debbie raise the lid and pull off the front panel. They set it carefully down on the carpet and leaned it against the wall.

Debbie pulled the tuning hammer out of her waistband, the tuning fork and wedges out of her pocket, and sat down at the piano, looking at the strings. There were two strings for each note.

She hit the tuning fork against her knee, held it to a part of the metal frame, listening to it carefully, and then tried the piano: *C! C! C! C!*

"Would you like to have some cookies and a glass of milk, Debbie?"

"Maybe later," Debbie said. She fitted her tuning hammer onto the pin that held the first string for middle C and put a wedge between the other C string and the first C-sharp string.

She hit the tuning fork against her knee again, and held it to the metal frame, and listened very, very closely. *C! C!* she played, and pushed the hammer. *C! C! C! C!* The gray felt wedge fell out, and Debbie put it back. *C! C! C! C! C! C! C!* She wished that Mrs. Perlman wouldn't keep standing right beside her.

Luckily, Mrs. Perlman, who had always been a great admirer of Isaac Lipman, felt that she could not wait another minute to decide what to wear to his concert. She patted Debbie on the shoulder and ran upstairs.

As Reuben Weinstock finished tuning the bass notes on the grand piano in the auditorium, he thought to himself that Debbie should be back any moment. He moved his tuning hammer and screwdriver up to the top of the piano, pushed wedges between the strings, and started tuning the treble notes.

He kept looking at the door while he worked. By the time he had finished tuning the treble and testing the whole keyboard up and down, and Debbie still had not come, he felt very, very worried. He put his tools back into his black bag, shut it, and sat back down on the piano bench, with his eyes on the door.

"Reuben," said Isaac Lipman, coming onto the stage behind him, "if only I had known what a comfortable couch there is in the dressing room in this auditorium, I would have come here before. I just had such a wonderful sleep!"

Mr. Weinstock turned to look at him but did not smile.

"What's the matter?" asked Isaac Lipman. "Where did that little granddaughter of yours go? I want to hear her play."

Mr. Weinstock stood up. "I sent her to ask one of our neighbors, who lives only a block away from here, if I may tune her piano tomorrow instead of today, because you are here. Debbie should have been back here an hour ago."

"She probably stayed there to tune it herself," said Mr. Lipman. "Let me try the piano while we are waiting for her. Then I want to take you and your granddaughter out to lunch."

He sat down and began to play. "Bravo!" he said. "Bravo, Reuben. There are few enough good piano tuners in the world, but there is only one Reuben Weinstock."

But Mr. Weinstock had left the stage and was standing in front of the first row of seats, putting on his coat and hat. "Thank you," he said. His hands were shaking, and he could hardly button his overcoat.

"Are you going out to find your little granddaughter? Just wait a minute, Reuben, and I'll come with you. I think a little walk would be good for me after that nap." Isaac Lipman went backstage to get his things from the dressing room.

"She hasn't come back yet? All right, let's go," he said, coming down from the stage wearing his coat and scarf and a brown fur hat.

"I'm so sorry this had to happen today, while you are here — and before your concert," Mr. Weinstock said to him as they walked up the aisle. They went through the lobby and outdoors.

"I'm only sorry because of you," said Isaac Lipman. "You don't look well, Reuben. You seem very tired. I'm afraid it has been hard on you, taking care of that little girl."

"She is my son's child," said Mr. Weinstock. "He and his wife died two years ago."

"I'm sorry, Reuben."

"Now Debbie is all I've got," said Mr. Weinstock. "But she is so much!"

The two men walked up the block in silence, looking all around for Debbie, or for anyone who might have seen her.

A minute later they came to Mrs. Perlman's house, and Reuben Weinstock stopped. "This is where she was supposed to come," he said.

A and E! A and E! A and E! they heard in the damp air. *A and E! A and E! A and E!*

"Ah," said Isaac Lipman. "You see, I was right!"

"But how ——" began Mr. Weinstock. "But she will ruin the piano!" he said. "She doesn't know how to tune a piano. She has never tuned one before."

"If she has been living with you for two years, then I'm sure she knows how. But, Reuben, she is very naughty!"

Mr. Weinstock put his hand on his friend's arm. "Don't say that. Thank goodness, she is safe. Whatever she has done to the piano, I can fix. She probably meant to help me. She always wants to help me!"

"She *should* help you, Reuben."

"She is only a little girl. I don't want her to help me; I have to help her. I am giving her piano lessons — that is all I can give her. I have been hoping that she will be a concert artist someday."

"When I was her age, I had already played for the Empress of Russia," said Isaac Lipman. "Reuben, your little granddaughter may be as talented as I am, but if she doesn't want to be a pianist more than anything else in the world, she will certainly never be one. She says she wants to be a piano tuner, so let's see how well she is tuning that piano." And taking Mr. Weinstock's arm, he marched up the walk to the front door and pressed the bell.

They stood on the steps and listened to Debbie's tuning until Mrs. Perlman opened the door. "Oh!" she gasped.

"Mrs. Perlman, may I present Mr. Isaac Lipman," said Mr. Weinstock.

"How do you do. I'm so thrilled to meet you! I recognized you from your picture. Do you know, I have your autograph? I've kept it for twenty years. Debbie said you were here. She's in the living room, tuning my piano. Come in, come in!"

They wiped their feet on the mat and took off their boots. Then they followed Mrs. Perlman into the living room, wearing their coats and holding their hats.

Debbie was standing between the piano bench and the keyboard, looking impatient and unhappy. "I've only done two octaves," she said.

"You shouldn't have done any," said her grandfather. "You should have come right back to the auditorium. I was very worried about you."

"Won't you take off your coats and sit down?" Mrs. Perlman was asking.

"Mr. Lipman can't ——" began Mr. Weinstock.

But Isaac Lipman took off his coat and scarf and handed them to Mrs. Perlman. "Thank you very much," he said. "I am sorry to trouble you."

"It's not any trouble. It's an honor!" said Mrs. Perlman. "Let me take your coat, Mr. Weinstock."

"Get out of there for a minute," Mr. Lipman said to Debbie, "and let me see if you are doing a good job."

"I've only done two octaves," Debbie repeated, but she

took the wedges out of the strings, picked up the tuning hammer, and slid out.

Mr. Lipman sat down and began to play.

"On my piano!" marveled Mrs. Perlman, coming back from hanging up the coats in her hall closet. "Isaac Lipman, playing on my piano!"

Mr. Lipman smiled. "Now, Debbie," he said. "I have traveled all over the world giving concerts, and I have played on pianos tuned by hundreds of different piano tuners ——"

"And Grandpa Reuben was the best?" asked Debbie.

"That's right."

"Well, it's very, very hard to get every note dead on, the way he does," she told him.

"It would be almost impossible with that kind of tuning hammer," said Mr. Weinstock. "It's no good. The handle is too long. I'm surprised you didn't break any strings."

"Then I think she did pretty well!" said Mr. Lipman.

"And what tuning fork did you use?" her grandfather asked her. "This? It's all rusted." He hit it against his shoe and held it to his ear. "It doesn't play a true C any more, Debbie."

Debbie's eyes filled with tears.

"Come," said Mr. Lipman, getting up from the piano. "I want to take you all out to lunch."

"My husband will be coming home for lunch soon," said Mrs. Perlman. "I've got a big meal ready, so please stay and eat with us."

"Ah," said Isaac Lipman. "A home-cooked meal . . ."

"It would be a great honor to have you."

"Thank you."

"It is very kind of you, Mrs. Perlman," said Reuben Weinstock, "and I am sorry about your piano. I'll come and tune it first thing tomorrow."

Mrs. Perlman put her arm around Debbie. "Please don't say anything more about it," she said.

"And now," said Isaac Lipman, "I would like to hear Debbie play."

"Play the Mendelssohn *Reverie,* Debbie," said Mr. Weinstock. "We will all remember that the piano is out of tune."

Mrs. Perlman and the two men sat down, and Debbie went to the piano.

"Is there anything you would rather play?" Isaac Lipman asked her when she was done. "Is there any other piece that you like to play better than this one?"

"No," said Debbie.

Mr. Lipman shook his head sadly, smiling at Mr. Weinstock.

"I think she will be a very lovely piano teacher someday," Mrs. Perlman said kindly, getting up to go to the kitchen.

"The world would be a better place if people who did not like to play the piano did not teach the piano," said Mr. Lipman. "People should take the responsibility for finding out what it is they really want to do."

"I want to be a piano tuner," said Debbie. "And I want to be as good as my grandpa."

"Right now, you had better go home and put on a dress," Mr. Weinstock told her. "And don't stop to tune any more pianos on the way. Come straight back here, because we must have lunch in plenty of time before the concert."

"Wait until she hears you play!" he said to Isaac Lipman, after he had helped Debbie on with her coat and hat and opened the front door for her. "And if that doesn't inspire her . . ."

"I think it *will* inspire her," chuckled Mr. Lipman. "I think it will inspire her to want to tune grand pianos for concert pianists."

Mr. Weinstock laughed. "If that's the case," he said, "then maybe I had better teach her how."

"Well, I think you should, Reuben. It seems to me she has a real talent for it."

"Yes, I was amazed at how well she was doing! But, you know, I wanted something better for her."

"What could be better than doing what you love?" asked Mr. Lipman.

At the concert, Debbie and Mr. Weinstock and Mr. and Mrs. Perlman sat in the first row of seats, a little bit over to the left, so they could watch Isaac Lipman's hands.

Everybody in town seemed to have heard that he had come, and all the seats in the auditorium quickly filled with dressed-up and excited people, who rose to their feet clapping and shouting "Bravo!" when the lights went down and the famous pianist walked out onto the stage.

He bowed to the audience and, sweeping back his long coattails, sat down at the piano. No one in the audience breathed while Mr. Lipman sat with his head bowed and his hands in his lap. After he had raised them to the keyboard and began to play the first piece on the program, a long fantasy and fugue by Bach, everyone began to breathe again.

They clapped loudly when it was over, and Mr. Lipman stood beside the grand piano and bowed. Then he swept back his coattails and sat down again, looking at his hands in his lap. The audience waited quietly, and he began to play a sonata in three movements by Beethoven.

At the end of the first movement, Mr. Perlman and Debbie clapped, but Mrs. Perlman and Mr. Weinstock did not. Debbie was amazed. "Didn't you think it was good?" she asked her grandfather.

"It isn't over yet," he said.

After the second movement no one clapped, but after the third, which was really the end of the piece, everyone clapped and shouted "Bravo! Bravo!" Mr. Lipman bowed and left the stage, but the clapping and calling continued until he came back to bow two more times. Then the lights came on, and everybody got up to walk around.

"That was good," said Debbie.

"You liked it!"

"Yes. No matter how hard he played, the piano stayed in tune. You did such a good job," said Debbie.

"It sounds as if you've got an assistant there, Mr. Weinstock," said Mr. Perlman.

"Sh-h," whispered Mrs. Perlman. "He doesn't want her to be a piano tuner! He wants her to be a pianist."

"What's wrong with being a ——" began Mr. Perlman, but the lights started to dim, and everyone went back to their seats.

On the second half of the program, Isaac Lipman played two rhapsodies by Brahms, and *Carnaval* by Schumann. At the end of the concert the audience clapped and clapped and called "Encore! Encore!" until he came out on the stage again and sat back down at the piano. He looked out at the audience and said, "A waltz by Chopin."

"Ah-h-h," said the audience.

They clapped and clapped when it was over. Mr. Lipman bowed and left the stage. The audience kept clapping, and he came back, bowed, and left the stage again. The audience kept on clapping until he came back and sat down at the piano again: *"Reverie,* by Mendelssohn."

"Oh-h-h," murmured the audience, and Isaac Lipman played the same piece Debbie had played that morning. After he finished, bowed, and left the stage, Mr. Weinstock, still clapping, said to Debbie, "Wouldn't you like to be able to play it like that?"

"No," said Debbie. "Grandpa Reuben ——"

Mr. Lipman came back onto the center of the stage, bowed again and again, and went out. Then the lights came on in the auditorium, and the concert was over.

"Grandpa Reuben, please let me be a piano tuner."

"We must go backstage and say goodby to Mr. Lipman now," said Mr. Weinstock. "He will be leaving right away."

The whole audience was pushing backstage to shake hands with the great pianist. "Please, Grandpa Reuben," said Debbie. "Please teach me how to be a good piano tuner!"

"What's wrong with being a piano tuner?" asked Mr. Perlman. "Especially a good one!"

"Nothing," said Mr. Weinstock. "Debbie ——"

They had come near Mr. Lipman by this time, and even though he was talking to some other people, he reached out and took Debbie by the hand. "You must come to the city and tune my piano sometime," he said.

"Yes, but first I am going to teach her how to do it," said Mr. Weinstock. "I was just about to say so."

Isaac Lipman was as delighted as Debbie. "So even after hearing one of my concerts, you would rather tune pianos than play them," he said. "Well, I was just like that at your age. I could only think of one thing. For me, of course, it was playing! When I get back to the city, Debbie, I am going to send you a leather bag of your own, filled with good tuning instruments."

"Thank you very much!" said Debbie. "And ——"
"Yes?"

"And regulating tools too, Mr. Lipman? Key pliers and bending pliers and a key spacer and parallel pliers and a

capstan screw regulator and a capstan wrench and a spring adjusting hook and a spoon bending iron and ——"

Some of the people who were standing near them were laughing.

"Everything!" cried Mr. Lipman. "I will ask the head of the piano factory for one of everything."

"Except the tools that I invented," put in Mr. Weinstock. "But I am going to make those for her, and she will be the only other piano tuner to have them."

Debbie put her hand into his. "I'll be just like you," she said.

Author

Marilyn Brooke Goffstein says that in her books she tries to show the beauty and dignity of a life of hard work to make something good. Because her husband is a concert pianist, Mrs. Goffstein is familiar with the world of music she wrote about in *Two Piano Tuners*. Several of her books have received awards, and *Fish for Supper* was a Caldecott Honor Book.

Thinking It Over

Comprehension Questions

1. Why was Debbie successful in convincing her grandfather that she should be a piano tuner?
2. Why did Debbie go home before going to the Perlmans'?

3. What did Mrs. Perlman think when Debbie wanted to tune her piano?
4. Why was Debbie unsuccessful at tuning the piano?
5. What did Isaac Lipman think about Debbie's career choice?

Vocabulary

The author of "Two Piano Tuners" used the boldface words below to add interest.

What are the base words of the boldface words? What suffixes have been added to them?

a **grassy** lot
a **wonderful** sleep
a **rusty** hammer

Write a sentence for each pair of words below. Underline the base words.

grouchy dog   **healthy cat**
careful doctor   **hopeful boy**

Writing a Paragraph

Choose a stringed instrument such as a violin or guitar. Look it up in an encyclopedia or reference book. Write a paragraph about the invention of the instrument. Share your paragraph with your classmates.

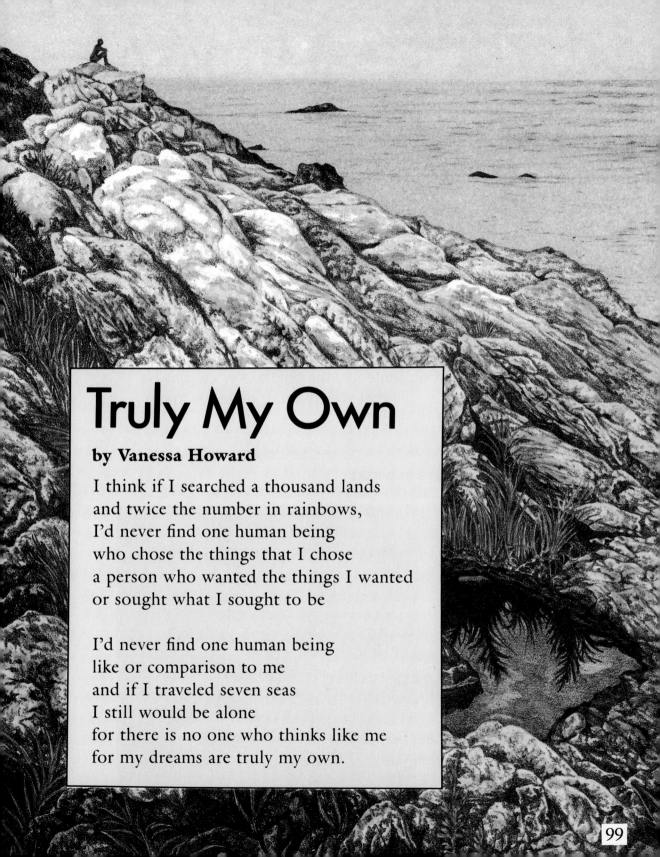

Truly My Own

by Vanessa Howard

I think if I searched a thousand lands
and twice the number in rainbows,
I'd never find one human being
who chose the things that I chose
a person who wanted the things I wanted
or sought what I sought to be

I'd never find one human being
like or comparison to me
and if I traveled seven seas
I still would be alone
for there is no one who thinks like me
for my dreams are truly my own.

Pronunciation Key

As you read, you may come to a word that you have never seen before. You know that you can get the meaning by reading the other words and sentences around it, or you can use a glossary or a dictionary. What should you do if you don't know how to say the word? You should study the special spelling that is given in a dictionary.

What Is a Special Spelling?

In the following sentence, the boldface word may be new to you. Use the other words in the sentence to get the meaning of the word.

With its long, black-striped tail, a *cacomistle* looks very much like a raccoon.

The other words in the sentence help you to know that a cacomistle is a kind of animal, but you may not be sure how to say the word. One way to find out how to say the word would be to look it up in a dictionary. A dictionary gives a special spelling for each entry word to help you know how to say the word. This is how the word **cacomistle** and its special spelling might look in a dictionary:

cac·o·mis·tle (kăk′ə mĭs′əl)

The letters and marks in the special spelling tell you how to say the word. You will need to use a pronunciation key to understand some of the sounds shown in the special spelling.

What Is a Pronunciation Key?

A pronunciation key is the rows of letters and words at the bottom of every page or every other page in a glossary or a dictionary. It shows you how to pronounce some of the sounds shown in the special spelling. The Glossary in this book uses the pronunciation key shown at the bottom of this page.

Use this pronunciation key with the special spelling to say the word **cacomistle**.

cac·o·mis·tle (kăk′ə mĭs′əl)

Look at the first syllable in the special spelling. The first letter is **k**. There is no letter **k** in the pronunciation key. That is because the letter **k** in the special spelling stands for its usual sound.

ă pat / ā pay / â care / ä father / ĕ pet / ē be / ĭ pit / ī pie / î fierce / ŏ pot / ō go / ô paw, for / oi oil / o͝o book / o͞o boot / ou out / ŭ cut / û fur / *th* the / th thin / hw which / zh vision / ə ago, item, pencil, atom, circus

The second letter in the special spelling is ă. Find ă in the pronunciation key. Notice that the word p**a**t comes after the ă. The **a** in p**a**t is in boldface. Pat is called a key word because it is the key to the sound that ă stands for. The sound ă that you hear in p**a**t is the sound that ă stands for in the special spelling.

Softly say to yourself the sound for **k**, followed by the sound for **a** in p**a**t, followed again by the sound for **k**. Those three sounds together make the sound for the first syllable in *cacomistle*.

cac·o·mis·tle (**kăk′**ə mĭs′əl).

Now look at the second syllable in the special spelling. There is only one mark in that syllable — (ə).

This mark is called a schwa. It stands for a sound that many different vowels may stand for. Find the ə in the pronunciation key. There are five words after ə: **a**go, it**e**m, penc**i**l, at**o**m, and circ**u**s. Notice that the letters **a, e, i, o,** and **u** are in boldface in those words. Say those five key words softly to yourself, and listen to the sound that those five letters stand for. The letters are different, but they all stand for the same sound — the schwa sound.

Now softly say the schwa sound to yourself. That is the second syllable of *cacomistle*.

cac·o·mis·tle (**kăk′**ə mĭs′əl)

Look at the third syllable in the special spelling. You know the sound that **m** stands for. Find ĭ in the pronunciation key. The key word that follows it is p**i**t. You know the sound that the third letter, **s**, stands for. Use the sound you know for **m**, followed by the sound for ĭ in p**i**t, followed by the sound you know for **s** to say the third syllable.

Now look at the last syllable in the special spelling. This syllable has the schwa sound. You know the sound that **l** stands for. Say **əl** softly to yourself.

There is something else that you need to know to be sure that you are saying the word **cacomistle** correctly. You need to understand the stress marks that are shown in the special spelling.

What Are Stress Marks?

When you pronounce a word that has more than one syllable, you say one syllable with greater stress, or force, than the others. Say the words **camel** and **canoe** to yourself, and listen to the stress on the syllables. You can hear the greater stress on the first syllable in **camel**. In **canoe**, the greater stress is on the second syllable.

In some words, more than one syllable is stressed. One of these will usually have more stress than the other. Say the word **telephone** to yourself, and listen to the stress that you put on each syllable. The first syllable of **telephone** has more stress than the others, but the last syllable has more stress than the second syllable.

cac·o·mis·tle (kăk′ə mĭs′əl)

Now look again at the special spelling for **cacomistle**. The heavy dark mark after the first syllable is called a primary stress mark. It tells you that the first syllable is said with more force than the other syllables in the word.

The mark after the third syllable shows that this syllable also is stressed. This mark, which is not as heavy as the primary stress mark, is called a secondary stress mark. This mark shows that you should say the third syllable with less stress than the first one.

Now use what you know about the sounds for the marks in a special spelling to say the word *cacomistle* softly to yourself. Be sure to put the correct stress on the syllables.

Using the Pronunciation Key

Use the pronunciation key on page 101 to get the correct pronunciation of the words shown in boldface below. Then answer the question that follows the sentence.

1. For Beth, being short was no *hindrance* (hĭn′drəns) to playing basketball. How many syllables are there in *hindrance*?
2. After the roller coaster ride, Ben's stomach felt *queasy* (kwē′zē). Which key word tells you the sound for **ea** in *queasy*?
3. The dark clouds and drizzle created a *melancholy* (mĕl′ən kŏl′ē) mood. Which syllable in *melancholy* has the secondary stress mark?
4. The raindrops fell with a *rhythmical* (rĭth′mĭ kəl) sound. Which key word tells you the sound for **th** in *rhythmical*?

Skill Summary

- In a dictionary, special spellings and the pronunciation key help you to pronounce words.
- If a letter or mark in the special spelling is in the pronunciation key, a key word tells how to say that sound.
- A primary stress mark in a special spelling shows that a syllable should be pronounced with greater force than the other syllables.
- A secondary stress mark shows that a syllable should be spoken with force, but with less force than the syllable with primary stress.

The Wish at the Top

**written by
Clyde Robert Bulla**

**illustrated by
Chris Conover**

Happy with life as it is, Jan, the blacksmith's son, has no reason to listen to his friend's tale about the golden ball on top of the church steeple. Why should he try an almost impossible climb to rub the golden ball to make a wish come true? Then one day something changes Jan's mind, and so begins award-winning author Clyde Robert Bulla's exciting story.

The reader shares Jan's hope and fear as he starts the dangerous climb toward the top in a faraway time and place where wishes may come true.

The Wish at the Top

by Clyde Robert Bulla

illustrated by
Chris Conover

In a far city, there once lived a boy named Jan. His father was Anton the blacksmith. The family's home was a little house next door to the blacksmith shop, in the shadow of a great church.

Jan was small and quick and strong. He helped his father shoe the horses that were brought to the shop. He was not afraid when they stamped their feet and blew their breath in his face.

Jan helped his mother too. He carried firewood and water for the house. Sometimes he went to market to buy something she needed at home.

Often his friend Viktorin went with him. The two boys liked to wander about the city together.

Sometimes they climbed to the top of the city wall. There they could look out over forests and fields to the mountains beyond. Always they shook their fists at the mountains and shouted, "Hah! Laszlo!" This was their way of saying, "Laszlo! We're not afraid of you!"

Laszlo was their enemy. He lived in the mountains. He and his men waited there to rob anyone who went too far outside the city wall.

"Laszlo is a giant," Viktorin told Jan. "He has a black beard that comes down to his belt. He has sharp teeth and big, round eyes. He climbs the highest mountains because he likes the danger. He is a strange and terrible man."

"But we're not afraid of him," said Jan.

"The old governor was once afraid of him," said Viktorin. "This is what I have heard. Laszlo had so much land and such power that he might have ruled all the country if our soldiers hadn't driven him out. He went into the mountains, and the wild mountain men made him their leader."

Jan said, "We're not afraid of him and all his men."

"No," said his friend, "because our soldiers and our city wall will keep us safe."

Viktorin was older than Jan. He knew many things that Jan did not know. If the new governor went by in his carriage, Viktorin told a story about him. If the two boys stopped to drink at a fountain, Viktorin was ready with a story about the fountain.

One day they were playing in the churchyard, and Viktorin began to tell Jan about the church.

"Did you know it took five thousand men five thousand days to cut the stones and bring them here? See how they fit together to make this wall. You couldn't put a knife blade between these stones."

"I know," said Jan.

"But that isn't the most wonderful thing about the church, though," said Viktorin. "The most wonderful thing is *there*."

He pointed. Jan looked up and up to the golden ball on top of the steeple. Against the blue sky it shone like a small sun.

"You can wish on it," said Viktorin, "and your wish will come true."

"How do you know this?" asked Jan.

"I've heard the old ones tell it to one another," said Viktorin. "The old have secrets from the young. I listen and hear what they say."

"Have you wished on the golden ball?" asked Jan.

Viktorin shook his head. "You can make your wish only at the top of the steeple."

Jan was puzzled. "At the *top?*"

"Yes," said Viktorin. "Before you wish, you must rub the ball. You must rub it with your hand."

Jan gazed at the golden ball. It looked as high as the sky. "But — but —— " he began.

"Ah, now you understand," said his friend. "No one ever wishes on the golden ball, because who could climb so high?"

"Well, then —— " said Jan. "Well, then, it doesn't matter, does it?"

"It is a great wonder, all the same," said Viktorin. "If you could have your wish, what would it be?"

Jan thought. He thought for so long that his friend began to laugh. "I once heard of a man so rich he had nothing left to wish for. Are you like him?"

It was a joke, because Jan was not rich at all. Yet there was truth in the joke. All he really wanted was a horse, and he would have one within a year. His father and mother had promised it to him.

"Yes, I am like that man," he said, and he laughed with Viktorin. "I have nothing left to wish for!"

Then one day his world changed.

His mother had sent him to market to buy some yarn. He was halfway there when he found he had forgotten the money. He ran home and into the house. He came upon his mother with her head bowed over the kitchen table.

She tried to hide her face, but he saw that she was weeping.

"Mother ——" he began.

"It's nothing," she said. But as he stood looking at her, she told him, "It's just — just that today is my mother's birthday."

He waited for her to go on. "Is that all?" he asked.

"Is that *all?*" Suddenly her voice rose, as if she were angry. "Isn't it enough? When I was a girl at home, this was a great day for us all. The family was together, everyone was happy — and now ——!" She was weeping again.

He stared at her.

"It is ten years since I have seen my mother and father," she said. "Ten long years! You have *never* seen them, even though they are your own grandmother and grandfather. I may never see them again. In all your life, *you* may never see them!"

"Why?" he asked.

"You know as well as I. Because they live on the other side of the mountains. We are shut inside these city walls as if we were in prison. Here we are, and here we must stay, and all because of Laszlo. Laszlo and his men wait to rob and kill anyone who takes the road through the mountains."

"I never knew you wanted to go ——" he said.

"I know," she said. "Because you were happy, you thought everyone else was happy too." She tried to smile. "I'm all right now. Forget what I said."

Jan could not forget, though. He saw what he had never seen before. He saw that his mother's eyes were often sad. He saw his father look at her with eyes that were sad too.

Many times a day Jan looked up at the church steeple. On clear nights he sat by his window where he could see the golden ball. It began to seem nearer. The steeple did not seem as high as before.

One day he stood in the churchyard. It was the first day of autumn, and he had on his red yarn cap. For a while he looked up at the steeple. Then he went into the church.

No one saw him as he went up the stairs to the loft. He found a small door that led to the roof. He looked out.

He could see the steeple. He was closer to it than he had ever been before.

He saw the stone figures on the steeple. They were figures of saints and angels. From below they looked small, but now he could see that each one was larger than a person. Each figure was inside a frame. The frames were rows of small, square stones.

He had never been close enough to see the stones before. They were set like pegs in the steeple. He thought, "I can climb them. I can climb them like a ladder."

He walked out across the roof to the steeple. He put his foot on one of the square stones. He took one step, then another. He was climbing!

Birds flew below him. He heard the brush of their wings, and it pleased him to think that he was higher than the birds. The climb was not hard. He had only to take care.

Still, he was tired when he came near the top. He could feel his heart pounding. Sometimes one of the stones moved a little under his feet. When this happened, he leaned closer to the steeple, and sweat came out on his forehead.

He climbed to the very top. On an iron rod just above him was the golden ball. It was nearly within reach.

He caught the rod and drew himself up and touched the ball. He rubbed it and made his wish. He began to climb down.

But the downward climb was different. When he tried to see where to put his feet, he could not help looking down. He saw the city below. It seemed to be turning slowly, and it was so far. . . .

He grew dizzy. His foot slipped, then his hand. He was falling.

Something broke his fall. It was the arm of a stone saint. He was caught between the arm and the side of the steeple.

There he lay, with his face toward the sky. He could move neither up nor down.

Jan's mother had gone to the blacksmith shop. She was asking, "Where is Jan?"

"I thought he was with you," said the blacksmith.

"He must be with Viktorin," said his wife.

"But Viktorin was just here," said the blacksmith. "He was looking for Jan."

They saw a man stop outside. He was looking up into the sunlight. Another man looked up. The two stood together. They began to talk, and they sounded excited.

The blacksmith and his wife went outside. They looked up to where the men were looking.

Near the top of the steeple was a tiny figure. It looked like a doll — a doll in a red cap.

The blacksmith cried out, "It's Jan!"

His wife cried after him, "It's Jan — it's Jan!"

118

More people gathered. "It's the blacksmith's son!" they said. "He's like a cat up a tree. Now he doesn't know how to get down."

The miller asked, "Why did he climb the steeple?"

Viktorin was there. "I think I know," he said. "He wanted to rub the golden ball and make a wish."

"The golden ball doesn't grant wishes," said the miller's wife. "Who told him that?"

"I — I told him," said Viktorin. "I heard people say it was true."

"I don't believe you heard anyone say it," said the woman. "I think you made it up out of your own head. Everybody knows you and the tales you tell. You shall be whipped!"

"No," said Jan's father. "That won't help now."

Bells were ringing. People were crowding into the square.

"What's to be done?" they asked one another.

"I'll climb the steeple," said the blacksmith.

"You could not even begin to climb it. You are too big and too heavy," said the miller. "We need someone small and light, but he must be strong enough to carry the boy down."

A merchant had the idea of bringing many ladders and tying them together. But when the ladders were placed against the church, they broke apart and came tumbling down.

120

"A scaffold!" said a baker. "Let us build a wooden scaffold as high as the steeple."

"That would take a year," said a weaver.

Jan's mother stood weeping in the square. The blacksmith stood beside her. "All I own," he said, "to anyone who will save my son!"

And while many people came and many words were spoken, it seemed there was not one who could help.

In the crowd there was a man who wore the ragged robe of a beggar. When evening came, he made his way to the city gate. There he threw off his rags and began to run. In truth, he was no beggar, but a spy for Laszlo.

Late at night he came to Laszlo's camp. "I bring news," he said. "A boy has climbed the church steeple and cannot get down. The people keep watch below. There is hardly a guard left on the city wall. Now is the time for us to attack and take the city."

"No," said Laszlo. "We are too few, and we fight best in mountain passes."

He began to ask questions, though. "The son of Anton the blacksmith, you say? Once I knew Anton when we were both very young. His son could be the age of my own son. Why does someone not bring the boy down?"

"The footholds are small — not large enough for a man," answered the spy.

Laszlo was thinking. An idea had come to him.

He was a strange man, but not all the tales told about him were true. He was no giant. He was slim and rather small. His eyes were no bigger than those of any other man, and his teeth were no sharper. He did have a long beard, and it was true that he climbed mountains because he liked the danger.

"How would it be," he said, "if I brought the boy down?"

"No!" said his men.

"There is no mountain peak I cannot climb," he said. "Surely a church steeple is not too much for Laszlo."

"Why should you help people who took your land and drove you into the mountains?" asked the spy.

"Surely the blacksmith's boy is not my enemy," said Laszlo.

"They will kill you if you go there," said the spy.

"I think they will not know me," said Laszlo.

He cut off his beard. He dressed himself in a goatskin suit. He threw a rope over his arm and rode away on his fastest horse.

By morning he was at the city gate.

A guard called down from the wall, "Who are you?"

"A farmer from the plains," said Laszlo. "I have heard of the boy on the steeple. I have come to help if I can."

123

"The blacksmith will give all he owns to anyone who can save his son," said the guard.

He led the way to the church. Laszlo looked up at the steeple. He saw the boy there, looking no larger than a doll.

People were still gathered in the square. Most of them had not slept all night. They were warming themselves at small fires.

"There is no fire to warm the blacksmith's boy," said a woman.

The blacksmith looked at Laszlo with the rope about his shoulders. He asked, "Have you come to help me? Do you know a way?"

"It may be," said Laszlo, and he disappeared into the church.

The people saw him move out across the church roof. They saw him put his hands on the steeple.

He made a noose in the rope and threw it up to the hand of a stone angel. He climbed a little way. He found a foothold and threw the rope again.

The people watched from below. They grew very still.

Jan lay on his back, behind the arm of the stone saint. The night had gone by. He had looked at the stars and thought of his mother and father and home.

By morning he was numb and cold. He could not turn his head far enough to look down. He wondered

124

if his mother and father could see him now, if he could make them hear him.

He tried to shout, but his voice sounded faraway. He could hardly hear himself.

He felt as if he were turning to stone.

A sound came to him. It was like a voice. "Jan," it seemed to say.

He listened.

The sound came again. It was nearer, and it *was* a voice. "Can you hear me?" it said. "If you can hear me, move your foot."

Jan moved his foot.

Something touched his knee. Something pushed him up from behind the stone arm.

"Now," said the voice, "hold out your hands."

He held out his hands. For a moment he looked into a man's face — a face he had never seen before. It was long and dark, more young than old, with straight, black eyebrows. Then he was lying over the man's shoulder.

"Don't move," said the voice, "and try not to look down."

Jan closed his eyes. He felt himself being carried down, now slowly, now quickly.

They were on the roof. They were inside the church. Jan saw his father and mother, and he was caught in their arms.

He forgot the long night on the steeple. He forgot how cold and afraid he had been.

"Listen to me!" he said. "I rubbed the golden ball. I rubbed it and made a wish. I wished the mountain road would be open so we could go to the other side. Now we can see my grandmother and grandfather!"

They were outside the church. Jan's father was shaking the stranger's hand and saying over and over, "Thank you — thank you!"

People were asking, "Who is this man?"

"Only one in the land could climb up the steeple and down," someone said. "It is Laszlo."

Others began to cry, "Laszlo!"

Soldiers were there. They pushed forward. But before they could seize the stranger, the blacksmith blocked their way.

"This man has saved my son," he said. "He risked his life, and you shall not lay a hand on him."

"Whoever this man may be, he has done what none of you could do," said Jan's mother, and she stood beside her husband.

The soldiers stopped. Some of them looked ashamed. While they talked about what should be done, the shout went up, "He is gone!"

Laszlo had slipped through the crowd and back to his horse. There was no one to stop him as he rode off across the plain.

The next day a guard found an arrow fixed to the city gate. Tied to the shaft of the arrow was a letter to "Anton the Blacksmith."

The blacksmith read the letter:

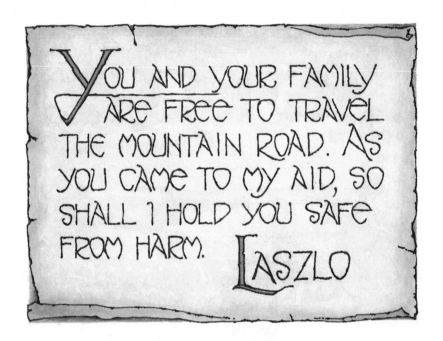

You and your family are free to travel the mountain road. As you came to my aid, so shall I hold you safe from harm. Laszlo

He read the words to his wife and son.

"Can this be true?" she said.

"Of course, it is true," said Jan. "This was my wish when I rubbed the golden ball."

Some of the neighbors shook their heads.

"It is a trick," they said. "Don't go outside the wall."

The blacksmith and his family did not listen. One morning they set out on three horses. No one stopped them as they rode through the mountain pass. And on the other side there was a joyful meeting with Jan's grandmother and grandfather.

Not once, but many times, the blacksmith and his family took the mountain road. Sometimes they talked with Laszlo and his men. Jan and Laszlo's son met and became friends. Jan took Viktorin with him into the mountains, and the three boys rode their horses together.

One day the new governor asked to meet Laszlo. They met on the plain near the city, and friendship grew out of the meeting.

Laszlo was given a farm on the edge of the forest. In the spring he and his family came to live in their new home. Jan and his father and mother were waiting to welcome them. Others were there from the city, and many of Laszlo's men had come too. Everyone joined in a celebration, and for a long time afterward there was peace in the land.

Author

Clyde Robert Bulla grew up on a Missouri farm. He went to a one-room school where his sister was the teacher. There he began writing stories and songs. Later, while working on a newspaper, he started to write for children. His first children's book was published in 1946. Since then Mr. Bulla has written more than fifty books and received many awards — for *White Bird, Shoeshine Girl,* and others. Mr. Bulla says, "I write, I travel, I come home to write again."

Illustrator

Chris Conover, born and raised in New York City, has always loved to paint and draw. Both of her parents were artists, and they sent her to New York's High School of Music and Art. She later attended the State University of New York. Her successful career in book illustration began with *The Wish at the Top,* an exciting project that took advantage of her love for researching costumes, scenery, and history.

Comprehension Questions

1. How did the kind of person Jan was help him to make his wish come true?
2. How did Viktorin's description of Laszlo differ from his actual appearance?
3. What did Jan do to help his parents?
4. Townspeople who saw Jan on the steeple said, "He's like a cat up a tree." What did the people mean?

Vocabulary

In "The Wish at the Top" it was **autumn**. The **merchant** suggested ladders, and the baker suggested a **scaffold** to rescue Jan. Everyone had a **celebration** when he was safe. In a dictionary, look at the special spelling of the boldface words in order to pronounce them correctly.

Writing a Thank-You Note

Pretend you are Jan. Write a note to Laszlo and thank him for rescuing you.

Magazine Wrap-up

Literary Skill: Major and Minor Characters

There are two kinds of characters in a story. There are one or more main characters who are the most important. They have a lot to say and do. They are very involved with what happens in the story. Minor characters have less to say and do and usually are not very important to the story.

In "The Third Avenue Elevated," Anna and Grandpa are the main characters because they say and do the most things and their adventure in the storm is the most important part of the story. All the other people in the story are minor characters.

For each of the following stories tell who are the main and minor characters and why:

- "The Code in the Mailbox"
- "Hurdles"
- "The Wish at the Top"

Vocabulary: Prefixes

Number your paper from 1 to 5. Then choose a prefix from the list to complete each boldface word in the following sentences. Write the word on your paper. You may use a prefix more than once.

over-	"above, over; too much"
mis-	"wrong, wrongly"
pre-	"before, earlier"
de-	"remove"
non-	"not"

1. When Grandpa came in from the storm, he removed his ____**shoes**, which had kept his shoes dry.
2. Tina hoped that Mr. James could ____**code** the Braille message she had put in his mailbox.
3. Grandpa Reuben's efforts to make Debbie a pianist were ____**directed** because she wanted to be a piano tuner.
4. Isaac Lipman had ____**arranged** for Debbie and her grandfather to sit with the Perlmans.

5. Vicente trained ____stop until he was able to skate well.

Writing: A Paragraph

Suppose you could invite one of the story characters in Magazine One, such as Anna, Vicente, Debbie, Jan, or Laszlo, to visit you for a weekend. Write a paragraph telling whom you would invite and why. Tell some of the things you would like to do with your guest.

Books to Enjoy

Where the Buffaloes Begin
by Olaf Baker

Little Wolf, a Native American, travels to the lake where the buffaloes come from in this adventure with handsome pictures.

Give Us a Great Big Smile, Rosy Cole
by Sheila Greenwald

Rosy, who takes violin lessons but cannot play well, is in trouble when her photographer-uncle tries to make her famous.

I Would If I Could
by Betty Miles

Patty tries to ride a new kind of bike and finds out about true friendship.

The Upside-Down Cat
by Elizabeth Parsons

Because Joe loses his cat, he forms a special friendship with an old lobsterman.

Flights
Magazine Two

Contents

Stories

The Arrival of PADDINGTON

by Alfred Bradley
and Michael Bond

The tag around his neck said, "Please look after this bear." What happens when the Browns take their polite but messy guest home with them?

Characters

Mr. Henry Brown   **Paddington Bear**
Mrs. Mary Brown   **Refreshment Man**

Judy Brown
Mrs. Bird
Jonathan Brown

Props

At Paddington Station:

*Cardboard boxes for
    parcels and luggage*
Sign saying
    PADDINGTON
    STATION
Suitcase
*Jar of marmalade —
    almost empty*
Tea trolley or tray
Cakes on paper plates
Plastic or paper cups
Drinking straw
Cake wrapper

At No. 32
    Windsor Gardens:

Table and chairs
*Tray with teapot
    and cups*
Towel
*Possibly some cushions
    and anything else
    that helps make the
    set look like the
    Browns' living room*

Scene One

When the play begins, Paddington *is hidden by a pile of parcels and luggage.* Henry *comes across the platform, closely followed by his wife.*

Mr. Brown: Well, Mary, after all that rushing about, we're here early.

Mrs. Brown: What's the time now?

Mr. Brown: It's just a quarter past four, and Judy's train doesn't arrive until half past.

Mrs. Brown: Are you sure?

Mr. Brown: She told me in her letter, and she doesn't often make mistakes.

Mrs. Brown: I'll just go and check which platform. . . . *(Goes off) (Left to himself,* Mr. Brown *walks slowly around the platform.* Paddington, *hidden behind the parcels, pops up like a jack-in-the-box and quickly down again.* Mr. Brown *is looking surprised.* Mrs. Brown *returns.)*

Mrs. Brown: It's platform five. And you're quite right. The train doesn't arrive until half past four.

Mr. Brown: Mary, you won't believe this, but I've just seen a bear.

Mrs. Brown: A what?

Mr. Brown: A bear.

Mrs. Brown: A bear? On Paddington Station? Don't be silly, Henry. There can't be.

Mr. Brown: But there is. I saw it clearly. Over there. Behind those parcels. It was wearing a funny kind of hat. Come and see for yourself.

Mrs. Brown *(Humoring him)*: Very well. *(She peeks behind the parcels.)* Why, Henry, I believe you were right after all. It is a bear!
(Paddington stands up suddenly. He is wearing a bush hat with a wide brim and has a large luggage tag around his neck.)

Paddington: Good afternoon. *(He raises his hat.)*

Mr. Brown: Er . . . good afternoon.

Paddington: May I help you?

Mr. Brown: Well . . . no . . . er, not really. As a matter of fact, we were wondering if we could help you.

Mrs. Brown *(Taking a closer look)*: You're a very unusual bear.

Paddington: I'm a very rare sort of bear. There aren't many of us left where I come from.

Mr. Brown: And where is that?

Paddington: Darkest Peru. I'm not really supposed to be here at all. I'm a stowaway.

Mrs. Brown: A stowaway?

Paddington: Yes. I emigrated, you know. I used to live with my Aunt Lucy in Peru, but she had to go into a Home for Retired Bears.

Mrs. Brown: You don't mean to say you've come all the way from South America by yourself?

Paddington: Yes. Aunt Lucy always said she wanted me to emigrate when I was old enough. That's why she taught me to speak English.

Mr. Brown: But what ever did you do for food? You must be starving.

Paddington (*Opening his suitcase and taking out an almost empty jar*)*:* I ate marmalade. Bears like marmalade. And I hid in a lifeboat.

Mr. Brown: But what are you going to do now? You can't just sit on Paddington Station waiting for something to happen.

Paddington: Oh, I shall be all right . . . I expect.

Mrs. Brown: What does it say on your tag?

Mr. Brown (*Reading it*)*:* "Please look after this bear. Thank you."

Mrs. Brown: That must be from his Aunt Lucy. Oh, Henry, what shall we do? We can't just leave him here. There's no knowing what might happen to him. Can't he come and stay with us for a few days?

Mr. Brown: But, Mary, dear, we can't just take him — not just like that. After all . . .

Mrs. Brown: After all, what? He'd be good company for Jonathan and Judy — even if it's only for a little while. They'd never forgive us if they knew you'd left him here.

Mr. Brown: It all seems highly irregular. I'm sure there's a law against it. *(Turning to* Paddington*):* Would you like to come and stay with us? That is, if you've nothing else planned.

Paddington *(Overjoyed):* Oooh, yes, please. I should like that very much. I've nowhere to go and everyone seems in such a hurry.

Mrs. Brown: Well, that's settled then. And you can have marmalade for breakfast every morning. . . .

Paddington: Every morning? I only had it as a very special treat at home. Marmalade costs a lot in Darkest Peru.

Mrs. Brown: Then you shall have it every morning starting tomorrow.

Paddington *(Worried)*: Will it cost a lot? You see I haven't very much money.

Mrs. Brown: Of course not. We wouldn't dream of charging you anything. We shall expect you to be one of the family, shan't we, Henry?

Mr. Brown: Of course. By the way, if you *are* coming home with us you'd better know our names. This is Mrs. Brown and I'm Mr. Brown.

Paddington *(Raises his hat twice)*: I haven't really got an English name, only a Peruvian one which no one can understand.

Mrs. Brown: Then we'd better give you an English one. It will make things much easier. *(Thinking hard)*: It ought to be something special. Now what shall we call you? I know! We found you on Paddington Station, so that's what we'll call you . . . Paddington.

Paddington *(Savoring it)*: Paddington. Pad-dington. Pad-dington. It seems a very long name.

Mr. Brown: It's quite distinguished. Yes, I like Paddington as a name. Paddington it shall be.

Mrs. Brown: Good. Now, Paddington, I have to meet our young daughter Judy off the train. I'm sure you must be thirsty after your long journey, so while I'm away Mr. Brown will get you something to drink.

Paddington: Thank you.

Mrs. Brown: And, Henry, when you get a moment, take that tag off his neck. It makes him look like a parcel. (Paddington *doesn't much like the thought of looking like a parcel.*) I'm sure he'll get put in a luggage van if a porter sees him. (*She goes off, almost bumping into a man pushing the refreshment cart.*)

Mr. Brown (*Removing the tag*): There we are. Ah! The very thing. Now I can get you something to drink. (Paddington *puts the luggage tag into his suitcase.*)

Man: What would you like — tea or coffee?

Paddington: Cocoa, please.

Man (*Annoyed*): We haven't got any cocoa.

Paddington: But you asked me what I would like. . . .

Man: I asked you what would you like — tea or coffee!

Mr. Brown (*Hastily, trying to avoid an argument*): Perhaps you'd like a cold drink?

Man: Lemonade or orangeade?

Paddington: Marmalade.

Mr. Brown (*Before the man loses his temper*): I think some orangeade would be a good idea — and a cup of tea for me, please. (*The man serves them.*) And perhaps you'd like a cake, Paddington?

Paddington: Oh, yes, please.

Man: Cream-and-chocolate, or cream-and-jam?

Paddington: Yes, please.

Man: Well, which do you want?

Mr. Brown: We'd better have one of each. (*The man puts them on a plate.* Mr. Brown *pays him and hands the plate to* Paddington.) How's that to be going on with?

Paddington: It's very nice, thank you, Mr. Brown. But it's not very easy drinking out of a cup. I often get my nose stuck.

Mr. Brown: Perhaps you'd like a straw. *(He takes one from the man and puts it into* Paddington's *drink.)*

Paddington: That's a good idea. *(He blows through the straw and makes a noisy bubbling sound.)* I'm glad I emigrated. *(He takes a bite from one of the cakes.)* I wonder what else there is? *(He puts the plate of cakes on the floor in order to look at the trolley, and promptly steps on the cake. In his excitement, he upsets the rest of the cups on the trolley, scattering them in all directions. Trying to keep from falling, he knocks* Mr. Brown's *tea out of his hand, slips over, and ends up lying on the platform. As* Mr. Brown *bends to help him up,* Paddington *staggers to his feet. They bump into each other and* Paddington's *cream cake ends up all over* Mr. Brown's *face. Just at this moment,* Mrs. Brown *returns with* Judy.*)*

Mrs. Brown: Henry! What are you doing to that poor bear? Look at him! He's covered all over with jam and cream.

Mr. Brown: He's covered with jam and cream! What about me? *(He begins to tidy up the mess.)*

Mrs. Brown: This is what happens when I leave your father alone for five minutes.

Judy *(Clapping her hands):* Oh, Daddy, is he really going to stay with us? *(Paddington stands up, raises his hat, steps on the cake, and falls over again.)* Oh, Mummy, isn't he funny!

Mrs. Brown: You wouldn't think that anybody could get into such a state with just one cake.

Mr. Brown: Perhaps we'd better go. Are we all ready?

Judy: Come along, Paddington.

(Paddington picks up his suitcase and puts the remains of the cakes in it. The cake wrapper sticks to his paws, but he

doesn't notice it.) We'll go straight home, and you can have a nice hot bath. Then you can tell me all about South America. I'm sure you must have had lots of adventures.

Paddington: I have — lots. Things are always happening to me. I'm that sort of bear. *(He goes off with Judy.)*

Mr. Brown *(To his wife):* I hope we haven't bitten off more than we can chew.

Man: Well, if you have, you'll just have to grin and bear it. *(He laughs loudly at his own joke and goes off.)*

Scene Two

(This scene takes place at No. 32 Windsor Gardens. Judy *and* Paddington *have just walked into the living room.)*

Judy: Here we are. Now you are going to meet Mrs. Bird.

Paddington: Mrs. Bird?

Judy: Yes. She looks after us. She's a bit fierce sometimes, and she grumbles a bit. But she doesn't really mean it. I'm sure you'll like her.

Paddington *(Nervously):* I'm sure I shall, if you say so. *(The door opens and* Mrs. Bird *appears.)*

Mrs. Bird: Goodness gracious, you've arrived already, and I hardly finished the washing up. I suppose you'll be wanting tea?

Judy: Hello, Mrs. Bird. It's nice to see you again. How's the rheumatism?

Mrs. Bird: Worse than it's ever been. *(She stops talking as she sees* Paddington.*)* Good gracious! Whatever have you got there?

Judy: It's not a whatever, Mrs. Bird. It's a bear. His name is Paddington.

(Paddington raises his hat.*)*

Mrs. Bird: A bear . . . well, he has good manners. I'll say that for him.

Judy: He's going to stay with us. He's come all the way from South America, and he's all alone with nowhere to go.

Mrs. Bird: Going to *stay* with us? How long for?

Judy: I don't know. I suppose it *depends!*

Mrs. Bird: Mercy me! I wish you'd told me he was coming. I haven't put clean sheets in the guest room or anything.

Paddington: It's all right, Mrs. Bird. I didn't have any sheets in the lifeboat. I'm sure I shall be very comfortable. (*He shakes hands with her. When he lets go, the cake wrapper is sticking to her hand. She tries with no luck to get it off, and finally it sticks to her other hand.*)

Judy: Let me help, Mrs. Bird. (*Judy takes it from her but then finds that it is glued to her own hand. At this moment,* Mr. *and* Mrs. Brown *arrive with* Jonathan.) Hello, Jonathan. (*She shakes hands with* Jonathan *and passes the sticky paper on to him.*) You haven't met Paddington yet, have you? Paddington, this is my brother, Jonathan.

Jonathan: How do you do?

Paddington: Very well, thank you.

(Paddington *shakes hands with* Jonathan *and receives the sticky paper.*)

Mrs. Bird: Whatever is going on?

Paddington: I'm afraid I had an accident with a cake, Mrs. Bird. It's left me a bit sticky.

Mrs. Bird: I think a good hot bath will do you the world of good.

Judy *(Confidentially)*: She doesn't mind really. In fact, I think she rather likes you.

Paddington: She seems a bit fierce.

Mrs. Bird *(Turning around suddenly)*: What was that?

Paddington: I didn't hear anything.

Mrs. Bird: Where was it you said you'd come from? Peru?

Paddington: That's right. Darkest Peru.

Mrs. Bird: Humph. Then I expect you like marmalade. I'd better get some more from the grocer. *(She leaves the room.)*

Judy *(Happily)*: There you are! What did I tell you? She *does* like you.

Paddington: Fancy her knowing that I like marmalade.

Judy: Mrs. Bird knows everything about everything.

Mrs. Brown: Now, Judy, you'd better show Paddington his room.

Judy: Come on. It used to be mine when I was small. There is a bathroom as well so you can have a good cleanup.

Paddington: *A bathroom*. Fancy having a separate room for a bath. (Paddington *and* Judy *leave the room*.)

Mr. Brown: I hope we're doing the right thing.

Mrs. Brown: Well, we can hardly turn him out now. It wouldn't be fair.

Mr. Brown: I'm sure we ought to report the matter to someone first.

Jonathan: I don't see why, Dad. Besides, didn't you say he was a stowaway? He might get arrested.

Mr. Brown: Then there is the question of pocket money. I'm not sure how much money to give a bear.

Mrs. Brown: He can have twenty pence a week, the same as Jonathan and Judy.

Mr. Brown: Very well, but we'll have to see what Mrs. Bird has to say about it first.

Jonathan: Hurrah!

Mrs. Brown: *You'd* better ask her then. It was your idea. (Mrs. Bird *comes in with a tray of tea, followed by* Judy.)

Mrs. Bird: I suppose you want to tell me you've decided to keep that young Paddington.

Judy: May we, Mrs. Bird? *Please*. I'm sure he'll be very good.

Mrs. Bird: Humph! (*She puts the tray on the table.*) That remains to be seen. Different people have different ideas about being good. All the same, he looks the sort of bear who means well.

Mr. Brown: Then you don't mind, Mrs. Bird?

Mrs. Bird: No. No, I don't mind at all. I've always had a soft spot for bears myself. It will be nice to have one about the house. *(She goes.)*

Mr. Brown: Well, who would have thought it?

Judy: I expect it was because he raised his hat. It made a good impression.

Mrs. Brown *(Pouring the tea)*: I suppose someone ought to write and tell his Aunt Lucy. I'm sure she'd like to know how he's getting on.

Mr. Brown: By the way, how is he getting on? *(There is a loud gurgling noise from the bath, followed by a splashing sound.* Paddington *begins to sing.)*

Judy: Oh, all right, I think. At least, he seemed all right when I left him.

(Mr. Brown suddenly feels his head.)

Mr. Brown: That's funny. I could have sworn I felt a spot of water.

Mrs. Brown: Don't be silly, Henry. How could you?

Mr. Brown *(Another drop lands on his head.)*: It's happened again!

Jonathan *(Looks up at the ceiling)*: Hey! *(He nudges* Judy.) Look!

Judy *(Looks up too)*: Oh, my! The bath!

Jonathan: Come on!

Mr. Brown: Where are you two going?

Judy: Oh . . . *(Pretending to be casual)*: We're just going upstairs to see how Paddington's getting on. *(She bundles* Jonathan *out of the room.)* Quick!

Mrs. Brown: What was all that about, I wonder?

Mr. Brown: I don't know, Mary. I suppose they're just excited about having a bear in the house. . . .

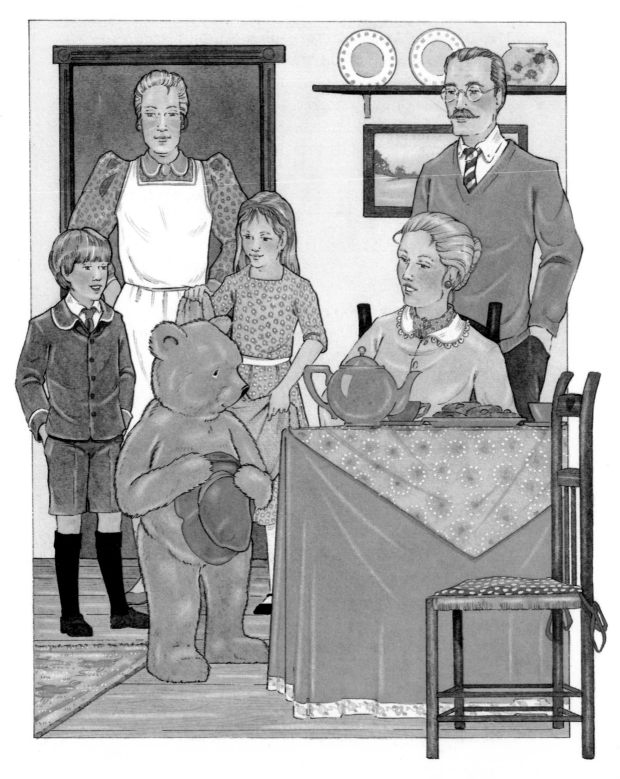

Judy (*Calls offstage*): Are you all right, Paddington?

Paddington: Yes, I think so.

Judy: Oh, oh! Look at this mess!

Judy: Why on earth didn't you turn the tap off? No wonder all the water flowed over.

Paddington: I'm afraid I got soap in my eyes. I couldn't see anything. (*As he is led back into the room by* Jonathan *and* Judy, *he squeezes water out of his hat.*) It's a good thing I had my hat with me. I used it to bail the water out. I might have drowned otherwise.

Mr. Brown: No wonder I thought I felt some water.

Judy: Now you just dry yourself properly, or you'll catch cold. (*She puts a towel round him.*)

Paddington (*Proudly as he looks at himself*): I'm a lot cleaner than I was.

(Mrs. Bird *enters.*)

Mrs. Bird: You'd better give me your hat, Paddington. I'll put it on the line.

Paddington (*Puts his hat back on*): I'd rather you didn't, Mrs. Bird. I don't like being without it. It's my special bush hat, and it belonged to my uncle.

Mrs. Brown: In that case, perhaps you'd like to tell us all about yourself and how you came to emigrate.

Paddington (*Sits down in a chair and makes the most of his audience*): Well . . . I was brought up by my Aunt Lucy. (*He closes his eyes.*)

Jonathan: Your Aunt Lucy?

Paddington (*Sleepily*): Yes. She's the one who lives in the Home for Retired Bears in (*SNORE*)ima. . . .

Mr. Brown (*Puzzled*): In (*SNORE*)-ima! Where is that?

Paddington: It's in Peru, Mr. Brown. (*SNORE*): *Dark-est* Peru.

Judy: Paddington . . . wake up.

(Paddington *gives a longer snore*. Mr. Brown *pokes him gently*.)

Mr. Brown: Well I never. I do believe he's asleep.

Mrs. Brown (*Drapes the towel round him to make him more comfortable*): I'm not really surprised. I don't suppose there are many bears who have had quite such a busy day!

Jonathan and **Judy** (*In chorus*): Especially from (SNORE)-ima.

Curtain

Author

British author Michael Bond wrote his first children's book, *A Bear Called Paddington,* about a small toy bear he had given his wife. Other books about Paddington followed. Alfred Bradley put some of them into play form.

Thinking It Over

Comprehension Questions

1. What funny chain of events began when Paddington went home with the Browns?
2. What happened when Paddington took a bath?
3. Will Paddington fit into the Brown household? Why?

Vocabulary

Tell how you would divide these words into syllables. Then pronounce the words.

scatter   **parcel**   **humor**

Writing a Letter

Pretend you are Paddington. Write a letter to Aunt Lucy telling her about meeting the Browns.

Synonyms

"I'm a rare sort of bear," Paddington chuckled.

"I'm a rare sort of bear," Paddington sighed.

In a play, you can tell how a speaker feels by the way the person playing the part says a line. Speakers can be angry, sad, surprised, or happy. When you read a play, you can tell how a speaker feels by reading the stage directions and by what the other speakers say. The stage directions are the words that are in parentheses beside a person's name. How does Paddington feel when he says this line from the play *The Arrival of Paddington*? How can you tell?

Paddington (*Happily*): I'm a rare sort of bear.

If you wrote a play, you would use stage directions after the person's name. If you wrote a story, you would use a speaker's exact words to show how that person feels.

Paddington said, "I'm a rare sort of bear."

Paddington exclaimed, "I'm a rare sort of bear!"

In these sentences, the words *said* and *exclaimed* show that Paddington was talking, but *exclaimed* gives a better idea of how Paddington felt. *Exclaimed* and *said* are synonyms, or words that mean almost the same thing. By using synonyms for *said,* you can show how a speaker in a story feels.

At the top of the next column are some words you can use in place of *said* to show feelings.

angry: shouted, yelled, grumbled
surprised: gasped, sputtered, stammered
joking: chuckled, joked, jested
sad: sighed, groaned, sobbed
questioning: questioned, asked, wondered
glad: cheered, laughed, rejoiced

Read the lines below from the play *The Arrival of Paddington.* Think how the characters in the play felt when they said the lines. Look back at how Paddington's line was made into sentences using synonyms for *said.* Then write each line as if it were in a story instead of in a play. Use words from the list above or think of others.

Mr. Brown: Mary, you won't believe this, but I've just seen a bear.
Man *(Annoyed)*: We haven't got any cocoa.
Paddington: Things are always happening to me.
Mr. Brown: He's covered with jam and cream! What about me?
Judy *(Happily)*: She *does* like you.

Word Parts

Tom and Jenny had to make two dozen clay animals to sell at the craft fair. "Well," said Tom, "I've counted them all, but I want to be sure I didn't miscount them. Will you recount them, Jenny?"

To understand the sentences you just read, you had to know the meaning of every word. The base word *count* was used several times. Do you know the meaning of *miscount*? Do you know the meaning of *recount*? If you know what *mis-* and *re-* mean, then you know that *miscount* means "count wrong" and *recount* means "count again."

When you read, you need to know how to use word parts called prefixes and suffixes. These word parts are added to base words to form new words. If you come to a word you don't know in your reading, look to see if you already know the base word. Then, if you also know the meaning of the suffix or prefix that is added to the base word, you can often figure out what the word means.

How Are Word Parts Used?

You know that a base word is a word to which prefixes or suffixes may be added. In the word *miscount, count* is the base word.

A prefix is added to the beginning of a base word. Which one is added to make the word *miscount?* The prefix *mis-* changes the meaning of the base word *count.*

A suffix is added to the end of a base word. Which one is used in the word *darkness?* The suffix *-ness* changes the meaning of the base word *dark*, as in this sentence:

The children heard a noise in the darkness.

Because *-ness* means "state of being," you can figure out that *darkness* means "state of being dark."

What suffix is used in the word *cloudy?* The suffix *-y* changes the meaning of the base word *cloud*. Because *-y* means "full of," *cloudy* means "full of clouds."

Sometimes both a prefix and a suffix are added to a base word, as in this sentence:

The baseball player thought the coach showed unfairness in picking his team.

Un- means "not" and *-ness* means "being." So you know that the player thought that the coach was not being fair.

How Do You Use Context with Prefixes and Suffixes?

Some prefixes and suffixes have more than one meaning. For example, the prefix *in-* can mean "not" or "in." To decide which meaning is the right one, read the other words in the sentence. You can tell that *in-* means "not" in the sentence below by the sense of the other words.

The puzzle was incomplete because the children had lost some of the pieces.

In the next sentence, the other words make it clear that *in-* means "in."

That train goes inland from the ocean to the mountains in the center of the state.

Now look at the sense of the other words in the sentence below, and decide which meaning of *in-* is the right one here.

Most butterflies are inactive after dark because their flight muscles are too cold without sunlight.

How Can Word Parts Help Your Understanding?

If you learn what prefixes and suffixes mean, you can figure out many words. Here is part of a news story. Read it, and look for words that have prefixes and suffixes. Be ready to answer a few questions about them.

Yesterday a police officer went to Carey School to talk to the pupils about seat belts. The officer said that seat belts are very useful and that people who wear them have a better chance of being unhurt in a car

crash. Seat belts are easy to wear, but some people still misunderstand the good they do. The police think their work has been unsuccessful even though they have been talking about wearing seat belts for many years. Over half of all people still don't wear them.

How many words with prefixes and suffixes did you find? Write them down, and circle the prefixes and suffixes. Then see if you can answer these questions. Try to use words with prefixes in your answers. Why do the police think their work has been unsuccessful? Why don't some people use seat belts?

Which word in the story was made up of a base word and two word parts? The word *unsuccessful* is made up of the prefix *un-,* the base word *success,* and the suffix *-ful.* The word means "not having success."

Because you knew what the prefixes and suffixes meant in the news story, you were able to understand it. As you read, always look for word parts that may change the meaning of base words.

Using Prefixes and Suffixes

Read the movie review below. For each boldface word, name the prefix or suffix. Then give the meaning of each word. For example, the meaning of the first boldface word is "not safe." To help you, each word part and its meaning are listed in the box at the top of the next page.

The Blue Planet tells the story of the passengers on a star ship that must land on an **unsafe** planet. As the **unlucky** people wait for help, they are scared by the **strangeness** of the planet. They see **unusual** animals and **harmful** plants. One person wanders away from the others and becomes lost. She must then fight off a huge beast before she can **rejoin** her friends.

At times, this is a good space story, but it seems **incomplete**. We need to know more about the passengers and the strange place they landed. At the end, the captain seems to **mishandle** the ship as they leave, but we never find out what happens after that. *The Blue Planet* could have been better.

Prefixes

re-	"again"
un-	"the opposite of," "not"
in-	"not"
in-	"in"
mis-	"wrong," "wrongly"

Suffixes

-y	"full of," "like"
-ness	"quality or state of being"
-ful	"full of," "having"

Skill Summary

To understand words that you read, it helps to know the meanings of word parts.

- A prefix is a word part that is added to the beginning of a base word.
- A suffix is a word part that is added to the end of a base word.
- Sometimes both a prefix and a suffix are added to a base word.
- If a prefix or suffix has more than one meaning, the sense of the other words in the sentence can help you to decide which meaning to use.

Hamilton Hill

by Jean Fritz

How did a surprising visitor, who came up the road from Gettysburg, change Ann's mind about her new life as a pioneer?

In the early 1780's, Ann Hamilton left her comfortable Gettysburg home east of the Allegheny Mountains. She moved with her parents and brothers to a cabin in Hamilton Hill on the western frontier of what is now Pennsylvania. Ann found herself homesick for Gettysburg. She missed her home and school, her cousin Margaret, and the friends and good times she had had there. She found life hard in the Western Country, where her father had little free time and where good times and special things had to wait for "some day." To amuse herself, Ann kept a diary, and when her friend, Andy McPhale, went back east, he gave her a deerskin cover for it. Ann often wrote in her diary in a special place at the side of the road that led from Gettysburg, a road that seemed to hold a special promise for Ann.

Ann fitted the new deerskin cover over the diary. It was very handsome, made from the soft underpart of a deer's skin where the brown shades into a honey color. It looked like a real frontier diary now, Ann thought as she stroked it. She began to turn the pages over, rereading parts she had written. All at once it struck her that on the inside her diary wasn't much like a frontier diary. For the first time she noticed that she had hardly written anything about the Western Country. Most of her entries were about Gettysburg, about Margaret, about her homesickness. If any outsiders were to pick up this diary and read it, they might not even know where it had been written.

She turned the pages more slowly. She had never mentioned what Hamilton Hill looked like. Ann jumped up. She didn't want to think about Hamilton Hill now.

She didn't care if her diary did have a handsome new cover; she didn't feel one bit like writing in it. She went inside the cabin and put the diary up on her shelf.

All day long as Ann went about her chores, she felt out of sorts and out of courage. It wasn't only that the McPhales had gone east while she was staying behind. She didn't know what was bothering her, but everything she did went wrong. She cut her finger when she was chopping pumpkin for her mother to make a pumpkin pie. She spilled half a pail of milk as she was taking lunch to the men in the field. She caught her dress on a prickly bush and tore it. And every time she picked up the baby, he cried.

"This just isn't your day," her mother said toward the middle of the afternoon. "Why don't you go on down the road and try to find some grapes? You'll like that. But mind you don't go too far."

It certainly wasn't her day, Ann thought crossly as she took an empty pail and went out the cabin door. But when she reached the road, she wondered. Maybe, after all, something might yet turn the day her way. The road seemed to have more magic to it than she had ever known. The sun's rays slanted down on it as though they were lighting up a stage where something important was going to happen. There was a difference in the mood of the road. It wasn't a happy, dancing mood, nor a mysterious, moonlight mood. Today there was a grandness to the road, as though it were a carpet unfurling over the hill before some glorious secret. As Ann stood in the middle of the road, holding her pail in front of her, two golden

leaves drifted down, turning slowly over and over in the air, and settled in the bottom of her pail. A wild goose dipped low, honking, from the sky, like a herald sent ahead with news.

Ann walked down the hill, captured by the spell of the road. As she rounded each bend, she found herself half expecting something wonderful to be waiting on the other side. She didn't know what, but something. From time to time she stopped to pick grapes that had survived the storm. On all the hill, the only sounds were the plopping of grapes in her pail and the occasional long honk of a passing goose. Ann followed the road as it wound its way down the hill, turning corner after corner, looking for grapes but secretly hoping for something she couldn't even put into words.

Her pail was almost full when she suddenly noticed where she was. She was almost to the bottom of the hill. Almost to the spot her brother David had pointed out as the site for the first church. She had let the road lead her farther than she had ever gone alone. Instead of something wonderful lying around the next corner of the road, there was probably something dreadful.

And then Ann heard hoofbeats. They were coming from the east — not just one horse but three or four, and they were not far away.

Ann ducked down behind some tall grass by the side of the road and made herself into the smallest ball she could possibly squeeze into, wrapping her arms tightly around her knees. She held her breath as the first horse rounded the bend of the road. She must not move — not even a finger. She kept her eyes on the road, counting the

legs of the horses as they came into sight. Now there were two horses . . . three . . . four. If four men were traveling together from the East to the West at this time of year, they were probably not settlers. They were likely up to no good. They must be the Doane gang that David had warned her about.

All at once Ann began to tremble all over. The first horses had stopped on the road in front of her. Then the other horses came to a stop. As Ann peeped out between the tall grasses, all she could see was a forest of horse legs. From some place way up high above the legs of the first horse came a deep voice. "Little girl," it said, "I wonder if you could tell me what your mother is having for dinner tonight."

The voice didn't sound like the voice of a horse thief. Slowly Ann lifted her eyes from the legs of the horse to the boots of the rider. Slowly she lifted them to the place where the voice had come from. Then she found herself looking into the most wonderful face she had ever seen.

It was a strong face, kind and good, and there was something strangely familiar about it. It was as if Ann ought to know this man, as if she almost knew him. No matter what David had said about strangers, somehow Ann knew deep inside that he hadn't been talking about this one. She stopped feeling afraid. She stood up.

"My mother is having peas and potatoes and corn bread for our evening meal," she said, "and she's baking pumpkin pie."

The man smiled. He leaned down toward Ann. "Would you tell her," he said, "that General George Washington would like to take supper with her?"

For a moment Ann could not believe her ears. General Washington on Hamilton Hill! Then all at once she knew it was true. This was the way she had pictured George Washington from what her friend, Arthur Scott, had said about him. This must have been just how Washington looked, riding among the men at Valley Forge. Suddenly Arthur Scott's words flashed into her mind. "He always seemed to be there just when our courage began to give out."

Ann swallowed hard. She tried to drop a curtsy, but it turned out to be just a stiff little bob. She tried to find her voice, but it didn't turn out any better than the curtsy. It was more like a squeak. "My mother will be pleased," she said. "I'll tell her."

Then Ann found herself and her pail of grapes up on the saddle in front of one of the men in General Washington's party. He said he was Dr. Craik, a friend of the

General's, but Ann didn't pay much attention. She didn't even look at the other men. All she could see was the white horse in front of her and the straight back of General Washington going up Hamilton Hill. The road itself seemed almost to be moving them up the hill in a kind of magic dream. Except it wasn't a dream, Ann reminded herself. It was true — gloriously, wonderfully true. For some unbelievable reason, General George Washington was on the western side of the mountains, and now he was going to have supper with her family on Hamilton Hill.

Suddenly Ann turned to Dr. Craik. "Why did General Washington come here?" she asked.

"He owns land in this county," Dr. Craik replied. "He's come to check on it."

"He owns land here — in Washington County?" Ann repeated.

Dr. Craik smiled. "Yes, he can't move here, but he bought land because he believes in this part of the country. Some day this land will be worth a great deal of money. He wants to do all he can to develop this side of the mountains."

Ann fell silent, her eyes on General Washington. Again she pictured him at Valley Forge. A lot of people hadn't believed in a free and independent country, she thought. But Washington had. And now he believed in the Western Country. It wasn't just fathers and brothers and settlers who believed in it and owned land here. *George Washington did too.*

Ann and Dr. Craik jogged up the hill. The other men called back and forth to each other, but Ann didn't hear them.

Afterward Ann could never remember just how she introduced General Washington and his friends to her mother. When she caught her breath again, they had started on a tour of the farm with David. Ann and her mother were alone in the cabin with supper to prepare.

Mrs. Hamilton's eyes were shining as she stepped away from the door. "Now is the time to use the linen tablecloth, Ann," she said, "and the lavender-flowered plates."

Ann was standing in the doorway, her head in the clouds, watching the men put up their horses. At her mother's words, she came quickly down to the world. What a wonderful world it was, she thought, as she flew over to her mother's chest for the linen tablecloth.

"The food is almost ready," Mrs. Hamilton said. "I'll take care of that while you set the table."

Ann spread out the white linen cloth on the table. She smoothed it gently over the rough boards. She pulled it to hang evenly on all sides. She unwrapped nine flowered plates and placed them around the table. She put knives, forks, and spoons at each place and set new tall candles in the center of the table.

Then Ann stepped back to look at what she had done. Somehow the whole room seemed changed; it seemed larger and more dignified. The clothes hanging awkwardly on hooks along the wall drew back into the shadows. All the light from the fire and from the open doorway fell on the gleaming white party table, waiting for General Washington.

"It's more beautiful than any table we ever set in Gettysburg," Ann whispered.

Mrs. Hamilton looked up from the hearth and smiled.

Later the table looked even more wonderful, piled high with steaming food — hot yellow corn bread, round bowls of green peas, roasted brown potatoes, a platter of cold venison, bowls of purple grape jelly, golden pumpkin pies. It was the same meal that they had had nearly every evening all summer on Hamilton Hill, but tonight with the lavender-flowered plates, it managed to look different.

"I hope I look different too," Ann thought as she fingered her two blue hair ribbons and hastily tied the sash of a fresh apron.

She felt different. General Washington and Mr. Hamilton led the others into the cabin, and suddenly Ann found herself feeling strangely shy. All the time they were taking their places at the table, she kept her eyes down. It was not until her father was asking the blessing that she stole her first look up from under half-closed eyelashes. When she saw George Washington's head bowed over the white tablecloth and lavender-flowered plate and the peas and potatoes, Ann thought she could hardly bear her happiness.

During the rest of the meal, Ann followed the conversation in a kind of daze. She didn't seem to hear anything that anyone said, except General Washington. Everything he said rang out clear, with a special meaning, it almost seemed, just for her.

"If I were a young man," General Washington said, "preparing to begin in the world, I know of no country where I should rather live.

"I am determined to find a way," he said again, "that we can join the waters of the West with those of the East so that the two countries may be close together."

Ann held onto every word, turned them over in her mind, locked them away in her heart. It was after the evening meal, after all the thank-you's had been said and General Washington and his party were preparing to leave, that he said what Ann was to treasure forever afterward. He stood at the doorway, looking toward the west, his eyes resting on Hamilton Hill, yet somehow going beyond.

"The future is traveling west with people like you," he said to Mr. Hamilton. "Here is the rising world — to be kept or lost in the same way a battlefield is kept or lost."

General Washington turned to Ann and put his hand gently on her shoulder. "Through the courage of young girls as much as anyone's, you will live to see this whole

country a rolling farmland, bright with houses and barns and churches some day. I envy you, Miss Hamilton."

Ann felt her heart turning over within her. Even after General Washington had gone, she went on standing in the doorway, still feeling his hand on her shoulder. She looked out on Hamilton Hill. It seemed to her she had never seen it so beautiful — the trees more stately, the sky closer. She remembered the tea party she and her mother had had in the woods. The hill had been lovely that day too. And, of course, the part of the hill that went up and down with the road had always been wonderful.

Ann looked at her vegetable garden laid flat by an earlier storm. It seemed to her that again she could feel the rain beating down on her and her peas. She could feel her own helplessness and despair as the vines broke all around her and she had to fish pods out from the muddy water. Suddenly Ann knew what she had not known before. She had cried during the storm, but it was not really because she hated the Western Country. It was because she loved her vegetable garden.

Other thoughts began crowding in on Ann almost faster than she could take care of them. Maybe she had begun to love Hamilton Hill, too, without even knowing it. Perhaps that was one reason her thoughts had been so mixed up and she hadn't asked if she could go east.

Ann lifted her chin. Well, she was going to plant another vegetable garden in the spring. It was important for her to do it. She was important to the Western Country. George Washington had said so. And some day, she thought . . .

Ann caught herself and smiled. Here she was thinking "some day" just like the others.

Author

Jean Fritz says that she likes best to write about the Revolutionary period. "Hamilton Hill" was taken from *The Cabin Faced West*, which is based on the life of Ann Hamilton, Jean Fritz's great-great-grandmother.

Thinking It Over

Comprehension Questions

1. How did the visit from George Washington change Ann's feelings about her new life?
2. Why had Ann started a diary?
3. What did Ann use to make the dinner special?
4. Why had Washington come to the Western Country?

Vocabulary

These words are from the story: ***dreadful, remind, unwrap, grandness, helpless***. Write each base word, prefix, and suffix on a separate card. Add five more words with prefixes and suffixes, and make cards for them. Use the cards to play a game like Concentration. Match a base word with its prefix or suffix.

Writing a Letter

Look up *Pioneer Life* in the index of a reference book. Then use what you read about the topic to write an imaginary letter about your life as a pioneer.

So Will I

by Charlotte Zolotow

My grandfather remembers long ago
the white Queen Anne's lace that grew wild.
He remembers the buttercups and goldenrod
from when he was a child.

He remembers long ago
the white snow falling falling.
He remembers the bluebird and thrush
at twilight
calling, calling.

He remembers long ago
the new moon in the summer sky.
He remembers the wind in the trees
and its long rising sigh.
And so will I
    so will I.

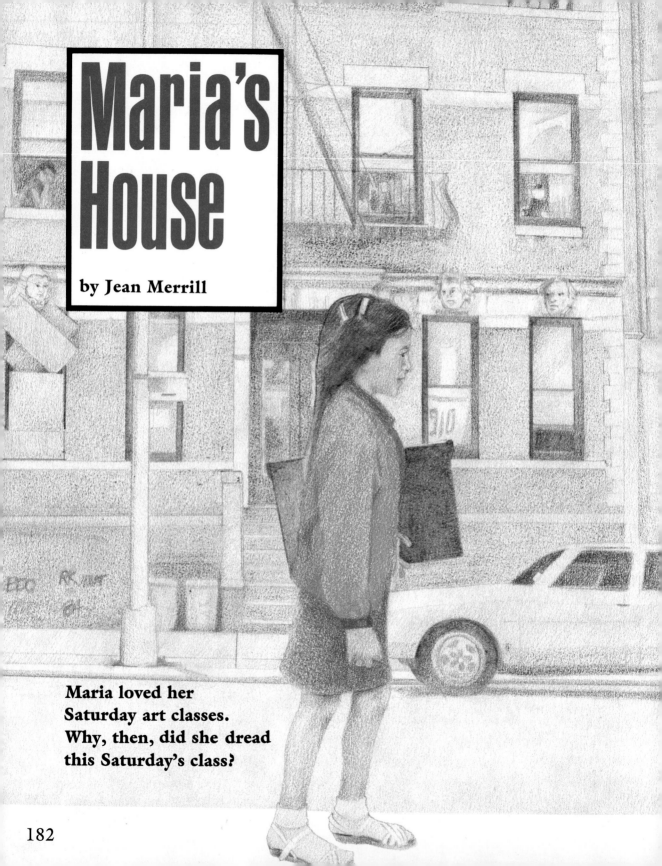

Maria's House

by Jean Merrill

Maria loved her
Saturday art classes.
Why, then, did she dread
this Saturday's class?

"Maria. Maria!"

Mama looked in the door of Maria's room.

"Today is Saturday," Mama said. "Wake up. You will be late for the art class."

Maria lay in bed staring at a crack in the ceiling. She did not want to go to her art class today.

Could she tell Mama that she was sick?

No. Mama would know.

Usually, Maria could not wait for Saturday morning. She loved her art class at the museum. And she liked Miss Lindstrom, her beautiful art teacher.

Usually, Maria was so excited on Saturday morning that she woke up even before the Sanitation Department started banging down the garbage cans outside her window. She would be up and dressed before the table was set for breakfast.

She would brush and braid her hair. Then it would take a long time to decide which of her three smocks she would wear.

Mama had made her three smocks for the art class — a blue one, a yellow one, and a tan one. "Art coats" Mama called them. They were exactly like the smocks Maria's art teacher wore, except that all Miss Lindstrom's smocks were blue.

When Maria came into the kitchen on Saturday morning, Mama would look up to see which smock she was wearing.

"Ah, pretty," Mama would say. "Pretty color on you."

Mama always said "pretty" — no matter which of the three smocks Maria chose.

Maria knew that Mama looked forward to Saturday as much as she did. Mama always looked very pleased with herself as she brought out the old teapot in which she kept the money she earned from ironing shirts for the Overnite Laundry.

Every Saturday morning, it was the same. Mama would count out three quarters from the teapot — two for Maria's bus fare to the museum and an extra one "just in case of something."

Mama would hand the quarters to Maria. Then she would stand at the kitchen door, holding Maria's portfolio, while Maria put on her coat.

"Art bag" Mama called the portfolio. Mama had bought the portfolio at an uptown art store for Maria's birthday.

"Special art bag, so pictures should not be damaged on the way to art class," Mama had explained.

Only two other girls in the class and Miss Lindstrom had portfolios. Maria was very proud of her portfolio.

Everything about Saturday morning made it seem a special day — the clean smock, the three quarters in her

coat pocket, Mama's handing her the portfolio. Maria always felt taller than usual as she walked down to the corner of Market Street to get the bus to the museum.

Maria even liked the long bus ride across town to the museum. She liked watching the city change from block to block.

Yes, everything about Saturday was wonderful. And knowing that Saturday was coming made the rest of the week wonderful too.

All week Maria would dream that the next Saturday might be the day that Miss Lindstrom would stop at her easel and admire the drawing there. She might even choose her drawing to go on the bulletin board that ran around two sides of the large room in which the art class was held.

That hadn't happened yet. Maybe it wouldn't for a long time.

Miss Lindstrom was always kind and encouraging, but she praised you only when your work was very, very good. If one small detail in a drawing pleased Miss Lindstrom, it was enough to make Maria happy all week.

Since Mama had been sending her to the classes at the museum, Maria had begun to draw with one purpose — to make a painting or drawing that Miss Lindstrom would find beautiful.

That was why she could not make herself get out of bed this Saturday. Maria did not want to show Miss Lindstrom the picture that she had finished last night.

Maria had been pleased last week when Miss Lindstrom gave them a special assignment. It wasn't until she got off the bus at Market Street that she realized that she could not do it.

Miss Lindstrom had asked the class to make paintings or drawings of the houses where they lived. As Maria walked down Market Street after class, she saw suddenly that she could not take Miss Lindstrom a picture of the building in which her family and fourteen other families lived.

Miss Lindstrom had said to draw a house. Maria did not think of the building in which she lived as a "house."

It was just an ugly, old building. It was squeezed into the middle of a block of ugly buildings, each one as tired and worn-out looking as the next. How could she make a beautiful picture of 79 Market Street?

Inside the building, the apartment where Maria lived looked bright and fresh. Mama and Papa scrubbed the kitchen floor every day and put new paint on the walls every year.

"Can't put up beautiful pictures on dirty walls," they said. Maria's best paintings and drawings were pinned up in every one of the apartment's three rooms.

The apartment looked nice enough. But from outside, the building looked terrible.

Maria was sure that when Miss Lindstrom said to draw a house, that she was thinking of a house where one family lived, a neat, freshly painted building set apart from other houses by grass, gardens, and shade trees. The kind of house that would have a front yard and a back yard with flowering bushes planted here and there. A house with a private driveway, and even a private sidewalk leading from the city sidewalk up to the front door.

The other children in the art class probably all lived in such houses, out on the edge of the city, just before you came to the country.

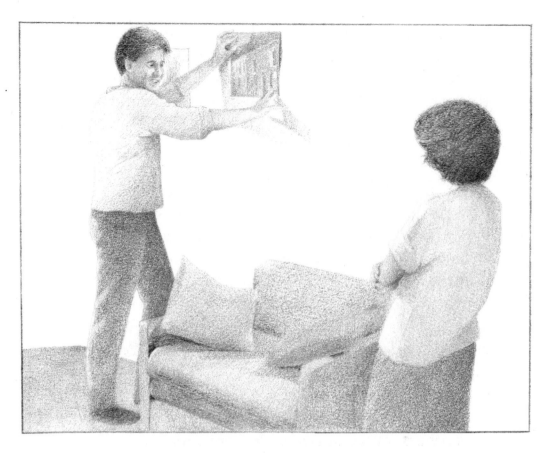

Why, of course. That was why the parents of many of them drove them to the museum on Saturday morning.

None of the other children in the art class lived in buildings like those on Market Street. Nobody on Market Street sent their children to art classes at the museum, except Mama and Papa.

Maria had worried all week about the assignment. How could she do it? There was no way of making a run-down tenement building look beautiful, if you drew it the way it was.

Maria had put off doing the assignment all week. Then last night, Friday night, she had opened her drawing pad on the kitchen table.

She had a new set of colored markers that Mama had bought her. She wanted to do a drawing with them.

She tried all the colors on the cover of the pad. Then she sat for a long time, staring at a clean sheet of drawing paper. Finally, she started to draw.

She drew a large white house with picture windows. The windows looked out over a wide lawn that sloped down to a pond.

Maria sketched in a winding driveway with trees on either side. To one side of the house, she drew a stone terrace and colored in some chairs, covered in a gay, striped cloth.

She wondered if she should put a car in the driveway — or a station wagon.

At the far end of the driveway, Maria drew a figure of a girl on a bicycle.

Mama looked over Maria's shoulder at the drawing.

"Pretty," Mama nodded. "Like a picture in the magazines. But what are you drawing for the art class?"

"This is for class," Maria said.

"A *magazine* picture?" Mama asked.

Mama had learned a lot about art, and she knew by now that art was not like a picture in a magazine. So when she asked about the house, Maria could not lie to her.

"We have to draw a house this week," she said.

"Just a house," Mama said. "Any house? Just a plain house?"

Maria did not answer for a minute. Then she told Mama, "It's supposed to be a picture of the house where we live."

"Oh," Mama said. She looked at Maria's picture again.

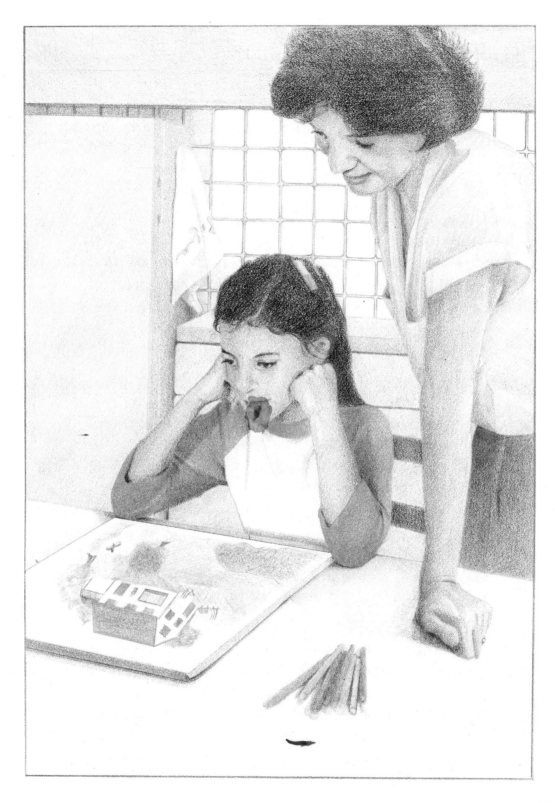

"Our house?" she said.

"No," Maria said. "I can't draw our house."

"Can't draw it?" Mama said. "Before you ever went to art class, you could draw a whole block of houses burning down and five fire engines and ten police officers and a hundred people in the picture. Now you can't draw one house?"

"That's not what I mean," Maria said.

Maria tried to explain to Mama that a three-room apartment on Market Street wasn't the same as a house. And so to do the assignment, she would have to imagine a house.

"But a three-room apartment is in a house," Mama said. "So it's a big house, an apartment house. Your teacher means for you to draw where you live."

Maria jabbed a pencil into the kitchen table.

"Oh, Mama!" she said. "This house is no good to draw. How can I make a beautiful picture of this house? I was trying to make a beautiful picture."

Mama looked down at the house Maria had drawn and shook her head.

"Maybe art should be beautiful," Mama said. "But it should also be true. Your teacher asks you to draw what you know."

Maria did not say anything. What was wrong with using her imagination? An artist should be able to imagine things too.

But the picture did look like a magazine picture. Mama was right about that.

Maria tore the picture from her drawing pad and slipped it into her portfolio. Then she started another drawing.

She sketched in the outline of the house she lived in. With angry slashes of a marker, she drew the rusted fire escape zigzagging down the front of the building. She drew the sagging window frames and the crumbling cement steps leading up to the front door.

There were the broken windows in Mrs. Sedita's apartment on the ground floor. The landlord had refused to fix them, and Mrs. Sedita had had cardboard tacked over the missing panes for a year.

On the windowsill outside the Durkins' apartment, Maria drew three milk cartons. The power company kept turning off the Durkins' electricity, and Mrs. Durkin had to put her milk on the windowsill to keep it cool.

Maria drew Mrs. Katz leaning out of a third-floor window, screaming at a bum slumped on the steps below.

Then she took a marker and lettered on the front of the building the words some kids had painted there in a nasty green color a long time ago.

She was drawing very fast. She put in all the things that made the building look so sad, old, tired, dirty, and ugly. Mama would see that she could not take a picture like this to Miss Lindstrom.

Maria paused and looked at her drawing.

It was 79 Market Street all right. And she hadn't had to go out and look at the building. She knew exactly how it looked.

Except that she had forgotten to put in the carved stone heads. They were the only thing she really liked about the building.

Between the first and second floors, just above the first-floor windows, were four carved stone heads. When the building was built, eighty or ninety years ago, the four stone heads had been set into the brickwork to decorate the building.

Under the heads were four names carved into the stone bases: BACH[1], MOZART[2], BEETHOVEN[3], and WAGNER[4]. Mr. Bocci, the super, had told Maria that they were the names of four famous musicians.

Maria chose a grey marker and carefully drew in the stone heads. She knew the exact expression on each musician's face and how each musician's hair was carved. She was just finishing Bach's funny little sausage curls when Mama came over to look.

---

[1] **Bach** (bäKH)

[2] **Mozart** (mōt′särt′)

[3] **Beethoven** (bā′tō vən)

[4] **Wagner** (väg′nər)

192

Mama studied the picture for a long time. "It's true," she said finally. "It's Market Street." Mama sighed. "Are you going to take it to art class?"

"Mama! I can't."

It was true. It was Market Street. And Maria was afraid she was going to cry.

She ripped the picture off the pad and stuffed it into her portfolio. She put away her markers and pencils, washed, and went to bed.

Now it was Saturday morning. Maria heard Mama calling her for the second time.

No, she could not tell Mama she was sick.

Maria dressed, braided her hair, and put on her yellow smock.

When Mama said "Pretty" as Maria came into the kitchen, Maria could not look Mama in the eye.

Mama did not say much at breakfast. And when she took down the old teapot and fished out the three quarters, Maria wanted to say, "Please, Mama, try to understand."

But she couldn't say it. And when Mama went to wake up Papa, Maria knew what she had to do.

She opened up her portfolio and took out the drawing of the white house with the picture windows. She looked at the drawing for a minute. The she tore it up and put it in the garbage can.

Mama must have known. She nodded her head in a proud stern way as Maria went out the door.

Maria felt better as she walked to the bus stop. But once on the bus, she began to think about Miss Lindstrom again and wished she had stayed home.

The city streets flashed by in the crazy way they do in a dream that is going too fast and is going to end in a terrible way. Suddenly the bus was at the museum.

Maria walked quickly through the big entrance room. Most of the kids in the class were already at their easels when Maria came in and were pinning up the drawings they had done during the week.

Coming in late, though, Maria felt as if everyone was watching her. Quickly, she opened up her portfolio and took out her drawing.

Her hands were clumsy as she tacked the drawing to her easel, afraid someone might laugh. But no one did.

Glancing over her shoulder, Maria saw that the other students were looking at their own work, some of them adding a few lines to their pictures. Others were trying to smudge out bits they didn't like.

Miss Lindstrom was already walking around looking at what everyone had done. At one easel, she would nod and smile. At another, she would ask a question. Now and then she would call the whole class to look at something unusual in someone's drawing.

Maria trailed behind the others, hardly hearing what Miss Lindstrom was saying.

Most of the drawings on the easels were of houses with yards and trees as Maria had expected, but many of the houses pictured were less grand than she'd imagined. None were as grand as the one she'd wanted to draw for Miss Lindstrom.

There was one picture that surprised Maria because the house in it looked quite old and shabby. The house was set in a big yard and had a funny tower on one side, which perhaps had made it look very handsome at one time. But the house looked now as if it needed painting, and there was one very messy-looking part of the yard with a lot of boards and boxes scattered around.

A redheaded boy named Jasper had painted the picture. Jasper pointed to the house in the painting.

"This is where I live," he told Miss Lindstrom. "But over here is where I'm going to live." He pointed to the boards and boxes.

"That's the most important part of the picture," he explained. "I'm building my own house out here. I'm designing it myself, and it's going to be really beautiful."

Miss Lindstrom laughed. "Is it going to have a tower?" she asked.

"Certainly not," Jasper said. "It's going to be a very modern house. With see-through walls that you can walk through to get outdoors."

The class laughed. Then Miss Lindstrom talked about how it was clear from the way Jasper had placed the house off to one side in the picture that the messy pile of boards was the most important part of the picture.

There was always something funny in Jasper's paintings, a kind of crazy way of looking at things. But Miss Lindstrom seemed to like Jasper's work.

Maria was puzzling over this when Miss Lindstrom moved over to her easel. Maria's hands felt cold. Her mouth felt dry. She wanted to run down the hall to the washroom and hide. But she just stood there by Jasper's easel, watching Miss Lindstrom.

There was a brief look of surprise on Miss Lindstrom's face, and Maria wished she could sink through the floor.

Miss Lindstrom did not say anything for a minute. Then she looked around for Maria.

"Maria," she called. "Come." She put an arm around Maria's shoulder.

"Everyone come here," she called.

The rest of the class crowded around Maria's easel.

Miss Lindstrom was saying, "Look what she's done."

Miss Lindstrom stepped back to let everyone see.

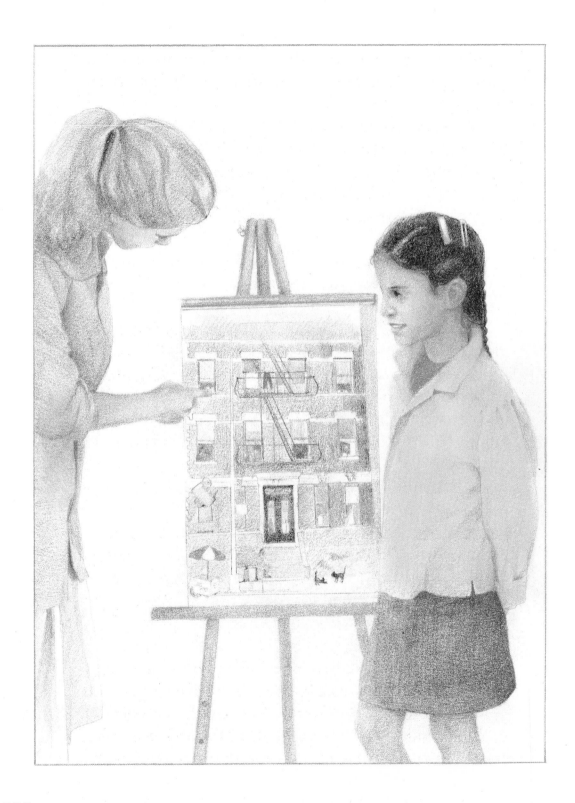

"I'd meant for you to draw your own house," Miss Lindstrom said to Maria. "But what you've done is very interesting."

Miss Lindstrom asked the class whether any of them had ever driven through Carpenter Street, Market Street, or Water Street — the old part of town down near the river.

"I have," Jasper said. "My uncle goes there to buy fish."

"If any of you have," Miss Lindstrom said, "you will see how perfectly Maria has caught the feeling of the crowded tenements in that part of town.

"Look." Miss Lindstrom bent over Maria's drawing. "See here," she said, " — and here — and here — " The art teacher's beautiful hands touched the paper lightly.

"So many beautiful things," she said.

Miss Lindstrom pointed to the laundry strung across the fire escape on the third floor, to the cats fighting over a spilled garbage can in front of the house, to a tired figure leaning on a windowsill, to the milk cartons on another sill.

"I can almost hear the kids yelling in the street," Miss Lindstrom said. "I can hear people yelling, laughing, and crying inside the apartments. I can smell spaghetti cooking. And chicken soup."

"Not me," Jasper said. "I smell fish."

Miss Lindstrom laughed. "You're right, Jasper. I can smell that too. There's so much going on in this house."

Now Miss Lindstrom was looking at the stone heads.

"And these heads," she said. "Look at these. When this building was built years ago, someone lovingly carved those heads, and Maria has drawn them so lovingly that you can feel the care the stonecutter took in carving them. Does everyone see what is so good about Maria's drawing?"

"All those little details," one girl said. "The heads, the cats, the milk cartons, and even the writing on the front of the building."

"No," another girl said. "All those bits are nice. Maria can draw anything. What's really good is that her picture isn't just a picture of a building. You feel as if you know the people who live in it."

"Yes," Miss Lindstrom said. "That's it. It's a beautiful drawing, Maria. Full of life and feeling. The nicest thing you've done this year." She gave Maria a hug and moved on to another easel.

Maria stood staring at her picture.

Miss Lindstrom had hugged her and told her that her picture was beautiful. But it wasn't Miss Lindstrom with her spun-gold hair that Maria was seeing as she stared at her picture.

She was seeing Mama. Mama was saying stubbornly, "Art must be true." Mama standing and nodding gravely as Maria would tell her what Miss Lindstrom had said about her drawing today. . . .

Then Maria heard Miss Lindstrom say her name again.

"Maria," she said, "maybe you would like to draw your own house next week."

Maria felt as if Mama's grave eyes were on her as she looked up at her art teacher and said in a clear, sure voice, "But that *is* my house in the picture."

Author

Jean Merrill worked as an editor in New York City. The description of Maria's apartment house comes from the author's knowledge of a big city. The popular *Toothpaste Millionaire* is another of Jean Merrill's books.

Thinking It Over

Comprehension Questions

1. Why did Maria not want to go to art class?
2. What had Mama given Maria for her art classes?
3. Why was the teacher excited about Maria's picture?
4. Why was Maria surprised when she saw the other students' pictures?

Vocabulary

These homographs are from "Maria's House": *lawn, plain, down, stern*. Look them up in a dictionary and write a sentence for each entry.

Writing a Descriptive Paragraph

Find a picture in color. Look closely at the picture and write an accurate description of it.

Main Idea

A good author puts sentences about the same idea together in one paragraph. The author uses details to explain the idea or gives examples to make the idea clearer. When ideas are presented in this orderly way, it is easier to understand what the author is saying.

A good reader learns to decide what the main idea is in a paragraph. When you know that, you are able to understand and remember what you read.

How Do You Find the Main Idea?

The **topic** of a paragraph is the one thing that all or most of the sentences in a good paragraph tell about. The **main idea** is a sentence that sums up what the other sentences in the paragraph are telling about the topic.

When you read a paragraph, look for a sentence that sums up what all the sentences say about the topic. Read the following paragraph. Then find the sentence that states the main idea.

People keep some strange kinds of animals as pets. People have owned monkeys, chickens, turtles, and even snakes. Some brave people have owned alligators and tigers. Some own strange birds, such as the owl. Some pet lovers have tamed foxes and deer and lizards.

The topic of that paragraph is *Strange Kinds of Pets.* All the sentences tell something about strange kinds of pets. Which sentence states the main idea? Did you decide that the first sentence summed up the facts that were given in the other sentences? When the main idea is stated in a paragraph, that sentence may be found at the beginning, the middle, or the end.

Sometimes the main idea is not stated. When this happens, you must make up a sentence that sums up what all the sentences are about. These steps will help you to decide what the main idea is.

1. Find the topic. Do this by deciding what all or most of the sentences tell about.
2. Think about the way in which all of the sentences go together. Decide what one idea ties all the sentences together.
3. Then make up a main idea sentence that sums up what all the sentences are telling about the topic.

Now read the following paragraph. Then make up a sentence that will best tell the main idea.

Long ago, people built their homes from the wood and bark of trees. They used wood to build boats and canoes. Today, people build houses, furniture, and many other things out of wood. Newspapers and books are printed on paper made from trees. Wood is also used for making things that were not even thought of in earlier days, such as plastic. The plastic comb you use may have started as part of a tree.

Decide what main idea sums up the paragraph. First, what is the topic? The paragraph is about wood. Think about the facts that are given. What do they tell you about wood? Does each sentence tell you about the uses of wood?

A main idea for the paragraph might be stated in this way: *Wood has many different uses.* Another way to state the main idea might be *People use wood for many different reasons.*

What Are Supporting Details?

To support means "to help." **Supporting details** are the facts that tell something about the main idea. They help make the main idea clearer and easier to remember. They help in these two ways:

- They make the paragraph more interesting.
- They help you figure out the main idea because they tell many things about it.

In the paragraph about wood, the author gave important and interesting details about how people use it. The first and second sentences tell you that people long ago used wood to build homes, boats, and canoes. These are supporting details. The next three sentences tell you that people today use wood for houses, furniture, paper, plastic, and many other things. The last sentence tells about something made from plastic that may have come from wood. When you put all the supporting details together you have quite a few facts to help you figure out that the main idea is *Wood has many different uses.*

How Do You Find Supporting Details?

To help you find and remember supporting details, it is sometimes helpful to draw a wheel, as shown below. This wheel shows the main idea and supporting details for the paragraph about wood.

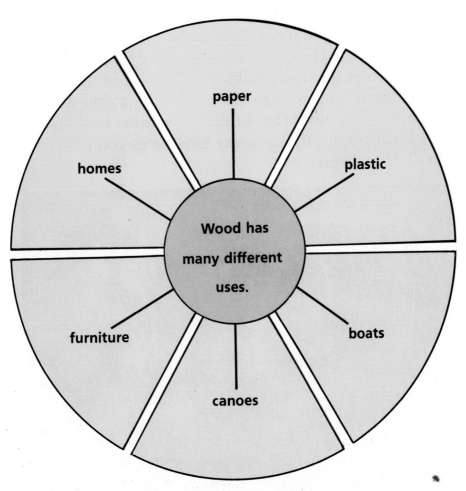

You can see that this wheel was easy to draw. The different uses were listed around the main-idea sentence. The wheel quickly shows you what the details are and how they support the main idea.

Determining the Main Idea

Read the following paragraphs, and use the steps you have learned to figure out the main ideas. Then answer the questions that follow each paragraph.

A. Some birds have very long songs. Other birds, like the bobwhite, have short, clear whistles. The songs of some birds, like the crow, are loud and high; but other birds, such as the dove, make a very low, cooing sound. The red-winged blackbird has its own song, but it can also copy the sounds that other birds make. It would take time to learn the different bird songs you could hear in any forest.

A pair of bobwhites.

1. What is the topic of this paragraph?
2. Write a sentence that best states the main idea of this paragraph.
3. What supporting details are given here?

B. Forest rangers help take care of forests. One of their important jobs is to protect the trees in the forests against insects and fire. They also check on people who cut trees for lumber. Rangers may even have to find lost or hurt visitors to the forests.

---

4. What is the topic of this paragraph?
5. Write a sentence that best states the main idea of this paragraph.
6. What supporting details are given here?

Skill Summary

- The topic of a paragraph is the one thing that all or most of the sentences in the paragraph tell about.
- The main idea of a paragraph is a sentence that sums up what the other sentences are telling about the topic.
- Sometimes the main idea is given in the paragraph. Look for a sentence that best sums up what all the sentences say about the topic. This sentence can be anywhere in the paragraph.
- If the main idea is not directly stated in the paragraph, make up one of your own. Decide what the topic is. Think about what each of the sentences tells about the topic. Then make up a sentence that sums up what all the sentences are telling about the topic.
- Supporting details help you to figure out the main idea.

HOW THE FOREST GREW

by William Jaspersohn

When you stand in a tall, dark forest, you may think that it has been there forever. How does a forest grow from seedlings to trees?

Have you ever wondered where forests come from, and how they grow? This article is about a hardwood forest in Massachusetts. It could be about a forest anywhere because most forests grow the same way. To find out how this Massachusetts forest grew, we must go back in time. We must see how the forest land looked two hundred years ago.

About two hundred years ago the land was open and green. Then the farmer and his family who had cleared and farmed the land moved away. But then changes began. The wind blew seeds across the fields. Birds dropped seeds from the air. The sun warmed the seeds. The rain watered them, and they grew.

In a few years the land was filled with weeds — with dandelions and goldenrod and chickweed. There was milkweed with its pods of fluff and ragweed and black-eyed Susans. Each spring new plants took root. The land began to look different. Burdock and briars grew among the weeds, making the land moist and brushy.

Blackberries grew. Birds came to eat them — song sparrows, bobolinks, and catbirds. Meadow mice and cottontail rabbits made their nests in the tall grass. Woodchucks, moles, and shrews dug their tunnels in the ground. Snakes came to feed on the small animals. Hawks and owls hunted over the land for their food. Time passed.

And then one summer five years after the farm family left, a tree seedling sprouted. It wasn't a cedar or a birch seedling, or a poplar or an aspen seedling, though it could have been because these trees like full sunlight. No, it was a young white pine, another sun-loving tree. The wind had blown its seed from a nearby forest. The seed sprouted.

That same summer more white pine seedlings came up. The land was speckled with tiny dots of green. Year after year, through weeds and low brush, the little trees pushed their way up. Tree scientists call the first trees that take hold on a piece of land *pioneer trees*. That is what these white pines were. No other sun-loving tree grows in such numbers, or so fast.

As the pine trees grew, brush-dwelling birds moved onto the land. They replaced the field dwellers. Towhees, warblers, and field sparrows made their homes in the thickets. But so did weasels and foxes who caught mice, rabbits, and birds for their dinner.

Twenty years after the first young pines sprouted, the land was covered with white pines. Their branches blocked the sun's rays. The old weeds and grasses died from want of light. What the pines did to the old weeds, they also did to their own kind. When new white pine trees tried to grow, they couldn't get sunlight, and they died.

Only those seedlings that liked the shade grew beneath the stands of white pines. Ash trees, red oak, red

maple, and tulip trees — these were the trees that the white pines helped the most. In less than fifteen years, the new trees were crowding the white pines for space. A struggle had begun; only the strongest trees would survive. Scientists call this change from one kind of tree or animal to a new kind *succession*. They say that one kind of tree or animal succeeds another.

As the new trees on the land began to succeed the old pines, the animal life on the land changed too. The meadow mice moved because their food supply was gone, and there was no more grass for them to build their nests. White-footed mice took their place. They made their nests in hollow stumps and logs. They ate seeds from the trees and shrubs.

For the first time deer came to live on the land. Now there were places for them to hide and tender shoots for them to eat.

Cardinals perched in the trees. So did redstarts, oven-birds, and ruffed grouse. Squirrels and chipmunks brought nuts onto the land. Some of these sprouted with the other seedlings.

Forty years had passed since the farmer and his family had left. And then one summer afternoon, fifty years after the farm family had gone, a storm broke over the land. Lightning struck the tallest pines, killing some of them and damaging others. Strong winds uprooted more pines, and lightning fires scorched branches.

But this is how forests grow. The death of some of the pine trees made room for new and different trees that had been sprouting on the forest floor. As time passed, insects and disease hurt the other pines. Every time one of them died, a red oak, white ash, or red maple tree took its place.

The forest grew. By the year 1860, more than eighty years after the farm family had left, the weeds were all gone. The pioneer white pines were nearly all gone. Red oaks, red maples, and ash trees were everywhere. The forest had reached its *middle stage*.

Now on the forest floor came the last of the new seedlings. These were the beeches and the sugar maples, trees that like the deep shade. The other young trees — the red oak, red maple, and ash — needed more light. And some of them needed more water and different kinds of soil to grow in. So they died, and the young beech and the sugar maple trees took their place.

Every autumn the trees lost their leaves. They fell to the ground with dead twigs and branches. All of these things decayed and made a rich layer of stuff called *humus*. Then slowly, bacteria, worms, and fungi turned the humus into soil from which the trees got food and water. Sometimes an animal or an insect died, and its body became part of the humus too.

One hundred years had passed since the farm family had moved. Now, whenever a red oak, red maple, or white ash tree died, it made room for the smaller beeches and sugar maples. These formed a layer below the older trees called an *understory*.

Every winter, snow blanketed the forest floor. Every spring, the ground was covered with wildflowers. Year after year, the beeches and sugar maple trees pushed their branches toward the sky. Hemlocks grew in their shade. Slowly, one by one, most of the red oak, red maple, and ash trees disappeared.

By the year 1927, which was one hundred and fifty years after the forest had begun, the beeches and sugar maples were kings of the forest. Today a family owns the land, and they love the peaceful forest. They built their house on the same spot where the farm family once built theirs. But they do not clear the land this time. Instead, they listen and look. What was once open fields is now a magnificent forest. It is home for many wild animals — for foxes, bobcats, wood turtles, chipmunks, bears, deer, squirrels, mice, porcupines, and many other creatures.

Its tree roots hold water and keep the soil from washing away. Birds of many kinds nest in its branches. Its humus enriches the earth's soil. All through the world other forests are growing like the one in Massachusetts. The kinds of trees in each forest may be different, but the way they grow is very much the same. Nothing in a forest ever stands still.

Author

William Jaspersohn knows New England well. It is the setting for his third children's book, *How the Forest Grew*. This book won the Boston Globe-Horn Book Award.

Comprehension Questions

1. What are the stages of growth of a forest?
2. What do scientists call the first trees that grow in an open space?
3. What is the sentence that gives the main idea of the third paragraph on page 209? What are some of the supporting details?
4. What is the main idea of the first paragraph on page 213? Give two supporting details.

Vocabulary

The words below are the names of birds and animals in the forest. Write each name on a card and sort them into categories.

sparrows	warblers	moles
grouse	woodchucks	cardinals
porcupines	shrews	chipmunks
foxes		

Making a Graph

Look up the main topic *Forest* or *Forest products* in a reference book. Make a line graph that shows the states that lead in forest products and how much wood is cut each year in those states. Write a caption for your graph.

Forest Alphabet

A forest is more than a group of trees. A forest is a home for many different plants, birds, insects, and animals. People live and work in the forest too. In fact, so many different things share the woods that there is likely to be something that lives in the forest for every letter from A to Z. If you try, you might be able to come up with a whole forest alphabet.

First list all the forest words that you can think of. Then put them into groups, such as the ones that follow.

218

Trees in the forest:
Ash, *walnut,* and *elm* are three that may be useful to you.

Plants in the forest:
Ferns and *Indian pipes* are two to start with.

Birds in the forest:
Kinglets, turkeys, and *owls* might be added to your list.

Other creatures in the forest:
Here you might want to add some insects and animals and maybe a snail or two.

People using the forest:
You might meet a *zoologist* studying the animals or a *botanist* gathering plants.
Hikers like to camp in the forest, and *rangers* are always on the watch for forest fires.

You could also add forest products to your list. Valuable amounts of *paper, rubber,* and *lumber* come from forests.

When you have thought of all the forest words you can, make a forest alphabet with the words from your list. If you can't think of a word for every letter, you may need to look in a book. Start your forest alphabet something like this:

A is for aspens.
B is for bears.
C is for chipmunks.

Something Extra

Choose a few of your favorite animals from the forest alphabet. Look them up in a reference book and write a paragraph about each animal. Draw pictures of the animals and make a forest encyclopedia with your classmates. Share the encyclopedia with other classes in your school.

Are Your Arms a Hundred Years Old?

by Sharon Bell Mathis

Michael was determined to save Aunt Dew's hundred penny box. Why did the old box mean so much to Aunt Dew and Michael?

Michael's great-great-aunt, Dewbet Thomas, has come to live with Michael and his parents. "Aunt Dew" has a precious old wooden box — her hundred penny box. The importance of this box is not understood by Michael's mother, but Michael feels that the box is very important. He knows how much it means to Aunt Dew. As this part of the story opens, Michael has just told Aunt Dew that he is going to hide the box to keep it safe.

"No, don't hide my hundred penny box!" Aunt Dew said out loud. "Leave my hundred penny box right alone. Anybody takes my hundred penny box takes me!"

"Just in case," Michael said impatiently and wished his great-great-aunt would sit back down in her chair so he could talk to her.

"What your momma name?"

"Oh, no," Michael said. "You keep on forgetting Momma's name!" That was the only thing bad about being a hundred years old like Aunt Dew — you kept on forgetting things that were important.

"Hush, John-boy," Aunt Dew said and stopped dancing and humming and sat back down in the chair and put the quilt back over her legs.

"You keep on forgetting."

"I don't."

"Do I forget to play with you when you worry me to death to play?"

Michael didn't answer.

"Do I forget to play when you want?"

"No."

"Okay. What your momma name? Who's that in my kitchen?"

"Momma's name is Ruth, but this isn't your house. Your house is in Atlanta. We went to get you and now you live with us."

"Ruth."

Michael saw Aunt Dew staring at him again. Whenever she stared at him like that, he never knew what she'd say next. Sometimes it had nothing to do with what they had been talking about.

"You John's baby," she said, still staring at him. "Look like John just spit you out."

"That's my father."

"My great-nephew," Aunt Dew said. "Only one ever care about me." Aunt Dew rocked hard in her chair then and Michael watched her. He got off the bed and turned off the record player and put the record back into the bottom drawer. Then he sat down on the hundred penny box.

"See that tree out there?" Aunt Dew said and pointed her finger straight toward the window with the large tree pressed up against it. Michael knew exactly what she'd say.

"Didn't have no puny-looking trees like that near my house," she said. "Dewbet Thomas, that's me, and Henry Thomas, that was my late husband, had the biggest, tallest, prettiest trees and the widest yard in all Atlanta.

"And John, that was your daddy, liked it most because he was city and my five sons, Henry, Jr., and Truke and

222

Latt and the twins — Booker and Jay — well, it didn't make them no never mind because it was always there.

"But when my oldest niece Junie and her husband — we called him Big John — brought your daddy down to visit every summer, they couldn't get the suitcase in the house good before he was climbing up and falling out the trees. We almost had to feed him up them trees!"

"Aunt Dew, we have to hide the box."

"Junie and Big John went out on that water and I was feeling funny all day. Didn't know what. Just feeling funny.

"I told Big John, I said, 'Big John, that boat old. Nothing but a piece a junk.' But he fooled around and said, 'We taking it out.'

"I looked and saw him and Junie on that water. Then it wasn't nothing. Both gone. And the boat turned over, going downstream.

"Your daddy, brand-new little britches on, just standing there looking, wasn't saying nothing. No hollering. I try to give him a big hunk of potato pie. But he just looking at me, just looking and standing. Wouldn't eat none of that pie. Then I said, 'Run get Henry Thomas and the boys.' He looked at me, and then he looked at that water. He turned round real slow and walked toward the west field. He never run. All you could see was them stiff little britches — red they was — moving through the corn. Bare-waisted, he was. When we found the boat

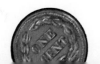

later, he took it clean apart — what was left of it — every plank, and pushed it back in that water. I watched him. Wasn't a piece left of that boat. Not a splinter."

"Aunt Dew, where can we hide the box?"

"What box?"

"The hundred penny box."

"We can't hide the hundred penny box, and if she got to take my hundred penny box — she might as well take me!"

"We have to hide it!"

"No — we don't. It's my box!"

"It's my house. And I said we have to hide it!"

"How you going to hide a house, John!"

"Not the house! Our hundred penny box!"

"It's my box!"

Michael was beginning to feel desperate. "Suppose Momma takes it when you go to sleep?"

Aunt Dew stopped rocking and stared at him again. "Like John just spit you out," she said. "Go on count them pennies, boy. 'Less you worry me in my grave if you don't. Dewbet Thomas's hundred penny box. Dewbet Thomas a hundred years old, and I got a penny to prove it — each year!"

Michael got off the hundred penny box and sat on the floor by his great-great-aunt's skinny feet stuck down inside his father's old slippers. He pulled the big wooden box toward him and lifted the lid and reached in and took

out the small cloth roseprint sack filled with pennies. He dumped the pennies out into the box.

He was about to pick up one penny and put it in the sack, the way they played, and say "One," when his great-great aunt spoke.

"Why you want to hide my hundred penny box?"

"To play," Michael said to her, after he thought for a moment.

"Play now," she said. "Don't hide my hundred penny box. I got to keep looking at my box, and when I don't see my box, I won't see me neither."

"One!" Michael said and dropped the penny back into the old print sack.

"18 and 74," Aunt Dew said. "Year I was born. Slavery over! Black men in Congress running things. They was in charge. It was the Reconstruction."

Michael counted twenty-seven pennies back into the old print sack before she stopped talking about Reconstruction. "19 and 01," Aunt Dew said. "I was twenty-seven years. Birthed my twin boys. Hattie said, 'Dewbet, you got two babies.' I asked Henry Thomas. I said, 'Henry Thomas, what them boys look like?'"

By the time Michael had counted fifty-six pennies, his mother was standing at the door.

"19 and 30," Aunt Dew said. "Depression. Henry Thomas, that was my late husband, died. Died after he put the fifty-six penny in my box. He had the double pneumonia and no decent shoes, and he worked too hard. Said he was going to sweat the trouble out his lungs.

Couldn't do it. Same year I sewed that fancy dress for Rena Coles. She want a hundred bows all over that dress. I was sewing bows and tying bows and twisting bows. Henry the one started that box, you know. Put the first thirty-one pennies in it for me and it was my birthday. After fifty-six, I put them all in myself."

"Aunt Dew, time to go to bed," his mother said, standing at the door.

"Now, I'm not sleepy," Aunt Dew said. "John-boy and me just talking. Why you don't call him John? Look like John just spit him out. Why you got to call that boy something different from his daddy?"

Michael watched his mother walk over and open the window wide. "We'll get some fresh air in here," she said. "And then, Aunt Dew, you can take your nap better and feel good when you wake up." Michael wouldn't let his mother take the sack of pennies out of his hand. He held tight and then she let go.

"I'm not sleepy," Aunt Dew said again. "This child and me just talking."

"I know," his mother said, pointing her finger at him a little. "But we're just going to take our nap anyway."

"I got a long time to sleep and I'm not ready now. Just leave me sit here in this little narrow piece a room. I'm not bothering nobody."

"Nobody said you're bothering anyone, but as soon as I start making that meat loaf, you're going to go to sleep in your chair and fall out again and hurt yourself. And John'll wonder where I was and say I was on the telephone, and that'll be something all over again."

"Well, I'll sit on the floor and if I fall, I'll be there already, and it won't be nobody's business but my own."

"Michael," his mother said and took the sack of pennies out of his hand and laid it on the dresser. Then she reached down and closed the lid of the hundred penny box and pushed it against the wall. "Go out the room, honey, and let Momma help Aunt Dew into bed."

"I been putting Dewbet Thomas to bed a long time, and I can still do it," Aunt Dew said.

"I'll just help you a little," Michael heard his mother say through the closed door.

As soon as his mother left the room, he'd go in and sneak out the hundred penny box.

But where would he hide it?

Michael went into the bathroom to think, but his mother came in to get Aunt Dew's washcloth. "Why are you looking like that?" she asked. "If you want to play, go in my room. Play there, or in the living room. And don't go bothering Aunt Dew. She needs her rest."

Michael went into his father and mother's room and lay down on the big king bed and tried to think of a place to hide the box.

He had an idea!

He'd hide it down in the furnace room and sneak Aunt Dew downstairs to see it so she'd know where it was. Then maybe they could sit on the basement steps inside and play with it sometimes. His mother would never know. And his father wouldn't care as long as Aunt Dew was happy. He could even show Aunt Dew the big pipes and the little pipes.

Michael heard his mother close his bedroom door and walk down the hall toward the kitchen.

He'd tell Aunt Dew right now that they had a good place to hide the hundred penny box. The best place of all.

Michael got down from the huge bed and walked quietly back down the hall to his door and knocked on it very lightly — too lightly for his mother to hear.

Aunt Dew didn't answer.

"Aunt Dew," he whispered after he'd opened the door and tiptoed up to the bed. "It's me. Michael."

Aunt Dew was crying.

Michael looked at his great-great-aunt and tried to say something, but she just kept crying. She looked extra small in his bed, and the covers were too close about her neck. He moved them down a little, and then her face didn't look so small. He waited to see if she'd stop crying, but she didn't. He went out of the room and down the hall and stood near his mother. She was chopping up celery. "Aunt Dew's crying," he said.

"That's all right," his mother said. "Aunt Dew's all right."

"She's crying real hard."

"When you live long as Aunt Dew's lived, honey — sometimes you just cry. She'll be all right."

Michael tiptoed into his room. "Aunt Dew?"

"What you want, John-boy?"

"I'm sorry Momma's mean to you."

"Isn't nobody mean to Dewbet Thomas — 'cause Dewbet Thomas isn't mean to nobody," Aunt Dew said, and reached her hand out from under the cover and patted Michael's face. "Your Momma Ruth. She move

around and do what she got to do. First time I see
her — I say, 'John, she look frail but she isn't.' He said,
'No, she isn't frail.' I make out like I don't see her all the
time," Aunt Dew said, and winked her eye. "But she
know I see her. If she think I don't like her that isn't the
truth. Dewbet Thomas like everybody. But me and her
can't talk like me and John talk — 'cause she don't know
all what me and John know."

"I closed the door," Michael said. "You don't have to sleep if you don't want to."

"I been sleep all day, John," Aunt Dew said.

Michael leaned over his bed and looked at his great-great-aunt. "You haven't been sleep all day," he said. "You've been sitting in your chair and talking to me, and then you were dancing to your record, and then we were counting pennies, and we got to fifty-six, and then Momma came."

"Where my hundred penny box?"

"I got it," Michael answered.

"Where you got it?"

"Right here by the bed."

"Watch out while I sleep."

He'd tell her about the good hiding place later. "Okay," he said.

Aunt Dew was staring at him. "Look like John just spit you out," she said.

Michael moved away from her. He turned his back and leaned against the bed and stared at the hundred penny box. All of a sudden it looked real *real* old and beat up.

"Turn round. Let me look at you."

Michael turned around slowly and looked at his great-great-aunt.

"John!"

"It's me," Michael said. "Michael."

He went and sat down on the hundred penny box.

"Come here so I can see you," Aunt Dew said.

Michael didn't move.

"Stubborn like your daddy. Don't pay your Aunt Dew no never mind!"

Michael still didn't get up.

"Go on back and do your counting out my pennies. Start with fifty-seven — where you left off. 19 and 31. Latt married that schoolteacher. We roasted three pigs."

"First you know me, then you don't," Michael said.

"Michael John Jefferson what your name is," Aunt Dew said. "Should be plain John like your daddy and your daddy's daddy — 'stead of all this new stuff. Name John and everybody saying 'Michael.'" Aunt Dew was smiling. "Come here, boy," she said. "Come here close. Let me look at you. Got a head full of hair."

Michael got up from the hundred penny box and stood at the foot of the bed.

"Get closer," Aunt Dew said.

Michael did.

"Turn these covers back little more. This little narrow piece a room don't have the air the way my big house did."

"I took a picture of your house," Michael said and turned the covers back some more.

"My house bigger than your picture," Aunt Dew said. "Way bigger."

Michael leaned close to her on his bed and propped his elbows up on the large pillow under her small head. "Tell me about the barn again," he said.

"Dewbet and Henry Thomas had the biggest, reddest barn in all Atlanta, G–A!"

"And the swing Daddy broke?" Michael asked and put his head down on the covers. Her chest was so thin under the thick quilt that he hardly felt it. He reached up and pushed a few wispy strands of her hair away from her closed eyes.

"Did more pulling it down than he did swinging."

"Tell me about the swimming pool," Michael said. He touched Aunt Dew's chin and covered it up with only three fingers.

It was a long time before Aunt Dew answered. "Wasn't no swimming pool," she said. "I done told you was a creek. Plain old creek. And your daddy like to got bit by a cottonmouth."

"Don't go to sleep, Aunt Dew," Michael said. "Let's talk."

"I'm tired, John."

"I can count the pennies all the way to the end if you want me to."

"Go 'head and count."

"When your hundred and one birthday comes, I'm going to put in the new penny like you said."

"Yes, John."

Michael reached up and touched Aunt Dew's eyes. "I have a good place for the hundred penny box, Aunt Dew," he said quietly.

"Go 'way. Let me sleep," she said.

"You wish you were back in your own house, Aunt Dew?"

"I'm going back," Aunt Dew said.

"You sad?"

"Hush, boy!"

Michael climbed all the way up on the bed and put his whole self alongside his great-great-aunt. He touched her arms. "Are your arms a hundred years old?" he asked. It was their favorite question game.

"Um-hum," Aunt Dew murmured and turned a little away from him.

Michael touched her face. "Are your face and your eyes and fingers a hundred years old too?"

"John, I'm tired," Aunt Dew said. "Don't talk so."

"How do you get to be a hundred years old?" Michael asked and raised up from the bed on one elbow and waited for his great-great-aunt to answer.

"First you have to have a hundred penny box," his great-great-aunt finally said.

"Where you get it from?" Michael asked.

"Somebody special got to give it to you," Aunt Dew said.

"And soon as they give it to you, you got to be careful 'less it disappear."

Author

The books of Sharon Bell Mathis have won many prizes. Her *Sidewalk Story* received an award from the Council on Interracial Books for Children. *The Hundred Penny Box,* part of which you have just read, was a Boston Globe-Horn Book Honor Book, a Newbery Medal Honor Book, and an American Library Association Notable Book.

Comprehension Questions

1. Why was the box so important to Aunt Dew and Michael?
2. Why didn't Michael hide the box?
3. What did Michael's mother tell him that explained why Aunt Dew was crying?
4. Do you think that Aunt Dew liked talking to Michael? Why do you think that?

Vocabulary

Anagrams are words made from some or all of the letters of another word. You can move letters around, but you don't need to use all of the letters. See how many anagrams you can find in the words from the story below. There is a definition for the first anagram of each word.

father	"the result of overeating"
splinter	"a metal used for pans"
sneak	"what happened to the old boat"
stubborn	"what you take a bath in"

Writing an Interview

Imagine that you are an expert who is being interviewed on the radio about collecting coins. Write down four or five questions and answers. Use quotation marks.

THE WRIGHT BROTHERS

by Quentin Reynolds

The Wright boys always talked over their ideas with their mother. How did she teach them to make their ideas come true?

Susan Wright liked to laugh and play games with her three youngest children: Wilbur, who was eleven; Orville, who was seven; and Katherine, who was four.

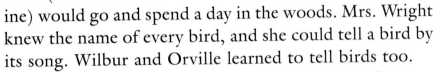

In the summer she'd pack a picnic lunch, and she, the two boys, and little Kate (no one ever called her Katherine) would go and spend a day in the woods. Mrs. Wright knew the name of every bird, and she could tell a bird by its song. Wilbur and Orville learned to tell birds too.

One day they sat on the banks of a river near Dayton, where they lived. Wilbur and Orville were fishing. Everyone called Wilbur "Will," and of course, Orville was "Orv." The fish weren't biting very well. Suddenly a big bird swooped down, stuck its long bill into the river, came out with a tiny fish, and then swooped right up into the sky again.

"What makes a bird fly, Mother?" Wilbur asked.

"Their wings, Will," she said. "You notice they move their wings, which makes them go faster."

"But Mother," Will said, not quite satisfied, "that bird that just swooped down didn't even move its wings. It swooped down, grabbed a fish, and then went right up again. It never moved its wings at all."

"The wind doesn't just blow *toward* you or *away* from you," she said. "It blows *up* and *down* too. When a current of air blows up, it takes the bird up. Its wings support it in the air."

"If we had wings, then we could fly, too, couldn't we, Mother?" Wilbur asked.

"Maybe," his mother said thoughtfully. "But I don't know. No one ever did make wings that would allow a boy to fly."

"I will some day," Wilbur said, and Orville nodded and said, "I will, too."

"Well, when you're a little older maybe you can try," their mother said.

That was another thing about Susan Wright. Most other people would have thought this to be foolish talk. Most other people would have said, "Oh, don't be silly; who ever heard of such nonsense!" But not Susan Wright. She knew that even an eleven-year-old boy can have ideas of his own, and just because they happened to come from an eleven-year-old head — well, that didn't make them foolish. She never treated her children as if they were babies, and perhaps that's why they liked to go fishing with her or on picnics with her. And that's why they kept asking her questions. She always gave them sensible answers.

They asked their father questions, too, but he was a traveling minister and was away a lot.

"It's getting chilly," Mrs. Wright said suddenly. "Look at those gray clouds, Will."

Wilbur looked up. "It's going to snow, I bet," he said happily.

"No more picnics until next spring," his mother said. "Yes, it looks like snow. We'd better be getting home."

As they reached home, the first big white snowflakes started to fall. They kept falling all that night and all the next day. It was the first real snowstorm of the year.

In the morning the wind was blowing so fiercely that Wilbur found it hard to walk to the barn where the wood was stored. The wind was so strong it almost knocked him down. He burst through the kitchen door with an armful of wood and told his mother about the wind.

"The thing to do is to lean forward into the wind," she said. "Bend over. That way you get under the wind."

That night when Wilbur had to make the trip for more wood, he tried his mother's idea. To his surprise it worked! When he was bent over, the wind didn't seem nearly so strong.

After a few days the wind stopped. Now the whole countryside was covered with snow. Wilbur and Orville, with little Kate trailing behind, hurried to the big hill not far from the house.

Orville's schoolmates were all there with their sleds. It was a good hill to coast down because no roads came anywhere near it, and even if they had, it wouldn't have mattered. This was 1878 and there were no automobiles.

Horse-drawn sleighs traveled the roads in winter. The horses had bells fastened to their collars, and as they jogged along, the bells rang, and you could hear them a mile away.

Most of the boys had their own sleds; not the kind boys have now, but old-fashioned sleds with two wooden runners. No one ever thought of owning a "bought" sled. In those days, a boy's father made a sled for him.

The boys who had sleds of their own let Wilbur and Orville ride down the hill with them. Ed Sines and Chauncey Smith and Johnny Morrow and Al Johnston all owned sleds, but they liked to race one another down the long hill. When this happened, Wilbur and Orville just had to stand there and watch. Late that afternoon the boys came home, with little Kate trailing behind, and their mother noticed that they were very quiet. She was wise, and she soon found out why they were unhappy.

"Why doesn't Father build us a sled?" Wilbur blurted out.

"But Father is away, Will," his mother said gently. "And you know how busy he is when he is at home. He has to write stories for the church paper, and he has to write sermons. Now suppose we build a sled together."

Wilbur laughed. "Who ever heard of anyone's mother building a sled?"

"You just wait," his mother said. "We'll build a better sled than Ed Sines has. Now get me a pen and a piece of paper."

"You are going to build a sled out of paper?" Orville asked in amazement.

"Just wait," she repeated.

Will and Orv brought their mother a pen and paper, and she went to the minister's desk and found a ruler. Then she sat down at the kitchen table. "First we'll draw a picture of the sled," she said.

"What good is a picture of a sled?" Orville asked.

"Now, Orville, watch Mother," said Will. She picked up the ruler in one hand and the pen in the other.

"We want one like Ed Sines has," Orville said.

"When you go coasting, how many boys will Ed Sines's sled hold?" she asked.

"Two," Wilbur said.

"We'll make this one big enough to hold three," she said. "Maybe you can take Kate along sometimes." The outline of a sled began to appear on the paper. As she drew it, she talked. "You see, Ed's sled is about four feet long. I've seen it often enough. We'll make this one five feet long. Now, Ed's sled is about a foot off the ground, isn't it?"

Orville nodded, his eyes never leaving the drawing that was taking shape. It was beginning to look like a sled now, but not like the sleds the other boys had.

"You've made it too low," Will said.

"You want a sled that's faster than Ed's sled, don't you?" His mother smiled. "Well, Ed's sled is at least a foot high. Our sled will be lower — closer to the ground. It won't meet so much wind resistance."

"Wind resistance?" It was the first time Wilbur had ever heard the expression. He looked blankly at his mother.

"Remember the blizzard last week?" she asked. "Remember when you went out to the woodshed and the wind was so strong you could hardly walk to the shed? I told you to lean over, and on the next trip to the woodshed, you did. When you came back with an armful of wood, you laughed and said, 'Mother, I leaned 'way forward and got under the wind.' You were closer to the ground, and you were able to lessen the wind resistance. Now, the closer to the ground our sled is the less wind resistance there will be, and the faster it will go."

"Wind resistance . . . wind resistance," Wilbur repeated, and maybe the airplane was born in that moment. Certainly neither Will nor Orville Wright ever forgot that first lesson in speed.

"How do you know about these things, Mother?" Wilbur asked.

"You'd be surprised how much mothers know, Will." She laughed. She didn't tell the boys that when she was a little girl at school her best subject had been arithmetic. It just came naturally to her. It was the same when she went to high school. And when she went to college, algebra and geometry were her best subjects. That was why she knew all about things like "wind resistance."

Finally she finished the drawing. The boys leaned over the table to look at it. This sled was going to be longer than Ed's sled and much narrower. Ed's sled was about three feet wide. This one looked as if it would be only half that wide.

"You made it narrow," Wilbur said shrewdly, "to make it faster. The narrower it is, the less wind resistance."

"That's right." His mother nodded. "Now let's put down the exact length of the runners and the exact width of the sled."

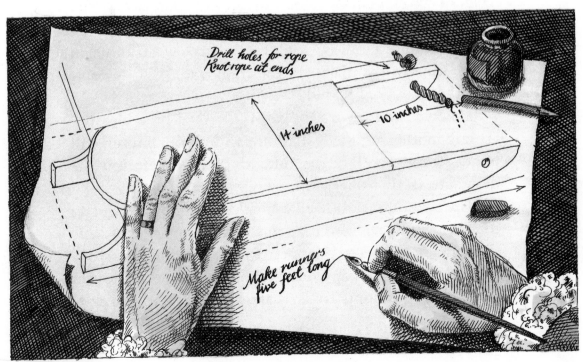

"But that's only a paper sled," Orville protested.

"If you get it right on paper," she said calmly, "it'll be right when you build it. Always remember that."

"'If you get it right on paper, it'll be right when you build it,'" Wilbur repeated, and his mother looked at him sharply. Sometimes Will seemed older than his eleven years. Little Orville was quick to give you an answer to anything, but as often as not, he'd forget the answer right away. When Wilbur learned something, he never forgot it.

"Mother, you make all your clothes," Wilbur said thoughtfully. "You always make a drawing first."

"We call that the pattern," his mother said. "I draw and then cut out a pattern that's exactly the size of the dress I am going to make. And . . ."

"If the pattern is right, it'll be right when you make the dress," he finished. She nodded.

"Now you two boys get started on your sled." She smiled. "There are plenty of planks out in the barn. Find the very lightest ones. Don't use planks with knots in them. You saw the planks to the right size, Will — don't let Orville touch the saw."

"May we use Father's tools?" Will asked breathlessly.

His mother nodded. "I don't think your father will mind. I know you'll be careful with them. Just follow the drawing exactly," she warned once more.

The two boys, followed by little Kate, hurried out to the barn. Both realized that this was an important occasion. Wilbur always chopped the wood for the stove when his father was away, but he had never been allowed to use the gleaming tools that lay in his father's tool chest.

Three days later their sled was finished. They pulled it out of the barn and asked their mother to inspect it. She had her tape measure with her, and she measured it. The runners were exactly the length she had put down in her drawing. In fact, the boys had followed every direction she had given them. Orville had polished the runners with sandpaper until they were as smooth as silk.

"We thought of one other thing, Mother," Will said. "We found some old candles in the woodshed. We rubbed the runners with the candles. See how smooth they are?"

Mrs. Wright nodded. She had forgotten to tell the boys that, but they'd thought it out for themselves. "Now try your sled," she told them.

Followed by Kate, the boys dragged their new sled to the hill only half a mile away to where their pals were coasting. They looked at the new sled in amazement. It

was long and very narrow. It looked as though it wouldn't hold anyone. The runners were thin compared to those on their own sleds.

"Who made that for you?" Ed Sines asked.

"Mother showed us how," Wilbur said proudly. Some of the boys laughed. Who ever heard of a boy's mother knowing how to make a sled?

"It looks as if it would fall apart if you sat on it," Al Johnston said, and he laughed too.

"Come on, we'll race you down the hill," another cried.

"All right, two on each sled," Wilbur said. He wasn't a bit afraid. He was sure the drawing had been right, and because he and Orv had followed the drawing, he knew that the sled was right.

They lined the four sleds up. Will and Orv sat on their sled, but it didn't "fall apart." Suddenly Wilbur got an idea.

"Get up, Orv," he said. "I'll lie down on the sled. Now you get on top of me. . . ." Orville flopped down on top of his brother. "Less wind resistance this way," Will whispered.

"Give us all a push," Ed Sines yelled.

And then they were off. It was an even start. The four sleds gathered speed, for at the top the slope was steep. Will looked to the right, then to the left. He brushed the stinging snow out of his eyes, but he couldn't see the other sleds. He looked behind. They were straggling along, twenty and now thirty feet in back of him. The new sled skimmed along, the runners singing happily. Both Will and Orv felt a strange thrill of excitement. They approached the bottom of the long hill. The other sleds were far, far behind now.

Usually when the sleds reached the bottom of the hill, they slowed down abruptly and stopped. But not this sled. It kept on; its momentum carried it on and on a hundred yards farther than any of the other sleds had ever reached. Finally it stopped.

Shaking with excitement, Will and Orv stood up.

"We flew down the hill, Orv," Will said breathlessly.

"We flew," Orv repeated.

Now Ed and Al and Johnny ran up, excited at what had happened. No sled had gone so far or so fast as the one Will and Orv had built.

"You *flew* down the hill," Ed Sines gasped. "Let me try it?"

Wilbur looked at Orv, and some secret message seemed to pass between them. They had built this sled together, and it was the best sled there was. They'd always work together building things.

"Orv," Will said, "I've got an idea. This sled can do everything but steer. Maybe we can make a rudder for it. Then we can make it go to the right or to the left."

"We'll get Mother to draw one," Orv said.

"We'll draw one, you and I," Wilbur said. "We can't run to Mother every time we want to make something."

By now little Kate had come running down the hill.

"You promised," she panted. "You said you'd take me for a ride."

"Come on, Kate." Will laughed. "The three of us will coast down once. And then you can try it, Ed."

They trudged up the hill, pulling the sled. Two words kept singing in Wilbur's ears. "We flew . . . we flew . . . we flew. . . ."

All through their lives Orville and Wilbur Wright planned and worked together. In the Wright Cycle Shop they made over and improved bicycles. They built a printing press on which they printed a newspaper. Together they planned and built a glider in which they flew at Kitty Hawk, North Carolina. Later they improved it and added an engine. For the first time, on December 17, 1903, a glider flew under its own power. That glider, which Wilbur and Orville had built, was the first airplane to fly with a man on board. Soon the Wright brothers were famous all over the world.

These men remembered well the lesson they had learned from their mother. They always worked by a plan. "Get it right on paper, and it'll be right when you build it," Susan Wright had said. That is exactly what they did.

Author

Quentin Reynolds, a well-known reporter, wrote many books for adults and children about his experiences as a war correspondent during World War II. He also wrote a book for children about the F.B.I. Because Mr. Reynolds loved planes, he wrote *The Wright Brothers: Pioneers of American Aviation*. The selection you have just read was taken from this book.

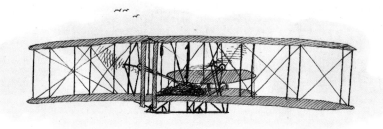

Comprehension Questions

1. How did Mrs. Wright help her sons to make their ideas come true?
2. What was Will's special ability that helped him greatly?
3. How was the Wright brothers' sled different?
4. What did the boys decide after the success of their sled?

Vocabulary

Many compound words, such as **outline** in the story, are formed with the base words **out** or **home**. Read the words below. How many more compound words can you think of which are formed with the base words *out* or *home*?

outside
outdoors
homesick

Writing Directions

Mrs. Wright gave her sons clear and accurate directions for building a sled. Imagine that a visitor is coming to your school. Write directions how to get from the school door to your room. Then give your directions to a classmate to try out.

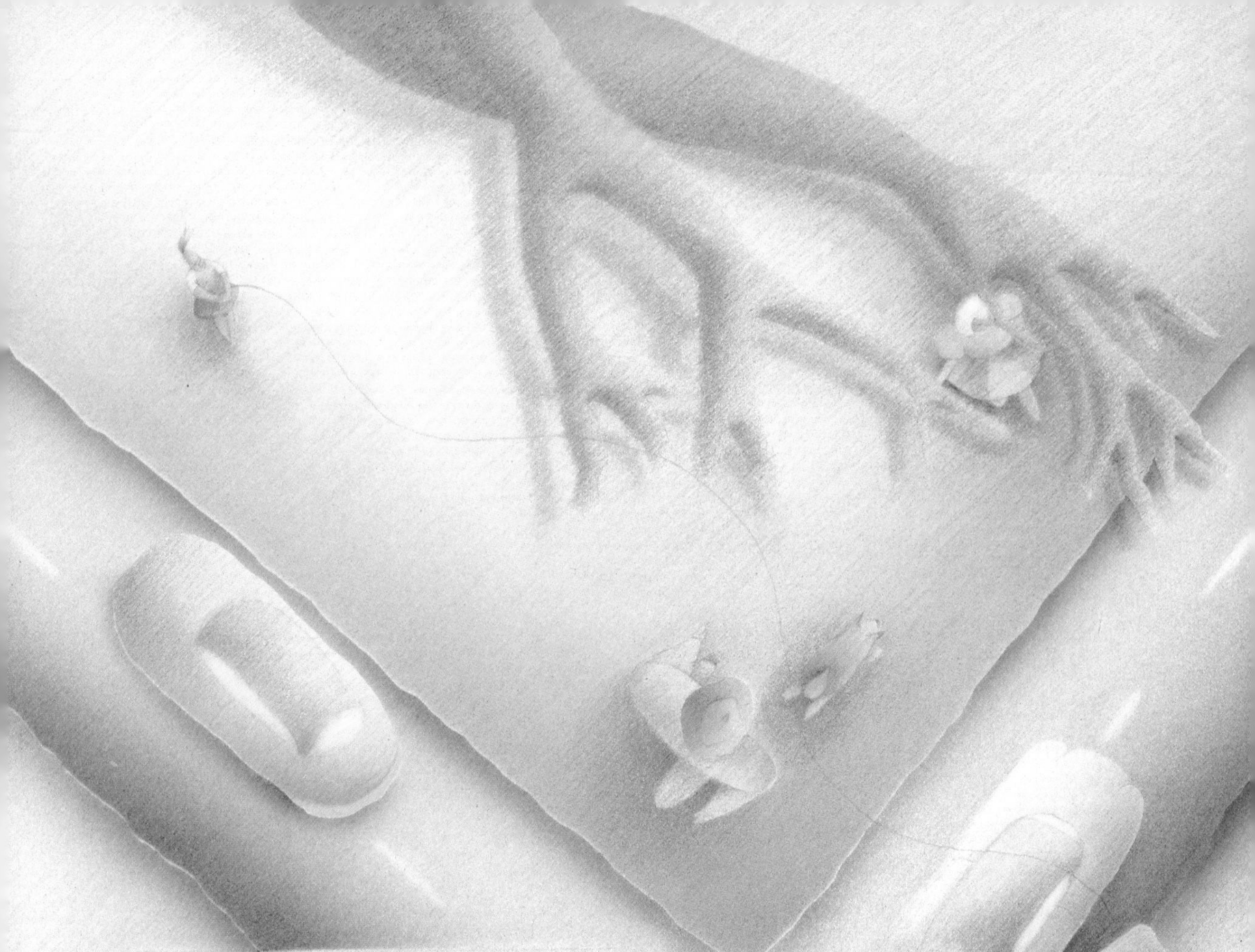

To Be a Bird
by Aileen Fisher

I wish I could fly
through the sky with ease
and try all the seats
in the boughs of trees,

And look from a perch
on the highest steeple
at streets full of
upside-down cars and people.

253

"My Town"

an excerpt from
Chester Cricket's Pigeon Ride

written by George Selden

illustrated by Lane Yerkes

After two weeks in the Times Square subway station, Chester Cricket is homesick for his Connecticut meadow. The moon shining through a subway grate reminds him of his country home, so he decides to find his way up to Times Square for a clearer view. Here Chester meets Lulu Pigeon, who takes him on a daring, high-flying tour over the New York City skyscrapers and harbor to the Statue of Liberty.

This story is one of a series about the adventures of Chester Cricket and his friends. The first book, *The Cricket in Times Square,* was a 1961 Newbery Honor Book.

Chester Cricket's Pigeon Ride

by George Selden

illustrated by Lane Yerkes

My Town

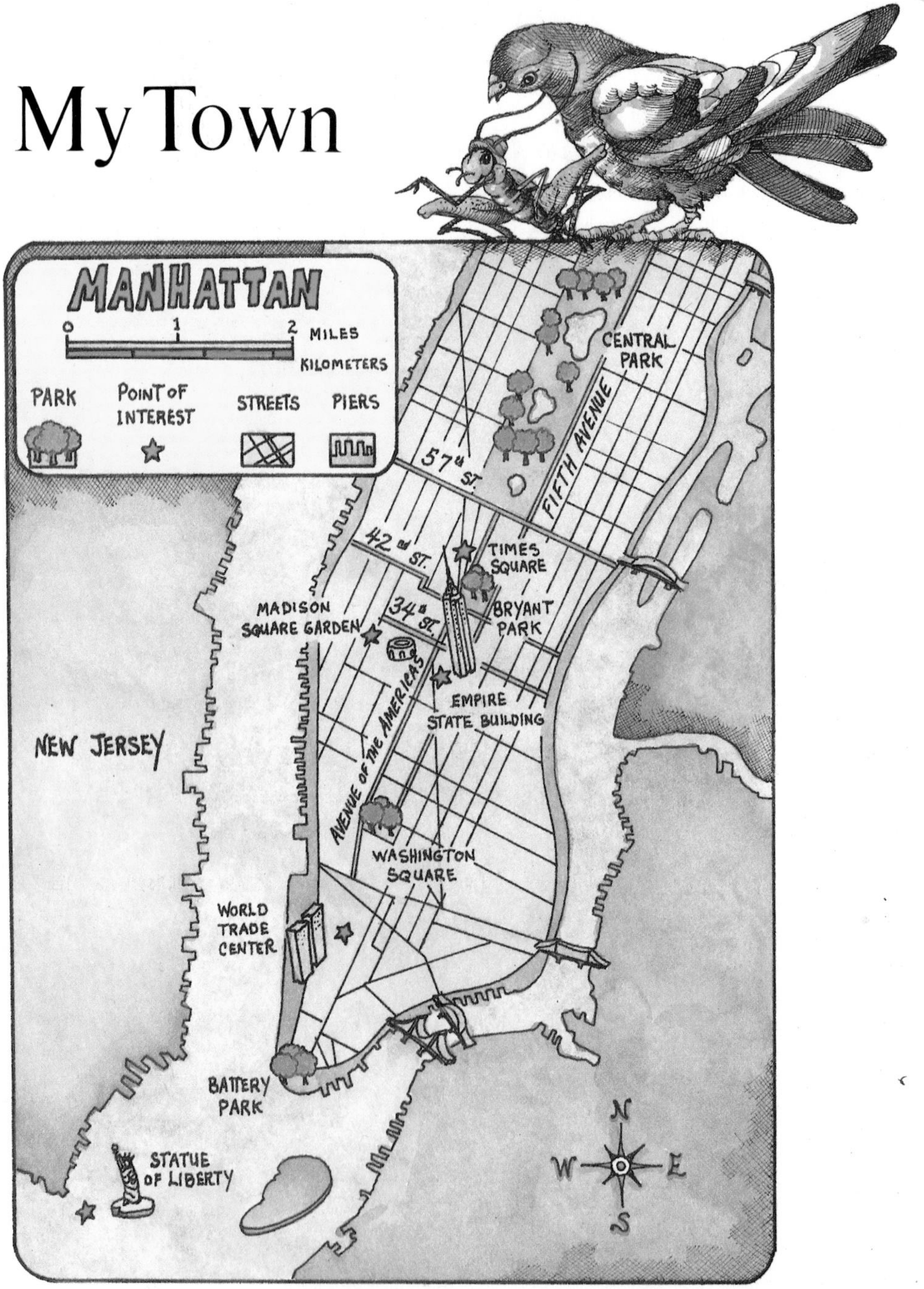

MANHATTAN

0   1   2   MILES
KILOMETERS

PARK   POINT OF INTEREST   STREETS   PIERS

CENTRAL PARK

FIFTH AVENUE

57ᵗʰ ST.

42ⁿᵈ ST.

TIMES SQUARE

34ᵗʰ ST.

MADISON SQUARE GARDEN

BRYANT PARK

AVENUE OF THE AMERICAS

EMPIRE STATE BUILDING

NEW JERSEY

WASHINGTON SQUARE

WORLD TRADE CENTER

BATTERY PARK

STATUE OF LIBERTY

N
W   E
S

Life in New York is very exciting. It was especially thrilling for a cricket named Chester from Connecticut who lived under the sidewalk in the Times Square subway station. He was accustomed to a quiet country life until the day that he met Lulu, a peculiar New York City pigeon. Their unlikely friendship led to a thrilling adventure.

Lulu said, "Come on, Chester C., let me show you some of my town" — by which she meant New York.

"Okay," said Chester, and he climbed on her claw.

"I want you to see it *all* now!" said Lulu. Her wings were beating strongly, rhythmically. "And the best place for that is the Empire State Building."

They rose higher and higher. And the higher they went, the more scared Chester got. Flying up Fifth Avenue had been fun as well as frightening, but now they were heading straight for the top of one of the tallest buildings in all the world.

Chester looked down — the world swirled beneath him — and felt as if his stomach turned over. Or maybe his brain turned around. But something in him felt queasy and dizzy. "Lulu — " he began anxiously, " — I think ——"

"Just hold on tight!" Lulu shouted down. "And trust in your feathered friend!"

What Chester had meant to say was that he was afraid he was suffering from a touch of acrophobia — fear of heights. (And perched on a pigeon's claw, on your way to the top of the Empire State, is not the best place to find that you are afraid of great heights.) But even if Lulu hadn't interrupted, the cricket couldn't have finished his sentence. His words were forced back into his throat. For the wind, which had been just a breeze beside the lake, was turning into a raging gale as they spiraled upward, around the building, floor past floor, and approached their final destination: the television antenna tower on the very top.

And they made it! Lulu gripped the pinnacle of the TV antenna with both her claws, accidentally pinching one of Chester's legs as she did so. The whole of New York glowed and sparkled below them.

Now it is strange, but it is true, that although there are many mountains higher than even the tallest buildings, and airplanes can fly much higher than mountains, nothing ever seems quite so high as a big building that's been built by people. It suggests our own height to ourselves, I guess.

Chester felt as if not only a city but the entire world was down there where he could look at it. He almost couldn't see the people. "Oh my!" he thought. "They look just like bugs." And he had to laugh at that: like bugs — perhaps crickets —

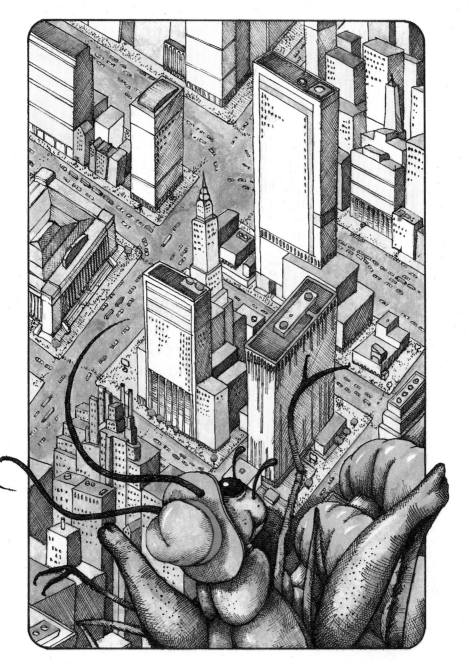

259

moving up and down the sidewalks. And the cars, the buses, the yellow taxis, all jittered along like miniatures. He felt that kind of spinning sensation inside his head that had made him dizzy on the way up. But he refused to close his eyes. It was too much of an adventure for that.

"Lulu, my foot," said Chester, "you're stepping on it. Could you please ——"

"Ooo, I'm sorry," the pigeon apologized. She lifted her claw.

And just at that moment two bad things happened. The first was, Chester caught sight of an airplane swooping low to land at LaGuardia Airport across the East River. The dip of it made his dizziness worse. And the second — worse yet — a sudden gust of wind sprang up, as if a hand gave them both a push. Lulu almost fell off the Empire State.

Lulu *almost* fell off — but Chester *did!* In an instant his legs and feelers were torn away from the pigeon's leg, and before he could say, "Old Meadow, farewell!" he was tumbling down through the air. One moment the city appeared above him — that meant that he was upside down; then under him — he was right side up; then everything slid from side to side.

He worked his wings, tried to hold them stiff to steady himself — no use, no use! The gleeful wind was playing with him. It was rolling him, throwing

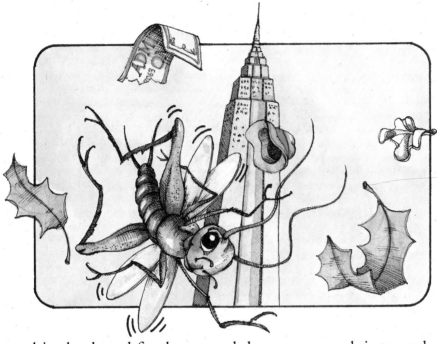

him back and forth, up and down, as a cork is tossed in the surf of a storm. And minute by minute, when he faced that way, the cricket caught glimpses of the floors of the Empire State Building plunging upward as he plunged down.

Despite his panic, his mind took a wink of time off to think: "Well, this is something that can't have happened to many crickets before!" (He was right, too — it hadn't. And just at that moment Chester wished that it wasn't happening to *him*.)

He guessed, when New York was in the right place again, that he was almost halfway down. The people were looking more and more like people — he heard the car engines — and the street and the sidewalk looked *awfully* hard! Then ——

Whump! He landed on something both hard and soft. It was hard inside, all muscles and bones, but soft on the surface — feathers!

"Grab on!" a familiar voice shouted. "Tight! Tighter! That's it."

Chester gladly did as he was told.

"*Whoooooey!*" Lulu breathed a sigh of relief. "Thought I'd never find you. Been around this old building at least ten times."

Chester wanted to say, "Thank you, Lulu," but he was so thankful he couldn't get one word out till they'd reached a level where the air was friendly and gently buoyed them up.

But before he could even open his mouth, the pigeon — all ready for another adventure — asked eagerly, "Where now, Chester C.?"

"I guess I better go back to the drainpipe, Lulu. I'm kind of tired."

"Aw, no — !" complained Lulu, who'd been having fun.

"You know, I'm really not all that used to getting blown off the Empire State Building ——"

"Oh, all right," said the pigeon. "But first there's one thing you *gotta* see!"

Flying just below the level of turbulent air — good pilot that she was — Lulu headed south, with Chester clinging to the back of her neck. He felt much safer up there, and her wings didn't block out as much of the view as they'd thought. He wanted to ask where they were going, but he sensed from the strength and regularity of her wingbeats that it was to be a rather long flight. And the wind was against them too, which made the flying more difficult. Chester held his peace, and watched the city slip beneath them.

They reached the Battery, which is that part of lower New York where a cluster of skyscrapers rises up like a grove of steel trees. But Lulu didn't stop.

With a gasp and an even tighter hold on her feathers, Chester realized that they'd flown right over the end of Manhattan. There was dark churning water below them. And this was no tame little lake, like the one in Central Park. It was the great deep wide bay that made New York such a mighty harbor. But Lulu showed no sign whatsoever of slowing. Her wings, like beautiful trustworthy machines, pumped on and on and on and on.

At last, Chester saw where the pigeon was heading. On a little island, off to the right, Chester made out the form of a very big lady. Her right hand was holding something up. Of course it was the Statue of Liberty, but Chester had no way of knowing that. In the Old Meadow in Connecticut, he never had gone to school — at least not to a school where the pupils used books. His teacher there had been Nature itself.

Lulu landed at the base of the statue, puffing and panting to get back her breath. She told him a little bit about the lady — a gift from the country of France, it was, and very precious to America — but she hadn't flown him all that way just to give him a history lesson.

"Hop on again, Chester C.!" she commanded — and up Lulu and Chester flew to the torch that the lady was holding. Lulu found a perch on the north side of it, so the wind from the south wouldn't bother them.

"Now, just look around!" said Lulu proudly, as if all of New York belonged to her. "And don't anybody ever tell this pigeon that there's a more beautiful sight in the world."

Chester did as he was told. He first peered behind. There was Staten Island. And off to the left, New

Jersey. To the right, quite a long way away, was Brooklyn. And back across the black water, with a dome of light glowing over it, the heart of the city — Manhattan.

And bridges! Bridges everywhere — all pricked out with tiny lights on their cables — that joined the island to the lands all round.

"Oh, wow! We're in luck!" exclaimed Lulu. With a flick of her wing, she gestured down. Almost right below them, it seemed, an ocean liner was gliding by, its rigging, like the bridges, strung with hundreds of silver bulbs.

An airplane passed over them. And even *it* had lights on its wings!

Through his eyes, Chester's heart became flooded with wonder. "It's like — it's like a dream of a city, at night."

"You wait till I fly you back," said the pigeon. "You'll see how that dream can turn real."

The wind, which had been a hindrance before, was a help now. Lulu coasted almost all the way back to Manhattan, only lifting a wing now and then to keep them on an even keel. But once or twice, just for the fun of it, she tilted her wings without warning. They zoomed up, fast — then dipped down, faster — a roller coaster in the empty air.

And all the while, the dream city drew nearer. It seemed to Chester like some huge spiderweb. The streets were the strands, all hung with multicolored lights. "Oh, Lulu, it's — I don't know — it's ——"

"Hush!" said the pigeon. "Just look and enjoy." They were flying amid the buildings now. "Enjoy, and remember."

Chester Cricket could not contain himself. He gave a chirp — not a song, just one chirp — but that single chirp said, "I love this! *I love it!*"

Then there was Times Square, erupting with colors. Chester pointed out the grating he'd come through — and Lulu landed next to it.

"How *can* I ever thank you?" said Chester.

"Don't bother, Chester C. Just glad to meet someone who loves New York as much as I do. And come on over to Bryant Park again. I'll be there — one branch or another. Night, Cricket."

"Night, Lulu."

She fluttered away.

Chester bounded through the grate and hopped as fast as he could toward the drainpipe. Tonight he had *really* had an adventure!

Author

George Selden started the adventures of Chester Cricket in *The Cricket in Times Square* when he heard a cricket chirp in a subway station one night. Later he wrote several books about Chester and his friends, including *Tucker's Countryside* and *Chester Cricket's New Home*. Mr. Selden writes for both adults and children and has received many awards and honors for his books. He now lives in New York City.

Illustrator

After four years in the United States Navy, Lane Yerkes attended the Philadelphia College of Art to study illustration. As a successful free-lance illustrator, he has worked on many magazines, newspapers, and children's books. He has also worked in the advertising industry and in fabric design. In his spare time, Lane Yerkes enjoys running, sailing, and tennis as well as painting and drawing.

Comprehension Questions

1. What especially thrilling sight did Chester see on his flight?
2. What did Chester try to tell Lulu as they started toward the Empire State Building?
3. According to the map on page 256, on which street is the Empire State Building that Chester and Lulu went to?
4. Lulu flew with Chester from Battery Park to the Statue of Liberty. According to the map on page 256, in which direction did they fly?

Vocabulary

Two of the compound words below came from "My Town." Make eight new compound words by adding the words in parentheses to each half of the compound word.

something (one, any)   **birddog** (bath, fish)
sidewalk (in, cat)   **catfish** (call, hook)

Writing a Description

Describe what you might see on a balloon ride over your home. How do things look from high up? From a balloon, a person standing under an umbrella would look like a giant flower.

Magazine Wrap-up

Literary Skill: Character Development

An author often uses a character's words to tell you how a character feels. For example, in "My Town," Chester says, "How *can* I ever thank you?" Chester's words show that he is very *grateful* to Lulu for the ride.

Write the numbers from 1 to 4 on your paper. Read each character's words. Then find a word in the list that describes how the character felt. Write the word next to the number on your paper.

1. Mrs. Wright in "The Wright Brothers": "It's getting chilly. Look at those gray clouds, Will."
2. Ann Hamilton in "Hamilton Hill": "It's more beautiful than any table we ever set in Gettysburg."
3. Mrs. Brown in *The Arrival of Paddington*: "Why, Henry, I believe you were right after all. It is a bear!"
4. Lulu in "My Town": "Come on, Chester C., let me show you some of my town."

surprised   **pleased**
friendly   **concerned**

Vocabulary: Synonyms

Each sentence below came from one of the stories in Magazine Two. Change each boldface word to another word, or synonym, that means the same thing. Choose from the list of words below, and write the new sentences on your paper.

awkward   **saw**
clean   **silent**
fastened   **strange**
following   **touched**
hurriedly   **used**
peaceful

1. He was **accustomed** to a **quiet** country life until the day that he met Lulu, a **peculiar** New York City pigeon.
2. "I hope I look different too," Ann thought as she **fingered** her two blue hair ribbons and **hastily** tied the sash of a fresh apron.

270

3. Her hands were **clumsy** as she **tacked** the drawing to her easel, afraid someone might laugh.
4. Late that afternoon the boys came home, with little Kate **trailing** behind, and their mother **noticed** that they were very **quiet**.

Comprehension Skills: Following Directions and Making a Graph

Start your own forest. Grow pine, oak, maple, or other trees. For each kind of tree, follow these directions:

- Fill a small plant pot with soil.
- Water it.
- Then plant the seed.
- Put the pot in a warm, sunny place.
- Water the seed regularly so that the soil does not dry out.

When the seeds start to sprout, make a graph for each kind of tree to show how much it grows each week. Measure the tree with a centimeter ruler on the same day each week. Then record the growth on a chart that shows the number of the week and the height.

Books to Enjoy

Mystery of the Disappearing Dogs
by Barbara Brenner

The Garcia twins, Elena and Michael, track dognapers in their city neighborhood.

Where the Bald Eagles Gather
by Dorothy Hinshaw Patent

This photo essay describes the yearly gathering in Montana of the bald eagle, our national bird.

Eleanor
by Mary Francis Shura

Chester's sister Eleanor saves the day for her Texas school in a funny sequel to *Chester*.

Flights
Magazine Three

Contents

Stories

PAUL BUNYAN

by Anne Malcolmson

At seventy pounds and more, Paul Bonjean was the biggest baby in Canada, and he got bigger and bigger. What problems did Paul have as the biggest, tallest, and strongest person in the world?

Even before he let out his first baby cry, it was clear that Paul Bonjean[1] was going to be a hero. He was a large baby, as babies go. Instead of the usual seven or eight pounds, *le petit*[2] Paul weighed seventy or eighty. He was born with a long, glossy black beard and a pair of beautifully waxed and curled mustaches. Furthermore, you could see him grow.

Monsieur[3] Bonjean, his father, nearly burst with pride. Before night came, however, he was worried. The baby had drunk up all the milk that Marie, the cow, could give. The little clothes that Madame[4] Bonjean had made were no longer of any use. The cabin bunk wouldn't hold him. Papa Bonjean wrung his hands in despair.

The neighbors did what they could to help. They gave the baby all the milk from their cows. They gave their sheets for diapers. They spread their blankets in the ox stall for him. Then they went home to bed.

In the morning the whole village stared in awe at the new baby. He had grown so fast during the night that his chubby little feet and hands stuck out through the doors and windows of the ox shed. The big double sheets were stretched to the ripping point across his tummy, and he was as hungry as a bear. He doubled his little fist and banged it down on the ground, crushing to pieces several racks for drying codfish. He waved his little legs in the air, knocking down two pine trees and a sea captain. Something had to be done.

The first problem was food. All the cows in New Brunswick were herded together to give milk. Several

---

[1]**Bonjean** (bōn zhŏn´)

[2]**le petit** (lə pə tē´): the little

[3]**Monsieur** (mə sûr´)

[4]**Madame** (mä däm´)

ships filled with cod-liver oil, meant for Boston, were put in storage for him. He had to have three barrels of it every day. The clothing problem was solved by a sailmaker from St. John. He cheerfully gave a pair of sails to be made into pants. The Ladies Aid Society offered to do the sewing. A wagon maker gave a dozen wheels to be used for buttons.

Still, there was no proper place for the little fellow to sleep. No hayloft would hold him. Papa Bonjean tried to rent a field from a farmer. "Think of my crops," cried the farmer. "They will all be crushed."

At last the problem was solved. A committee was sent to the shipyards in Maine. They found in one the half-built hull of a clipper ship. The ship was to be the largest in the China trade. As yet, no decks nor masts had been put in. "The very thing we want!" said the committee. So they bought it.

They asked the surprised shipwright to line the hold with feather beds. Then they towed it up to the Bay of Fundy. With the aid of a large steam crane, they lifted little Paul into his new cradle.

It was a perfect fit. The baby cooed and gurgled to show how happy he was, and soon he fell asleep. The gentle rocking of the sea and the slap of waves against the shore were his lullabies. He slept soundly for two weeks, with his little pink thumb resting against the glossy black of his beard and mustache.

Unfortunately, when the time came to give him his bottle, he would not wake up. People rowed out to his cradle and yelled at him. He slept right on. The light-house keeper sounded the foghorn. Little Paul only sighed in his sleep. What to do next? Papa Bonjean went

to the mayor. The mayor went to the provincial governor. The provincial governor went to the governor general. He had a bright idea. He knew that part of the British Navy was stationed off the coast of Nova Scotia, so he wrote to the admiral of the fleet. The admiral was very fond of children and agreed to help.

He ordered all his ships into the Bay of Fundy. He lined up the ships across from Paul's cradle. Then the ships fired their cannon over the baby's head.

That woke him up! It frightened him too! He opened his little mouth and screamed *"Maman[5]!"* which is French for "Mama!" His scream was heard in Boston by the Coast Guard Listening Station. Thinking that the whole North Atlantic fishing fleet must be in trouble, the Coast Guard sent out all its ships to see what was wrong.

The child trembled so in his fright that his cradle rocked from side to side, kicking up waves seventy-five feet high. Even after all these years, the water has not settled down completely. In some places in the Bay of Fundy, the tides are still fifty feet or more.

Even with many problems, which you can well imagine, little Paul grew up. His childhood was a happy one. His parents adored him, and he loved them in return; but something bothered him. His clear blue eyes grew dreamy. His thoughts wandered into far places. He seemed to know that some great task lay ahead of him, but what it was, he couldn't tell.

He went to school with other children. He was very bright for his age. Even so, he had his troubles. In penmanship, for instance, he could write only one letter

---

[5]**Maman** (mä män´)

on a page. His geography book was so large it had to be carried by a team of oxen. Once, in a careless moment, he sat on his lunch box. When he opened it later, he found the first of his many inventions — hamburger!

He had soon learned all that school could teach him. He loved to read, but he knew that he must learn other things. He had to find out what it was he had to do in life.

Papa Bonjean suggested that he try fishing. For a year, young Paul worked with nets and ships. He was a great help to his father. Every morning at sunrise, he towed a pair of three-masted schooners out into the fishing banks of the Atlantic Ocean. Before breakfast he waded back to the docks, a ship under each arm. Their holds were jammed with cod and other fish. Fishing was easy, but it didn't satisfy him. It was too easy. Surely this was not the great work he had to do!

Next he tried hunting and trapping. He went up into the Canadian woods to learn from the Indian guides. They taught him to follow the tracks of animals, of moose and bear and deer. He became so clever at this that his teachers were amazed. Once, he found the body of a dead moose. From the antlers he judged it to be fifteen years old. He set out to follow the big fellow's tracks — just for fun. He traced them as they grew smaller and smaller, until they became the tiny hoofprints of a baby moose. He didn't give up until he had reached the moose's birthplace.

Paul tried one thing after another. Nothing was right. At last the desire to find something big to do in a big way got to be too much. He became cross and sulky. He wouldn't eat his dinner, not even when his mother fixed his favorite dish — a roasted moose stuffed with wild boar and a dozen wild turkeys.

He had to get away from things. With a pack of books and provisions on his back, he trudged north into the wilds of Labrador. He was so absent-minded that he stepped across the St. Lawrence River without noticing. On and on he went. At last he found a cave big enough for him, on the coast. Here he settled for the winter.

All winter long he stayed there. He left the cave only to fish and to hunt for food. The rest of the time he lay by his fire, reading and dreaming and trying to figure out just what his lifework was meant to be. He thought so hard that he didn't notice the strange and wonderful snow that was falling on the world. Outside everything was hushed. Forests, fields, and paths, all were being covered with a bright blue blanket. It was as blue as Paul's eyes.

Unaware of the miracle, Paul lay dreaming in his cave. Suddenly a great noise made him wake up. He heard the thunder of snow slipping off the roof of his cave. With a rumble and a splash, something heavy tumbled over the cliff and fell into the ocean. Paul rushed out to see what it could be.

Sticking up from the cold black water were the horns and the head of a baby ox. The little calf lay still among the icebergs. For a moment Paul thought it was frozen or drowned. He dashed into the sea to pull it out, but it was heavy, much heavier than an ordinary calf. He had to struggle to carry it to the shore and into the warmth of his cave.

When he had finally laid it down before the fire and covered it with his blankets, he had a chance to admire it. The baby ox had bright blue hair the color of the strange snow. It was a big fellow, as big as Paul himself.

"Ah, Bébé[6]!" he said softly, as he petted its baby head. At that, it opened its big blue eyes and licked his face weakly with its big pink tongue. For days and nights Paul nursed the little calf back to health. What a remarkable beast it was! Paul himself had to go hungry, for Bébé ate everything in sight.

It was strong — fifty times as strong as any full-grown ox should be. It was playful. It loved to play hide

---

[6]**Bébé** (bā bāʹ)

and seek. It liked to lie down in the blue snow, which was almost the same color as its hide. Its horns stuck up like black trees. Then Paul would wander about calling, "Bébé, Bébé, where are you?" At last, Bébé, who had been lying in plain sight all the time, would jump up and charge at Paul.

When spring came, the lovely blue snow began to melt. As the sap began to stir in the trees, Paul's problem began to stir in his mind. Somehow or other, he began to feel that he was about to solve it. Night after night he dreamed the same dream. When he got up in the morning, it was gone. All that he could remember was that it had something to do with the United States.

He decided to go to the United States. Perhaps he could find there the kind of work he was meant to do. One morning he packed a little lunch and called Bébé. Together they set out. By evening they had reached the border. Off ahead of them stretched the state of Maine, with its miles of pine woods. As far as the eye could see, there were trees, nothing but trees.

Bébé romped on ahead. When a hundred-year-old pine got in its way, Bébé kicked it impatiently. It snapped and fell crashing to the forest floor.

Then Paul knew what it was he had to do in life. He had to go to the United States and invent logging. It was his job to cut down all those trees and to make room for all the Americans who were coming to plant farms and build cities.

He stepped proudly across the border. He started to call, *"Holà[7], Bébé!"* in French Canadian — but the words

[7]**Holà** (ô lä′)

wouldn't come. Instead he heard himself shouting a new language — "Hey, Babe!"

He stopped in amazement. He pinched himself all over. He discovered that he was a new man.

"By my old mackinaw!" he said, and he slapped his knee. "By the great horn spoon! I'm really in the United States. I'm going to log off this state before you can say 'Jack Robinson.'" With a shout and a holler, he started right in on his new job.

That is how Bébé became Babe, the blue ox, and that is how Paul Bonjean became Paul Bunyan!

Author

Anne Malcolmson met a man in New Hampshire who told stories he said he had heard while he worked as a lumberjack with Paul Bunyan. Later she wrote her first book of tall tales, *Yankee Doodle's Cousins*, from which this story of Paul Bunyan was taken.

Comprehension Questions

1. What were Paul's problems as a grown man?
2. When Paul was little, what woke him up?
3. How did Paul invent hamburger?
4. What details about Babe showed that this story was a tall tale?
5. What did Paul decide to do when the pine tree fell?

Vocabulary

In this story, the trees in Maine stretched "as far as the eye could see." Below are some idioms made with **hand**. Match the idioms with their meanings. Then make a list of idioms that use **foot**.

to have a hand in something	"to find"
to give someone a hand	"to take part in"
to put your hand on	"to help"

Writing a Description

Babe was Paul's only pet. Write a description of another pet that you might have if you were Paul Bunyan.

Prefixes and Suffixes

> I'd sure love to have those skates, but I could never afford to **pay** for them.

> Maybe you could make a small **payment** every week.

> That would take a long time. I might lend you the money—if you promise to **repay** me with interest.

Prefixes and suffixes are word parts that can be added to a base word to make new words. Look at the base word *pay* in the pictures. Now look at the words *payment* and *repay*. These words are made by adding the prefix *re-* or the suffix *-ment* to the base word *pay*.

When you add word parts like these, you change the meaning of the base word. For example, the base word *pleasant* can be changed into several other words by adding word parts. Each new word means something different from the base word.

pleasantness (base word with suffix -*ness*)
pleasantly (base word with suffix -*ly*)
unpleasantly (base word with prefix *un*- and suffix -*ly*)

Understanding how word parts are used can help you learn many new words.

In the following sentences, add a prefix or a suffix from the box to each base word to make new words.

Prefixes

re-	"again; back"
dis-	"not; opposite of"
un-	"not; opposite of"

Suffixes

-ment	"condition or state of being"
-ful	"full of; having"
-or	"person who"
-ly	"in a way that is"
-ness	"quality or state of being"

---

1. The person who was the best act____ got the largest part in the play.

2. Kyle did not ____act very well when another pupil got the lead.
3. Gale ____packed the make-up trunk before the dress rehearsal.
4. Melissa carefully ____packed the costumes after practice.
5. Mark did a skill____ job of spotlighting the singers.
6. The pupils in the play ____agreed about what time the play should begin.
7. We were all in agree____ that the cast deserved a big hand.

Something Extra

See how many words you can build with the word parts from the box on the left and the base words below. You might want to do this with a classmate and see who can make the most words within a time limit. Check your words in a dictionary.

enchant	**content**
flavor	**do**
quiet	

Ernie and the Mile-Long Muffler

by Marjorie Lewis

When Ernie was sick, his uncle showed him a good way to pass the time. Little did Ernie dream what would happen because of his hobby.

One October afternoon Ernie was home from school waiting for the scabs from his chicken pox spots to fall off. Even though nobody could catch the chicken pox from him anymore, he looked pretty awful. Now that he didn't itch and feel terrible, he was bored. Ernie was so bored he couldn't wait to get back to school. He wondered what exciting things his friends in the fourth grade and Mrs. Crownfeld, his teacher, were doing while he spent his time waiting for scabs to fall off. When the doorbell suddenly rang, Ernie was glad. Even answering the door was something to do.

When Ernie looked through the peephole in the door to find out who was there before opening it, he saw it was his Uncle Simon, his mother's brother, who was a sailor. Ernie and his mother hadn't seen Uncle Simon in two years because he had been away at sea. Ernie had thought of Uncle Simon often during those two years and had imagined Uncle Simon climbing the rigging, doing things with the mizzenmast, swabbing the deck, and standing watch with a spy glass — all the things that sailors did in the stories Ernie read.

Ernie and Uncle Simon sat and talked with each other while Ernie's mother made dinner. Uncle Simon showed Ernie pictures of the places he had been and of the ship he'd sailed on.

Then Uncle Simon asked Ernie what he liked best to eat. Ernie told him his best thing was a hamburger with red onion circles, lots of ketchup on the top part, lots of

mayonnaise on the bottom part, and a roll with seeds to hold it all together. Ernie told Uncle Simon his worst thing to eat was anything that shook. Uncle Simon said he didn't like shaky things either, especially tapioca pudding because the tapioca beads looked like fish eyes. Uncle Simon told Ernie all about the strange foods he had eaten all over the world: rattlesnake, turtle soup, candied grasshoppers, rabbit stew, cows' eyes, calves' brains, and chocolate-covered ants. Ernie began to feel sick.

Uncle Simon changed the subject and asked Ernie what kinds of things he liked to do. Ernie told him about reading comics and cereal boxes, trading baseball cards, making cookies, and shooting baskets.

Uncle Simon told Ernie he liked most to read mystery stories; next, to bake bread; and third, to knit. He told Ernie that on his ship, when he wasn't working, he had lots of time to do all three. Ernie said that he didn't know that men knitted. Uncle Simon said that men have knitted for hundreds of years, especially men in armies and navies who spent a lot of time waiting for things to happen. Uncle Simon opened his seabag and took out a sweater that looked like a rainbow and let Ernie try it on. Ernie thought it was the most terrific sweater he had ever seen. Then Uncle Simon took some knitting needles out of his bag and a big ball of yellow yarn. By the time Ernie's mother called them for dinner, Uncle Simon had taught Ernie to knit.

The next few days, while Ernie waited for the scabs to fall off and his spots to fade, he knitted a sweater for his dog Buster, socks for his father's golf clubs, a Christmas stocking for his canary, and a muffler for his mother for her birthday. The muffler was so beautiful and fit his

mother's neck so well that Ernie decided to make one for everyone he knew. Then he had a better idea. The idea came to him one morning while he was eating breakfast and reading his world-record book for the millionth time. Ernie decided that he would knit the world's longest muffler. He would make it a mile long! Ernie wrote a letter to Uncle Simon, who was back at sea, and told him about his plan.

He asked his mother to get all the record books she could find in the library. Ernie looked through all of them and found that none of them had a record for muffler-knitting. Ernie pictured himself holding the victorious knitting needles crossed in front of him, with foot after foot of muffler looping around the throne he would be sitting on when they took his picture for the record book.

Ernie told his mother about his idea. She told him that there were 5,280 feet in a mile. Then Ernie and his mother figured out that there were 63,360 inches in a

mile. Ernie's mother said that it would surely be a lot of muffler to knit!

Ernie asked his mother to ask her friends to give him all the extra yarn they had. By the time Ernie was well enough to go back to school, he had finished about two feet of muffler. Ernie thought that the two feet had been done so quickly that it wouldn't be hard at all to do a mile of knitting.

His first day back at school, Ernie packed his gym bag with his gym shorts, his T-shirt, and his knitting. He kept his knitting with him all morning. When he was sitting and waiting for late-comers to be present for morning attendance, or for the assembly program to begin, or for the fire drill to be over, Ernie knitted. Mrs. Crownfeld said she thought it was wonderful to be able to knit and asked Ernie if, after recess, he would show the class how to knit. Ernie said he would.

At recess, the class went outside. Ernie sat down on the bench to wait for his turn to shoot baskets. He took out his knitting.

"I can't believe you're doing that," said Frankie.

"I mean my *mother* does that!" said Alfred.

"So what," said Ernie. "Your mother bakes cookies, Alfred, and so do you. So do I."

"It's different," Alfred said. "Knitting is different."

Alfred watched while Ernie's fingers made the needles form stitches. When Edward came over, Frankie and Alfred moved away. Edward leaned over and watched Ernie.

"No boy I ever saw did that," Edward said. "Boys don't do that." Edward reached out and grabbed the ball of yarn, tearing it off from the knitting. Ernie watched

silently while Edward, Frankie, and Alfred played basketball with the yarn ball. Then they dropped it into a puddle. They fished it out and tossed it to Ernie.

Ernie looked at the ball of yarn with glops of mud and leaves tangled in it. Then he put his needles and the two feet of muffler on the bench and threw the ball of yarn away into the bushes.

The three boys, Frankie, Alfred, and Edward, formed a circle around Ernie. They began to run around madly with their thumbs in their ears and their fingers flapping, yelling, "Nyah, nyah, Ernie knits!" Over and over again. Then the three boys called Ernie a nitwit (or was it a *knitwit?* thought Ernie miserably). The other children in the class came over to watch. Some of them joined the group around Ernie.

"Hey, Ernie," called Richard. Raising his voice to a screech that sounded like a girl's voice, Richard said, "Oh, Ernie. Would you make me a pink sweater?"

By the time the bell rang for the end of recess, Ernie felt terrible. When Mrs. Crownfeld asked him to show the class how to knit, everyone began to giggle. Ernie walked up to the front of the classroom. In his hands, he held the needles and the two-foot piece of the record-making mile-long muffler. He took a deep breath and waited until the class quieted down.

He told them all about his Uncle Simon's being a sailor. He told them about the strange things Uncle Simon had eaten and the places Uncle Simon had been. He told them about Uncle Simon's terrific sweater. He told them that Uncle Simon liked best to read mysteries; next, to bake bread; and third, to knit. He told them what Uncle Simon had said about people in armies and navies having lots of time while they waited for things to happen, so soldiers and sailors for hundreds of years knitted to keep from being bored.

Finally, Ernie told the class that he was going to knit the longest muffler in the world, a mile long, and get his name and his picture in the record books. The class was absolutely quiet.

Mrs. Crownfeld said that she would be very proud to have one of her fourth-grade students be a record maker. Then Mrs. Crownfeld asked Ernie to demonstrate how to knit. Ernie said that he couldn't because he had lost his ball of yarn during recess. Ernie promised to show Mrs. Crownfeld and the class how to knit the next day.

At the end of the day, Ernie was walking home by himself with his knitting in his gym bag.

"Ernie, Ernie," called Frankie. "Wait up!"

Frankie walked along with Ernie. "Thanks for not telling the teacher what happened to your yarn," he said. "I think it's neat how you're going to win the muffler-knitting record."

Ernie and Frankie went to Ernie's house and ate some cookies that Ernie had baked when he was sick. Ernie showed Frankie all the stuff he had knitted when he had been home with the chicken pox. Frankie admired the dog's sweater most of all. Ernie next showed Frankie the bags of different-colored yarns that his mother's friends had given him for his muffler project.

"Say, Ernie," said Frankie. "I'll bet my mother's got some yarn left over from the sweater she knitted for my sister. I'll ask her if I can give it to you."

"That would be great, Frankie," said Ernie. "I'm going to need all the yarn I can get!"

The next day in school, Ernie showed the class how one needle went in front of the stitch to make a knit stitch and how it went in back to make a purl stitch. He showed them how the two kinds of stitches together made the bumpy ridges that kept the sleeves tight at the wrists. He showed the class how to make the pieces get bigger and smaller to fit next to each other, so that they could be sewn together to make a swell outfit. He offered to teach anyone in class who wanted to learn. Mrs. Crownfeld was the first to ask Ernie for lessons.

After a while, everyone in the fourth grade learned to knit. Mrs. Crownfeld made a deal with them: The class could knit during homeroom, fire drills (while they were outside waiting to go back in), or rainy-day recess, plus a special knitting time right after lunch each day when the class could knit while Mrs. Crownfeld put her knitting aside and read them a story from the library.

In return for all the knitting lessons from Ernie, the class brought in all the yarn they could get from anyone who would give it to them. Ernie kept the yarn in a big plastic garbage bag in the corner of the classroom. Each day, a knitting monitor measured Ernie's muffler and wrote the length in a notebook Mrs. Crownfeld had given the class as a present.

By Thanksgiving, Ernie's muffler was sixteen feet long, and Ernie was looking pale. He never went outside to play. He didn't do anything at all but go to school, do his homework, eat his meals, and knit. Cynthia, who was very good in math, subtracted the sixteen feet Ernie had finished from the 5,280 feet in a mile. That left 5,264 feet to go before the end of school. Since school would be over and summer vacation begin in twenty-eight weeks, Ernie would have to knit over 188 feet of muffler *every week,* or about twenty-seven feet *every day* (including

Saturday and Sunday) to finish the muffler by the end of fourth grade.

Ernie listened to Cynthia very carefully. He remembered the picture he had dreamed of: sitting on a throne, his knitting needles crossed in front of him, foot after foot of muffler looping around him. His name and photograph would be in the record books. Pride would be in the faces of his parents and his teacher. He would have the admiration of all his friends. Then Ernie thought of how long it had been since he played with his friends or baked cookies or read a book — or even a cereal box.

Ernie decided to take it easy. It wasn't important when the muffler got finished. He could finish it someday. So maybe it wouldn't be the longest muffler in the world. Mrs. Crownfeld would be disappointed not to have a fourth-grade record-breaker, but Ernie figured if he ever did finish it — in fifth grade maybe, or sixth — he would publicly thank her for her encouragement when he became famous.

Ernie told his mother, Mrs. Crownfeld, and his friends what he had decided. Now he could go out and shoot baskets during recess. He began to read his cereal boxes again. Sometimes, while he was watching television or waiting for the dentist to see him, or riding in the car for a long time, he would knit. He even had time to write to Uncle Simon and tell him everything that had happened since he learned to knit.

Ernie's class continued to bring in yarn for him. Ernie decided to give the yarn to the class because now that they all could knit, they could have a fair or something to raise money to buy games and books for children in the town hospital.

All the things sold at the fair were knitted by the fourth grade. Frankie was good at mittens and so was Edward. Frankie knitted all the right-hand ones and Edward all the left-hand ones. Between them, they made five pairs of mittens for the fair. Alfred made bean bags. Cynthia made pot holders. Other people made mufflers (the regular length). Mrs. Crownfeld made cat and dog sweaters. Someone else made pincushions. Everyone in the fourth grade made something. The fair was a huge success. They sold $173.42 worth of stuff, including six

pairs of slipper socks in bright colors that Ernie made and cookies that Frankie, Alfred, and Ernie baked and sold.

By the time spring came, the fourth grade was famous. Everyone in town knew about their knitting and Ernie's muffler, which was getting very long even if it wasn't anywhere near a mile. When the local paper did a story about the class and took a picture to go with it, on the front page right in the middle of the photograph was Ernie sitting on a chair, holding his knitting needles crossed in front of him. Ernie's muffler was looped

around each member of the class and Mrs. Crownfeld, with several feet left over. It made Ernie as happy as if he had finished his mile of muffler. Suddenly, Ernie decided the time had come. Even though people were always saying you should finish everything you start, Ernie knew better. Three hundred fourteen feet was long enough. Long enough, Ernie thought, is long enough.

He asked Mrs. Crownfeld, who was an expert fringe maker, to put fringe at each end of the muffler. When the muffler was done, it was exhibited all over school — in the fourth-grade room, down the hall, in the principal's office, and in the library. People came to see it and admire the way Ernie made all the colors of fuzzy and thin yarn come together into a multicolored muffler. People who had contributed yarn could recognize their bits and were very pleased to see them used in Ernie's muffler.

When summer vacation came, Ernie's mother took the muffler home. Ernie helped her wrap it and put it away in a box. Then he went out to ride bikes with Frankie, Alfred, and Edward.

Author

Marjorie Lewis says, "I believe in stories — in giving children delight. I believe in the power of words to create music, laughter, and tears." Mrs. Lewis, a school librarian, has written several books for young readers. Like Ernie, she enjoys knitting projects that don't take too long to finish.

Comprehension Questions

1. What happened to Ernie and his classmates because they learned how to knit?
2. Why did Ernie decide that he would make a record-breaking muffler?
3. How was Ernie a good sport at recess?
4. How did Ernie convince the class it would be fun to knit?
5. What did Ernie finally decide about the muffler?

Vocabulary

Ernie's friends called him a **nitwit**. More words that repeat sounds are in the box below. Look up the ones that are unfamiliar, and match the words with their meanings. Think of more words like this. Why are these words fun?

teeny-weeny	"completely confused"
razzle-dazzle	"dazzling excitement"
higgledy-piggledy	"very small"

Writing a Paragraph

Ernie's sailor uncle knitted to pass the time. Look up the main topic *Knitting* in an encyclopedia, and write a paragraph about the history of knitting.

Outlines

Why Is an Outline Useful?

Making an outline is useful when you want to remember what you have read. An outline will help you to pick out what is important. It also will help you to put the facts in order and to remember them. Later you will be able to use the outline to help you study.

Read the following article very carefully. After you read it, you will learn how to outline it.

Planting a Vegetable Garden

How Do You Choose a Spot?

For a good vegetable garden, choose a spot of ground where plants will grow well. The soil should be fairly rich. The place should get plenty of sunshine. Pick a spot where the plants will get enough water, but not too much.

How Do You Prepare the Soil?

After you have chosen the garden spot, get the soil ready for the planting you intend to do. Unless the soil is very rich, it is a good idea to spread plant food over the ground. Then turn the ground over with a shovel and break up any large lumps of soil. Then rake until the soil is fine. Be sure the garden is flat.

What Are the Steps in Planting Seeds?

When planting seeds, carefully follow the directions printed on the packages. If you think you won't be able to tell the young plants as they come up, write the name of the vegetable on a label, or take the empty seed package, and attach it to a pointed stick. Then push the stick into the ground at the end of the row. Be sure to leave enough space between rows. You want to be able to work among the plants later on.

How Are Main Topics Found?

To make an outline, first read the title of the article and think about its meaning. Then think of a question about the title that you expect the piece to answer. What question might you ask about the title "Planting a Vegetable Garden"? You might ask *How do you plant a vegetable garden?* Then read the article again to find answers to your question. Often you will find several answers to your question. For each paragraph or part, the answers that you find will become main topics in your outline. A main topic of a paragraph or part is the most important piece of information given there.

Sometimes the author will make it very easy for you to find the main topics. There will be a heading that states the main topic of each paragraph or part. In what you just read about gardens, each heading can be changed into a main topic.

How Are Headings Turned into Main Topics?

In "Planting a Vegetable Garden," each heading is stated as a question. Most of the time, questions are not used as main topics in outlines. Instead, you should think of a group of words that can be used without a period or a question mark. The first heading is *How Do You Choose a Spot?* To make it a main topic you would change it to a group of words such as *Choosing a spot.*

Look again at "Planting a Vegetable Garden." What main topics can you think of for the second and third headings? *Preparing the soil* and *Planting seeds* would be good main topics.

How Do You Write the Outline?

Here is how you would write a short outline for the garden article:

Planting a Vegetable Garden

  I. Choosing a spot
 II. Preparing the soil
III. Planting seeds

When you make an outline, write the title in the center of the first line. The words in this title all begin with capital letters, except for the word *a*. The first word and all the important words in the title should begin with capital letters.

The main topics are listed in the order in which they appear. Each main topic is numbered with a Roman numeral that is followed by a period. The main topic is written differently from the title. Only the *first* word in each main topic begins with a capital letter.

There are two other points to remember when you are writing main topics in an outline. First, do not begin your main topics with the words *The, A*, or *An*. Second, there is no period at the end of the main topics.

How Do You Check Your Main Topics?

To be sure you have the right main topics for your outline, you should check them. One way to do this is to make a sentence for each main topic by using your main topic and the title. For the first main topic in this outline you could make this sentence:

To plant a vegetable garden, you must choose a spot.

What sentences could you make with the other two main topics? Here are sentences for paragraphs 2 and 3:

To plant a vegetable garden, you must prepare the soil.
To plant a vegetable garden, you must plant the seeds.

Making an Outline

Read the following piece carefully. Then make an outline that has a title and main topics. Try to make your main topics as short as possible.

Camels

Why Are Camels Useful?

Camels are best known for carrying heavy loads across the deserts of Asia and Africa. On a long trip, a large camel can carry four hundred pounds on its back. On a shorter trip, the camel can carry many more

pounds. Also, the hair, meat, and milk of camels are important to desert people. The soft hair is woven into cloth. Both the milk and the meat are used as food.

Why Are Camels' Bodies Important?

A camel's feet, hump, and stomach are well suited for going across the desert. The feet are broad and padded. The camel's hoof is only at the tip of the toes. This helps a camel to walk on loose sand. Fat is stored in the hump. When there is not much food, the camel's body draws on the fat. Besides the water stored in the fat, some water may be stored in certain parts of the camel's stomach. Most camels can go about three days without water.

What Are Some Complaints About Camels?

Camels are bad tempered, ugly, and ungraceful. No matter how well they are treated, they never seem to love — or even notice — their masters. Also, it is costly to buy and keep camels. They can find some grasses and leaves for themselves, but they still must be fed such foods as hay and grain.

Skill Summary

Making an outline will help you to remember the information that you have read.

- Turn the title into a question.
- Look for answers to the questions. These answers will become main topics.
- Check main topics by using each one in a sentence with words from the title.
- If there are headings, use them to form main topics.

About Elephants

by Barbara Williams

Elephants are the biggest land animals, but that's not their only claim to fame.

A big stack of mail was waiting for Abraham Lincoln when he became President in 1861. One interesting letter was from the king of Siam. The king had learned some shocking news. Someone had told him there were no elephants living wild in American "jungles." There were no elephants to help farmers till the soil or to move the heavy logs to lumber mills. There were not even any elephants to ride into battle.

The king was sure no country could last without elephants, so he offered to help. He would send a few elephants to America. President Lincoln could turn them loose in the hot American "jungles." In time, the elephants' children and grandchildren could be caught and tamed.

This may sound silly, but the king was really trying to help. To him, the elephant was as important as the horse has been to North Americans.

North Americans have never used elephants for work, but they love elephants. At any zoo, people crowd around the elephant cages. At any circus, the people clap and cheer when the elephant act begins.

An Asian elephant with a rider. In some parts of Asia, elephants are used as work animals.

What Is Unusual About Elephants' Feet?

Elephants are bigger than any other land animal. Some grow to be twelve feet at the shoulder and weigh twelve thousand pounds. Hunters can tell the size of an elephant by its footprints. They measure all around one footprint; then they multiply by two. The number they get gives the elephant's height at its shoulder.

When you look at it, the elephant's foot seems flat and clumsy. However, you don't see the real foot. You see a cushion of flesh around it. Inside this cushion, the elephant walks gently on its toes.

Elephants walk very fast — up to twenty-five miles an hour. They move with ease through thick forests, up steep hills, along winding jungle paths. Ambling along, an elephant can keep up with the fastest track stars.

This may seem strange, for an elephant cannot run; nor can it jump. For this reason, farmers who live near jungles sometimes dig ditches around their land. An elephant can knock down almost any fence, but it cannot jump across a ditch.

Why Are Elephants' Trunks Important?

To hold up its big head and heavy tusks, the elephant needs a strong neck. Its neck cannot turn very well from side to side. If it wants to see

The forty thousand muscles and tendons in an elephant's trunk make it strong and flexible—and very useful!

something on one side, the elephant must turn its whole body. So the elephant needs another sense to tell it if it is in danger. It learns what it needs to know by smelling the world with its trunk.

An elephant can smell a person several miles away. It can even smell water. The leader of a herd of elephants will wave its trunk in the air for a few seconds. Then it will walk away. The rest of the herd will follow single file. Eating leaves as they walk, they will go straight to the water hole.

The elephant's trunk is more than a nose for smelling and breathing. It is an instrument for squealing and trumpeting. It is a weapon for fighting. It is a tool for lifting and breaking. It is a snorkel for swimming. It is a paddle for spanking. It is a hand for eating.

A baby elephant isn't born knowing how to use its trunk. It will wave its trunk in the air like a rubber hose, not knowing quite what to do with it. It may sit down and put the tip in its mouth to suck like a thumb. It may even hit itself on the back by accident.

At the tip of its trunk, an elephant has either one or two points, which work like fingers. In fact, the points are sometimes called the elephant's fingers. With them, an elephant can pick a blade of grass, crack a peanut, or take a lump of sugar from its trainer's pocket.

One unusual way the elephant uses its trunk is to take a shower. The elephant will suck up about two gallons of water in its trunk. Then it will lift the trunk above its head.

These young bull elephants in Samburu, Kenya, are using their trunks in a contest of strength.

With a splash, two gallons of water run down the elephant's back. By putting the tip of the trunk in its mouth instead, the elephant will get a cool drink. It needs to drink up to fifty gallons of water a day.

Showers keep an elephant cool. If an elephant gets too hot, it will die. In the heat of day, it just stands still in the shade. When there is a wind, it spreads its big ears to catch a breeze. When the air is still, it flaps its ears like fans. When there is no shade, no wind, and no water, the elephant can do a surprising thing. It can put its trunk deep down its throat and draw water from its stomach to spray on its body.

How Are Elephants' Teeth and Skin Special?

Hidden behind the elephant's trunk is a very large mouth. Just one tooth can be the size of a person's foot and weigh up to ten pounds. During its life the elephant gets six sets of teeth. First come the baby teeth. These are replaced by new ones at ages two, six, nine, twenty-five, and

An African elephant enjoys a bath in a waterhole at Etosha National Park in Namibia, Africa.

sixty. Scientists studying elephants have been able to look at their teeth and guess how old they are.

Some people believe that elephants live to be over one hundred years old. They think an elephant's wrinkles prove how old it is. The truth is that elephants live only about sixty or seventy years.

If an elephant does not meet up with a hungry lion, or fall down a mountain, or sink into a swamp, or come into shooting sight of a hunter, it may die of tooth wear. When its very last tooth is ground down, an elephant cannot eat the food it must have to go on living.

An elephant needs such big teeth and so many sets of them because it is always eating. Twenty hours out of every twenty-four, an elephant munches, munches, munches. It needs from two hundred to one thousand pounds of food every day, depending on its size and how hard it works. Elephants like grass, leaves, twigs, grain, nuts, and fruit. They do not eat meat.

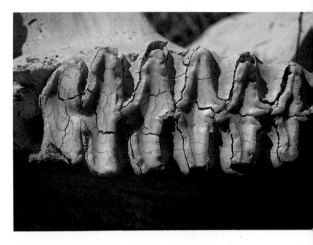

These elephant molars belong to one of the six sets of teeth an elephant has in its lifetime.

With all this eating, an elephant's stomach always growls. Sometimes people hear the growling stomachs before they see the elephants. Twenty or thirty growling elephant stomachs can sound like thunder.

The two big teeth that grow out from the elephant's upper jaw are called tusks. Elephants have no other front teeth. With the sharp points of its tusks, an elephant can strip the bark off trees to eat. It can also fight.

Elephant skin is thick and wrinkled, like the bark of a cottonwood tree. The hide is so thick it makes up about one sixth of the elephant's weight — or about two thousand pounds. Even so, elephants are ticklish. They hate crawling insects like flies and mosquitoes.

Elephants are gray, but they don't always look gray. The color of an elephant's skin depends on what it has been doing. If it looks white, the elephant may have been moving through the forest, raising clouds of white dust. If it looks red-brown, the elephant has been splashing in a mud pool. If it looks gray, it has just had a bath.

What Are the Kinds of Elephants?

There are two kinds of elephants. One kind comes from Asia; the other comes from Africa. African elephants are sometimes called *loxodonts*.

Some people say that African elephants are bigger than Asian elephants. This is not

This elephant herd at Etosha National Park shows a wide range of color. The white ones are actually the dirtiest, while those that look dark gray have probably just taken a bath.

exactly true. In Africa, some elephants live in open spaces where low bushes grow. Others live in the forest where high trees grow. The bush elephants are bigger than Asian elephants; but the forest elephants are smaller.

It is not hard to tell the difference between Asian and African elephants. African elephants have big ears that look like the two sides of a giant valentine heart. Asian elephants' ears are smaller and shaped more like a triangle. African elephants have sloping foreheads and sway backs. Asian elephants have foreheads that go straight up and down. Their backs are rounded at the top.

Among both Asian and African elephants, males are called bulls. Females are called cows. Babies are called calves. In Asia, only bulls grow tusks. In Africa, both bulls and cows grow tusks. African elephants have rings around their trunks and two "fingers" at the tips. Asian elephants have smoother trunks and one "finger" at the tips.

The Asian elephant (top) has smaller ears than the African elephant (bottom). What other differences do you notice?

How Do Elephants Help Each Other?

Elephants are good mothers. They take good care of their babies. When a cow is about

319

ten years old, she has her first calf. After that, she usually has one about every four years. She does not often have more than ten babies. She almost never has twins.

The cow carries the baby inside her about twenty-two months. During this time, a strange thing happens. Another cow senses that the first is going to be a mother. The second cow, known as the "auntie," starts to take care of the mother. She helps during the birth, and she helps the mother raise the baby. If the mother dies, the auntie raises the baby as her own.

When the time of birth is close, the mother and auntie choose a good spot. The best place is under a tall tree near a river. The tree will give them shade. The river will give them water to drink.

A new baby elephant has red, wavy hair and a short trunk. Its head has a squashed look. Its belly looks like a crumpled paper bag. Its two ears hug its body like leaves around the heart of a lettuce. The baby weighs about two hundred pounds.

This baby African elephant will be well taken care of by its mother and auntie, as well as by all the cows in the herd.

The mother uses her trunk to nudge the baby to its feet. This may take several hours. Then, the mother helps it get milk.

A baby elephant needs its mother's milk for about two years. And it needs a lot of it — about twenty-one gallons a day! During that time, the baby stands and walks under its mother's fat stomach. As it grows older, it roams farther away.

Even a calf one day old can walk. With weak, shaking legs, it balances on its soft round pads. After two days in the world, a baby can keep up with its family, walking about three miles a day in search of food.

Cow elephants and their calves live in groups called herds. They travel together and take care of one another. Sometimes there are as many as fifty elephants in a herd. Each herd has a leader, or several leaders. They are the oldest cows who have had the most calves.

When danger is near, the herd forms a circle. The cows

As danger approaches, these elephants form a tight defensive circle, with the calves safely hidden in the middle.

push the calves to the center where they can't be seen. All the mothers make a tight ring, facing out. Then the cow leader tries to scare off the enemy.

The bulls roam in very small groups or by themselves. Sometimes, the males will help a herd if it is in danger, but they usually stay away. As a rule, baby elephants do not know their fathers.

Elephants have always appealed to people's imaginations, and many stories have been told about them, some true, some false. This has been a true story.

Author

When Barbara Williams started reading to her own children, she found out how interesting children's books could be. Then she began writing for young readers.

Barbara Williams has written more than thirty books. Two of her picture books have won awards. "About Elephants" is from her book *Seven True Elephant Stories*.

Thinking It Over

Comprehension Questions

1. What is unusual about elephants besides their size?
2. How does an elephant use its trunk to keep cool?
3. Where in this selection is information given about the two kinds of elephants?
4. In what ways is an elephant herd like a family?

Vocabulary

From the groups below, pick the best word to go with each animal.

owl   "wise, smart, quick"
mouse   "small, tiny, little"
deer   "speedy, swift, fast"
elephant "big, large, huge"

Making an Outline

The incomplete outline below is based on the selection "About Elephants." Copy the outline that is given here, and fill in the rest of the main topics in the correct order. Follow the steps that you learned in the Skill Lesson on outlining.

About Elephants

I.
II.
III.
IV. Kinds of elephants
V.

Oliphaunt

by J.R.R. Tolkien

Gray as a mouse,
Big as a house,
Nose like a snake,
I make the earth shake,
As I tramp through the grass;
Trees crack as I pass.
With horns in my mouth
I walk in the South,
Flapping big ears.
Beyond count of years
I stump round and round,
Never lie on the ground,
Not even to die.
Oliphaunt am I,
Biggest of all,
Huge, old, and tall.
If ever you'd met me,
You wouldn't forget me.
If you never do,
You won't think I'm true;
But old Oliphaunt am I,
And I never lie.

The Once-a-Year Day

by Eve Bunting

Annie had tried hard to be
nice to her cousin Emma,
but Emma kept to herself.
One day, though, Annie
shared a piece of the sun
with Emma and found a
friend.

The bucket was almost filled with the wrinkled purple berries. Annie knew her mother would be pleased. She straightened her back, looking once again across the dark waters of the bay. Something moved in the stillness, but it was only a flock of ducks flying south, and as she listened she heard their honking clear in the empty air.

The short Alaskan summer was almost over. Already the grass beneath her feet was growing hard, and the tender summer moss was gone. Soon snow would fall, and the sea would freeze over, closing them in. Annie sighed. She touched the coins in her pocket, counting them one by one. They were there, waiting. Summer was not yet gone, not with the barges still to come. The radio had told them last week that the big ship was steaming north from Hooper Bay. Soon, soon the barges would come.

It was at that instant that she saw them, gliding like surfaced whales across the dark bay. There were two of them, flat-nosed, low in the water. Annie picked up her bucket and began to run. The barges had come! This was the day . . . the wonderful, wonderful once-a-year day!

She was almost halfway down the hill when she remembered. Anger rose in her, sudden and hot.

"Emma!" she called. "Where are you, Emma?" There was no answer. That silly Emma! Annie scrambled back up the hill. "Emma! Emma!"

She saw a bit of red against the brown of the grass. Emma sat without moving, her eyes closed, her face turned up to the pale coolness of the midday sun. Her berry bucket was beside her, a few berries on the bottom, not even a handful.

"Emma!" Annie heard the righteous anger in her own voice. What had Emma been doing all this time! No berries to speak of, and now, because of her, Annie was missing the barges.

Emma's eyes opened. Her face wore the sulky look that Annie knew so well. She rose slowly, without a word, and picked up the almost empty bucket.

"Is that all you've got?" Annie knew the answer, but the question helped ease the frustration she felt.

Emma nodded. She was one year younger than Annie, but she was much smaller. Her black braids trailed wisps, fine as feathers. Her sweater was buttoned wrong, so that one end hung down. Emma was Annie's cousin, and an orphan, and now that she had come to live at Annie's house, she was going to be the sister that Annie had never had. That was what Annie's mother had said.

"Well, hurry up." Annie emptied half of her berries into Emma's bucket. "You can at least help me carry them."

Emma shrugged, moving her thin shoulders. Her mouth turned down at the corners.

Annie began slipping and sliding back down the hill. "The barges have come," she said, and waited for Emma's question — but behind her there was only silence.

The village below was moving with excited people. They were running from their houses to the edge of the bay. Annie could see the crowd already gathered on the muddy banks. The first barge was almost in, its straight nose churning the water, touching the shore.

Emma's feet were slow and uncaring behind her. Annie wished she could run on by herself and leave her cousin, but that would make her mother angry. "Come on, come on, come on!" she urged, grabbing Emma's bucket and carrying it with her own. "Can't you hurry?" She felt like crying with impatience. She had been the first person in the village to see the barges, and she might be the last to reach them. It wasn't fair. Nothing was fair since Emma had come. Annie had to share her bed, her clothes, her father and brothers, and, worst of all, her mother.

"I couldn't let my own sister's child go all the way to the city, to the orphanage," her mother had said. "How could I, Annie? What we have we will share with her. You will have a sister to go egging with. She will be company for you on the goose drive. It will be good."

It hadn't been good. Emma *had* gone egging with them, yes. But her egg basket had been as empty at the end of that day as her berry bucket today. "Lazy Emma," Annie said to herself. "Thoughtless Emma. She wasn't a sister to Annie. She didn't belong in the Koonooka family."

The goose drive was worse. Emma had fallen behind, and when two of the geese escaped the net, she had let them run right past her. Didn't she know that geese were food and food was life? The smallest child in the village knew that. Annie couldn't understand her mother. No matter what Emma did, Annie's mother excused it with a gentle word. It was almost more than Annie could bear.

Emma's own mother had died the year before on the mail plane on the way to the hospital. Her father had been lost last winter when an offshore wind blew the pack ice on which he stood away from the floe. He had never been found. It was summer before Emma could be brought to them. "Bad enough," Annie thought, "to suffer through the short summer with sulky old Emma, who didn't want to play and didn't want to talk. How would it be in the winter when they would be together inside the small house for days and weeks at a time?"

"It will be all right," her mother said. "Emma is strange now. She doesn't care about anything, but as time passes, she will."

Sulky old Emma. Annie didn't believe she'd ever change. "I won't think about it now," Annie decided. "Not on the once-a-year day. I won't spoil it."

They were down the hill now and running along the short stiff grass in front of the houses. There was no one in sight. Even the dogs had gone down to the shore. The buckets banged against Annie's legs. She could feel their edges through her sealskin boots. From the bay came a drift of voices and the dull putt-putt of an outboard motor.

Annie opened the door of her house and dropped the two buckets inside — just inside — and then she was

running again toward the dark waterline and the laughing voices. Her hand closed tightly on the coins in her pocket, and she counted again. The one with the crinkled edge was the dime, the bigger one was the nickel, the other fifteen were the pennies. They were all there, safe, ready.

"Don't you even want to know about the barges?" she called to Emma over her shoulder.

Emma didn't answer.

"Once a year the big ship brings supplies from Seattle." Annie's fast-moving legs kept a rhythm with the words she threw back to Emma. "The ship can't come in here because the water's not deep enough. The barges bring the goods from the ship to us. We have to be quick. All the best things sell first."

Only the wind of her running answered her. "Sulky old Emma doesn't understand," Annie thought. "I don't know why I bother to tell her."

Mr. Odark, the storekeeper, had an old army truck, and it was waiting at the edge of the bay. Gordon Okukchuk's big tractor was there, too, with the drag sled behind it, hitched and ready to haul the supplies from the beach to the village.

Annie saw her mother standing with the other women. Her two brothers were knee-deep in the water, pulling on the first barge, helping to wedge it in the mud. The front gate was down; the slide from the deck to the dry ground was already in position. Annie could see that this barge carried only the big drums of fuel for heating

the school and the houses of those who had oil stoves — fuel for the snowmobiles and to run the boats next summer.

The second barge was coming in, and Mr. Odark stepped forward with his list. Annie felt a faint stirring, deep inside. Would it be on this one? No. These were the wooden boxes filled with fishnets, harpoons, and dog harnesses. There were bags of nails and lamps, carefully packed, and big bright boxes of washing soap. Here were the small boxes of shells and the cartridges for the hunters to use.

Everything was piled on the shore, and the smaller children ran to peek between the slats in the packing cases. "Not yet, not yet," thought Annie. With one part

of her mind, Annie sensed Emma motionless beside her, but there was no time to think about Emma now.

The second barge moved out. There would be a while to wait before the first one came back with another load from the big ship.

Daniel and Thomas and some of the other boys began rolling the heavy oil drums up the hill toward the store. The men lifted the big crates up onto the truck, piling them untidily, lashing them down with ropes so they wouldn't slide off. Mr. Odark rushed around, giving instructions, telling them to be careful of this and to be careful of that, but everyone was so excited, they paid him little attention.

When Annie looked again, she saw that the first barge was gliding back across the bay, humped high with the rest of the supplies. She felt a sudden rush of saliva to her mouth and a weakness inside of her. This must be it! She wanted to dive into the water and tow the barge behind her like a lead dog pulling a sled. "Hurry, hurry," she begged silently. Then it was there, nosing in, jamming itself on the shore.

Here were the sacks of flour, sugar, coffee, salt, dried peas and beans, baking soda, and powdered milk. It was hard for Mr. Odark to check with the people crowding around. Suddenly Annie saw it — the big slatted crate with the one word stamped in black on its side. It came bumping and sliding down the slide. Annie breathed deeply. It was here. No need to worry now. There was only the waiting till Mr. Odark got everything up to his store. The barge was empty. The second barge would stay out with the big ship. There was nothing else to bring ashore.

"Anyone for a ride?" one of the bargemen yelled, and he stood back as the children crowded up and crawled all over the boat.

"Come on, Emma," Annie called, running forward. But Emma stood still, not moving. "Let sulky old Emma stay!" thought Annie. From the back of the barge, Annie saw her mother speak to Emma and Emma shake her head. Then they were moving, sliding through the dark, clear bay, with the people on the shore getting smaller and smaller and the village itself disappearing from sight. This was the once-a-year ride on the once-a-year day. It didn't last long. When they got back, they watched as the barge disappeared behind the line of sea and sky, and for an instant everyone was very, very quiet. "Good-by," Annie thought. "Good-by barges, good-by big ship. Don't forget to come back next year."

The drag sled was filled; the truck was back for another load. Annie searched and found the wooden box with the bold black letters on the front of the sled. Not long now, not long.

The tractor ground its way up the hill, and Annie raced along beside it. She didn't see Emma, and she was glad. Nobody knew about the thirty cents. There was ten cents for minding Mrs. Ungatt's baby while she went to a meeting in the church, five cents from Mrs. Quavuk for carrying buckets of fresh water from the stream, and the rest had been saved, penny by penny. "This I will not share," she thought. "This is going to be all mine!"

Mr. Odark's store was crowded. Annie saw her father, bent over someone else's outboard motor, the same hungry look on his face that she saw on other faces around the room.

Jim Tulimak and his wife whispered together. They had gone to work in the fishery when the salmon were running, and they had money when they came back. Now they waited for the wood and the glass they had ordered. This winter they would have a new floor and good windows.

Mr. Odark was sorting and checking.

"Mr. Odark," Annie whispered, coming to stand beside him. The wooden box lay on the floor. The bands of metal around it gleamed in the last light from the window.

"Don't bother me now, Annie." Mr. Odark chewed the end of his pencil and frowned.

Annie pulled at his arm and pointed to the wooden box. "Will you open this one next?"

He paid no attention, crossing off words on the list he held. Then he sighed and smiled. "All right, Annie. We'll open it now."

"May I have the first one?" Annie took the dime and the nickel and the pennies from her pocket. They were hot and sticky from her tight fist.

Mr. Odark held out his big hand, and Annie poured the money into it, a shining ribbon polished by the rubbing. He got down on his knees beside the box and cut first one metal band, then another. With a piece of flat iron, he pushed up the lid.

It seemed to Annie that everyone in the room gasped at the sight. Big golden oranges lay, row on row, fat and gleaming in their own rich skins, trapping the light, holding it without reflection.

Ruby Bird stretched a hand into the box.

"Uh-uh!" Mr. Odark said. "Annie Koonooka has paid for one already. Take your pick, Annie."

Annie knelt by the box and took out one of the oranges. It was stamped with the same magic word that had been on the wood — CALIFORNIA.

She carried it outside into the early cold air. The air filled with the groans of the truck laboring up the hill with another load. Boys called to one another, their voices high and sharp as the bark of a fox in the night. Annie cradled the orange in her hands. She walked slowly behind the store and sat facing the bay. Then she closed her eyes, lifted the orange to her nose, and breathed of it. "California," she thought. In her hands, she held the sunshine, the warmth, the groves of orange trees, the

blue of the ocean, and the wonder of the land she had learned of in school but might never see.

The day was shimmering to an end, the special day. She bit into the peel, tasting the first bitter oil, feeling it sting her tongue. She remembered last year. Ruth Ormuk had eaten the skin and thrown away the inside. Annie smiled. Ruth had thought the outside was all there was! She nibbled at the white beneath the peel and then placed the piece of skin carefully in her pocket. Later, she could take it out, smell, and remember. Little by little, she peeled the orange till its pale, tender roundness lay free in her hand. She pulled off one section and sank her teeth in. Oh, it was good. It was good beyond believing! Drops stung her chin, stickied her fingers. It was like eating summer.

She ate another piece and another, stuffing it in her mouth, greedy as a tomcod for the bait on the line. It was half gone. She stopped, thinking back. Last year she had had four pieces, one fruit shared with her brothers. The memory had sharpened with the days between. She was going too quickly. Too soon it would be over.

That was when she heard the noise. It was a snuffling noise, a gaspy, raspy noise. Annie sat up and listened. Someone was coming around the side of the store. It was Emma. Annie heard a great gulping sob, and then, as Emma turned, she saw her face. Never in all of Annie's life had she seen such misery. The eyes were screwed up like a baby's. The mouth was open, moving, saying words without sound.

"Emma," Annie whispered.

Emma saw Annie. In an instant, every expression was gone from her face. She looked blankly at her cousin. She was sulky old Emma again.

Annie got up. Had she really seen Emma's face like that, or had she imagined it? "I saw it," she thought. "That I could never have imagined."

The night wind was coming up. She could hear it moving between them. The orange was sticky in her hand. She looked down — and all at once she knew. Emma's sulky face was what she showed to the world. It was like the orange skin, protecting, hiding everything beneath. "I didn't know," Annie thought. "Like Ruth Ormuk, I threw it away."

"Emma," she said. "I didn't know you felt so bad."

Emma stood looking over the bay. Her hair still feathered from its braids. Her sweater was still buttoned wrong. Her face still wore its sulky look.

Annie held out the half orange. "Here," she said.

"What is it?" Emma took the orange and smelled it suspiciously.

"It's an orange. I had one last year. Eat it." She watched as Emma took a small bite. "Isn't it good?"

Emma nodded.

A warmth crept around Annie, comforting as rabbit fur. "This," she thought, "is the first thing I have shared willingly with Emma since she came."

"Please, you have some too," Emma said. Her voice was shy. She broke off a piece of the orange and gave it back to Annie.

Annie put the orange in her mouth, keeping her teeth from it, storing the memory that she would have to hold in her mind for a whole year, till the next time the barges came. This piece tasted best of all — this little bit, shared. Annie smiled. Maybe this was how it was, and how it would be from now on, with Emma.

Author

Eve Bunting, who has written more than one hundred thirty books for young people, says, "Creating stories is the thing I enjoy most in the whole world." When Mrs. Bunting's children were almost grown, she took a course in writing for publication which started her on her career as an author. Since then she has taught courses for other would-be authors. One of her many award-winning books, *The Empty Window,* was chosen as an Outstanding Science Book for Children.

Thinking It Over

Comprehension Questions

1. How did Annie make friends with Emma?
2. Why was Emma so sulky?
3. What kinds of things were brought in the barges?
4. What did the word *California* mean to Annie?

Vocabulary

Similes and metaphors in a story help your imagination. Match these similes from the story with the words they are compared to.

like surfaced whales   "the taste of the orange"
like eating summer   "the barges coming"
like the orange skin   "Emma's face"

Complete this sentence with your own simile:

The sound of corn popping is like. . . .

Writing a Letter

Pretend you live in Annie's village. What would you most want the ship to bring you? Write a letter to Mr. Odark's store to order this thing.

Science Words

The people in the pictures above are studying wild animals. Many people like to study wild animals. For some people, it is their job. Other people study wild animals for fun. Here are some words with their meanings that are used in the study of animals.

behavior How people or animals act under certain conditions.

environment The surroundings in which something lives.

fieldwork Studies done outside of a classroom.

observe To notice; to watch in a careful way.

research Organized study of a subject or problem.

scientists People who are expert in one or more kinds of science.

Read the following piece about the study of animals. Be sure you understand the meaning of each boldface word.

Scientists use different ways to study how animals behave. Sometimes they put animals in pens that are much like the animals' own homes. There the scientists are close enough to watch the animals' habits. Scientists also do **fieldwork** to study animals.

They can then **observe** how an animal hunts for food, cares for its young, and fights its enemies in its own **environment.** Many interesting things can be learned from the **research** scientists do on animals they have caught and on animals in the field.

Now read these sentences about scientists at work. Which sentences are about scientists doing research with animals in pens? Which sentences are about scientists doing fieldwork? How do you know?

1. Looking through field glasses, Dr. Karl observed a lioness and her cubs near the far river bank.
2. To record how a gorilla acts when it is close to humans, Dr. Morse photographed it through the bars.
3. Although it was very hot, Sharon waited quietly in the brush to see the herd of wild elephants.
4. Dr. Robbins added salt water to the pond where the seals were kept.

Something Extra

Imagine that you are a scientist doing fieldwork. What animal will you study? Where will you go to find it in the wild? What kind of information do you want to learn about the animal? Write a paragraph with the answers to these questions, and read it to your classmates.

Sea Life

Many fascinating creatures live in the sea — from tiny one-celled animals to the great whales. One of the most interesting is the shark, which has a reputation for fierceness although it is not as dangerous as most people think. Scientists are seeking to learn more about the shark and its neighbors in the sea.

Reading in Science

Eugenie Clark: Shark Lady

by Ann McGovern

Can you imagine having a shark pen right outside your door? Eugenie Clark has one!

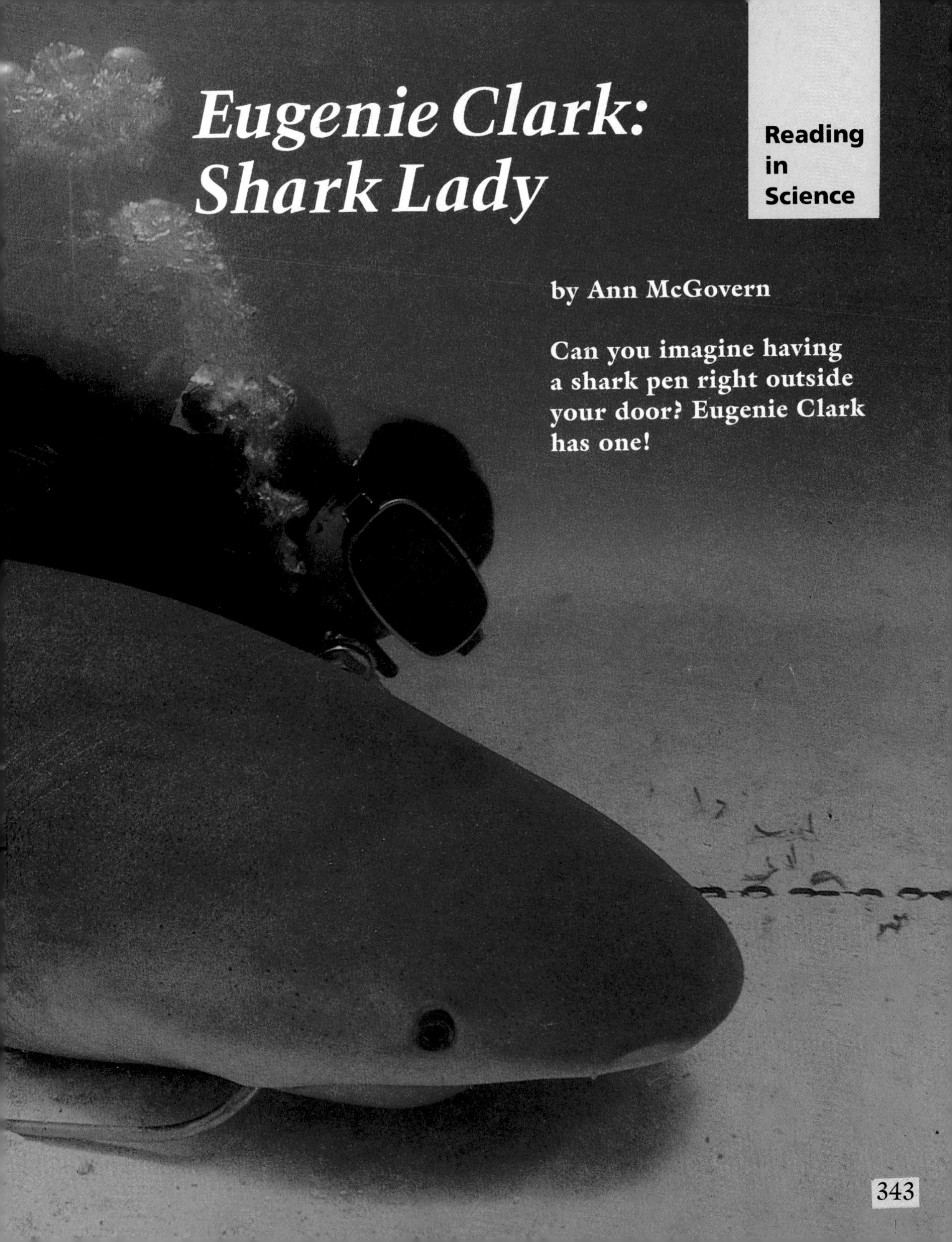

"Wake up, Genie," Mama called. "We have to go downtown soon."

Eugenie Clark sighed into her pillow. Who wants to go downtown on a Saturday? Saturdays were for climbing rocks and trees with Norma, her best friend. Saturdays were for digging up fat worms, bringing home bugs and snakes — making sure that Grandma didn't see them.

Those were the good Saturdays. But today was different. Her friend Norma had to go shopping with her mother. Grandma wasn't feeling well and needed to have peace and quiet. There was no place for nine-year-old Eugenie to be except with Mama at work.

Mama worked in a big building in downtown New York City. She sold newspapers at the stand in the lobby.

In the rumbling subway train speeding downtown, Mama looked at her daughter's sad face and wished there was something she could do to make Eugenie happier.

Eugenie's father had died when she was a baby. So Mama had to work extra hard to earn enough money to take care of the family. Working extra hard meant working Saturday mornings too.

The subway train pulled into their station and they got out. A sign at the top of the subway stairs said TO THE AQUARIUM.

"A good idea," Mama said. "I'll leave you at the aquarium, and I'll pick you up at noon. That will be more fun for you than sitting around the stand all morning."

Eugenie walked through the doors of the aquarium and into the world of fish.

She walked among the tanks filled with strange fish. Then she came to a big tank at the back. She stared at it for a long, long time. The green, misty water seemed to go on and on. She leaned over the rail, her face close to the glass, and made believe that she was walking on the bottom of the sea.

Eugenie went to the aquarium the next Saturday, and the next Saturday, and the Saturday after that. She went on all the cold Saturdays, the rainy and snowy Saturdays of autumn and winter. Sometimes her best friend, Norma, went with her, but often she went alone to be with the fish.

Eugenie read about fish too. She read about a scientist who put a diving helmet on his head and went deep under the waves. He walked on the bottom of the sea with the fish swimming around him.

"One day I'll walk with the fish too," she said.

In the summer, Mama took her to the beach. Mama had taught Eugenie to swim before she was two years old.

When Mama came out of the water, her long black hair streamed down her back. Eugenie thought Mama looked like pictures she had seen of beautiful pearl divers of the Orient. Mama was Japanese.

Mama was a good swimmer, and Eugenie loved to watch her swim with long, graceful strokes.

Now, in the autumn and in the winter, Eugenie watched the very best swimmers — the fish in the aquarium. She

In this tank are fish native to the Amazon River of South America. Among them are neon gobies, discus fish, and freshwater angelfish.

found all the fish exciting — the smallest fish glowing like tiny stars and the fish with fluttering fins that looked like fairy wings. But it was the biggest fish in the aquarium that she came back to again and again.

She watched the big shark swimming, turning, swimming, turning, never resting its long, graceful body. She watched it and lost track of time.

"Mighty shark," she thought. "One day I'll swim with sharks."

Eugenie kept visiting the aquarium and studying the fish there. Soon she convinced her mother that she could study fish better if she had an aquarium at home too. Her mother agreed. Throughout elementary and high school, Eugenie collected and studied all kinds of fish. By the time she began to think about college, she knew that she would become an ichthyologist — a person who studies and works with fish. She went on to college and graduate school, earning high honors in her chosen field.

Now she was Dr. Eugenie Clark. She had won scholarships to study fish in many parts of the world. She had married a doctor and they had Hera, a baby girl. She had also found time to write a book about her adventures. The book was titled *Lady with a Spear*.

In the book, she had written about a marine laboratory on the Red Sea, where she had studied and worked for a year.

Thousands of people read her book. Anne and William Vanderbilt of Florida read it too.

There was no marine laboratory in the western part of Florida where the Vanderbilts lived. They called Eugenie and invited her to meet with them.

"It would be great if we had a marine lab here like the one you described in your book," Mr. Vanderbilt said to her. "What do you think? Would you like to start one?"

Her own lab! It was a great thought.

Six months later, in early January, 1955, Dr. Eugenie Clark opened the doors of a small wooden building. A sign over the door said CAPE HAZE MARINE LABORATORY. Nearby were beaches, bays, islands, and the Gulf of Mexico. The sea was right outside the door!

Eugenie couldn't wait to see what treasures were in those waters. That very afternoon, she and Beryl Chadwick, a fisher who lived nearby, netted many fish. They even found some sea horses. Eugenie was eager to start the job of finding out about all the fish. Beryl said he would help her.

Eugenie also wanted to study sharks in captivity. The lab needed a place to keep sharks alive. So next to the lab's dock, a big pen was built for sharks and other fish.

The lab grew. From the beginning, scientists came to it to work on their research projects. There was a library just for books and magazines about sea life. There were thirty tanks for fish and other sea creatures. New shark pens were always being built.

Every day, people brought in buckets filled with some

Dr. Eugenie Clark diving in Japan.

swimming or creeping creatures of the sea. They brought in snakes and turtles. One man came in with an alligator almost as big as Eugenie. Beryl made a pond for it under the shade of a tree.

During the twelve exciting years she worked at the lab, Eugenie had more children. Now Hera had a little sister, Aya, and two brothers, Tak and Niki.

"I was doing what I always wanted to do most," she wrote later. "I was studying sharks and other fish, with everything in one place. I had the collecting grounds, the lab, and my home and family."

Eugenie had traveled widely, exploring the underwater world beneath many seas. She was learning and making important scientific discoveries.

One of those discoveries was made when Eugenie went to Israel to do research at the Marine Laboratory on the Red Sea. She was studying a little fish called the Moses sole.

The first time she caught the Moses sole in her net, she was surprised to see a bit of white milk-like fluid coming out along its fins. She reached out and touched the fins. The white stuff felt slippery. Her fingers felt tight and tingly. That white fluid might be full of poison!

Eugenie made tests in the lab. Then she began experiments in the sea. She put the Moses sole in a large plastic

Two divers, with a Moses sole in a plastic bag, are testing the effects of its poison.

bag that fit over a branch of coral where many little fish lived. Next she squeezed the Moses sole through the plastic bag. She squeezed until a few drops of milk came out. In minutes, every small fish that had been swimming in the bag was dead, killed by the poison of the Moses sole.

"What would happen to bigger, more dangerous fish?" she wondered. She began testing the Moses sole with sharks in the lab. She tied the little fish to a line in the shark tank.

First the sharks swam toward the Moses sole with their mouths open, ready to gobble the little fish. Then, with their jaws still wide open, the sharks jerked away. They leaped about the tank, shaking their heads wildly from side to side. All the while, the Moses sole kept swimming, as if nothing were happening.

Next, Eugenie put other live fish right next to the Moses sole on the line. The sharks kept away from those fish too.

For the next test, Eugenie washed the skin of a Moses sole with alcohol. She dropped

Dr. Clark studying the Moses sole in the Red Sea.

the fish into the shark tank. The little fish was swallowed by the shark in no time! Washing the fish with alcohol had removed its poison.

What was this powerful poison? The little Moses sole didn't look very special. It looked like any flat fish you might see in a fish store, but it certainly kept away sharks in the tanks. Now Eugenie wanted to find out what would happen when it came in contact with big sharks in the sea.

Eugenie and her helpers set out a shark line in the sea, far from shore. They put different kinds of fish on the line, some alive and some dead. All along the line, in between the other fish — but not too close — they hung the Moses sole.

They set the line during the day. Nothing happened as long as it was light. Then the sun began to set and the sea grew dark.

Eugenie and the others put on scuba gear and slipped into the water to watch.

The sea was calm and as smooth as glass. Suddenly the water moved over the shark line. One dark shadow, then another, drifted up from the deep. From the dark depths of the sea, sharks were swimming up. Silently, swiftly, they swam to the little fish wriggling on the line.

The sharks ate up all the fish one by one — all but the Moses sole!

Day after day Eugenie repeated the test. She noticed that the sharks came to the line most often just after sunset and again the next morning before the sun rose. Each time, they avoided the Moses sole!

Naftali Primor, one of Eugenie's students in Israel, also studied the Moses sole. He found that the poison from this little fish was better as a shark repellent than any other chemical. A very small amount of it could keep hungry sharks away for many hours — eighteen hours in one of the tests. It didn't wash away in the water as other chemicals did.

Eugenie is glad that a useful shark repellent might come from the little fish, but she doesn't think that the Moses sole should be used only for that. She says that sharks aren't as dangerous to swimmers and divers as most people think. There is another useful chemical in the milk-like fluid of the Moses sole. It can stop the action of the poison in some snake bites, scorpion bites, and bee stings. Eugenie Clark thinks that if research companies become willing to spend the time and money, they might find a way

to make this chemical. Then the lives of many people who have been bitten by animals and insects could be saved.

So many dreams have come true for Eugenie Clark. When she was a little girl, she dreamed of walking on the bottom of the sea with the fish. Eugenie Clark dreamed of

Dr. Eugenie Clark studying a hooked blacktip shark.

swimming with sharks. She dreamed of becoming a teacher. Later she dreamed of working at her own marine lab. She has done all these things.

Author

Ann McGovern, who is an author and an editor, has written more than thirty children's books. She also has founded a children's book club. Because of her interest in underwater photography, Mrs. McGovern has dived with sharks and sea lions. Her books, *Shark Lady* and *Underwater World of the Coral Reef,* reflect her interest in the ocean and its creatures.

Thinking It Over

Comprehension Questions

1. Why did Eugenie have a shark pen right outside her door?
2. Where did Eugenie first see sharks?
3. How did Mother encourage Eugenie's interest in fish?
4. What was Eugenie's first experiment with the Moses sole? Her second experiment with the sole?
5. How might Eugenie's study of the Moses sole be important to people someday?

Vocabulary

The following words have more than one meaning. Match the words with their meanings from the story. Then look up each word in a dictionary, and write three sentences for each word, using the other meanings you find.

marine	"a flatfish"
pen	"of the sea"
sole	"a small, fenced-in area"

Writing From a Different Point of View

Reread on page 349 about Eugenie's second experiment with the Moses sole in the shark tank. Write about what happened from the sole's point of view.

352

The Shark

by John Ciardi

My dear, let me tell you about the shark.
Though his eyes are bright, his thought is dark.
He's quiet — that speaks well of him.
So does the fact that he can swim.
But though he swims without a sound,
Wherever he swims he looks around
With those two bright eyes and that one dark thought.
He has only one but he thinks it a lot.
And the thought he thinks but can never complete
Is his long dark thought of something to eat.
Most anything does. And I have to add
That when he eats his manners are bad.
He's a gulper, a ripper, a snatcher, a grabber.
Yes, his manners are drab. But his thought is drabber.
That one dark thought he can never complete
Of something — anything — somehow to eat.

Be careful where you swim, my sweet.

Mighty Mini

by Chris Morningforest

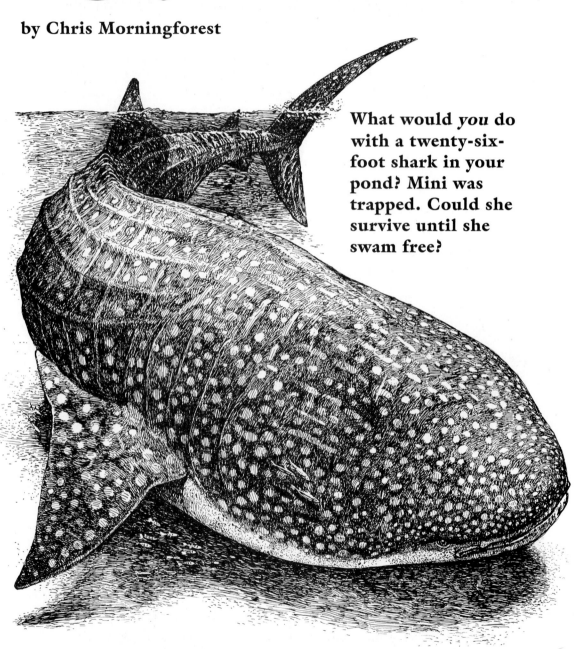

What would *you* do with a twenty-six-foot shark in your pond? Mini was trapped. Could she survive until she swam free?

Mini was a young whale shark — the largest kind of fish in the world. Most of the time, she swam peacefully in the open sea. Now she was upset by her strange surroundings.

Mini had swum into the lagoon, or big bay, of a South Seas island. High tides had swept her over a coral reef in the bay. Now she was lost in a maze of channels, with walls of coral all around.

Paths of water led to other paths that led to nowhere. Suddenly Mini saw an opening in the coral ahead. She squeezed her big body through it, but it did not lead back to the bay. Instead, it opened into a small saltwater pond right next to the island.

Mini didn't know it, but now she was a prisoner. The reef she had swum through separated her from the bay and from freedom. Now she was too frightened and upset to find her way back through the reef.

The next day a few island people went down to the beach to go fishing. There, cutting through the warm green water, was the tallest shark fin they had ever seen. It was Mini, swimming back and forth, back and forth, in the narrow pond.

The island people couldn't believe their eyes — and no wonder! Mini was only half-grown, but she was already longer than two living rooms. Pale-colored dots and long, narrow stripes covered her gray-brown body. Her huge mouth was nearly four feet across.

A week later, Mini was still there. She swam a regular route around the pond, but she always steered clear of the coral reef. People began to worry. How could such a big fish find enough to eat in such a small space? They didn't want Mini to die, so they decided to send for help.

A very excited team of scientists soon arrived from Hawaii. Few people had ever had the chance to see even a dead whale shark. Now they would be able to study a *live* one up close!

The scientists didn't waste any time. Two of them put on their scuba diving gear and flip-flopped down to the water's edge. Many of the island people were worried: Would the giant fish hurt the divers?

A scientist who stayed on shore explained that there was very little danger because huge whale sharks eat only very small fish and tiny floating plants and animals called *plankton*.

Mini swam toward the divers as soon as they were in the water. The people on shore held their breath, but she passed the divers by with barely a glance.

On her next lap around the pond, Mini found she had two "hitchhikers" on her back. The divers were trying to hold on to her as she swam. One of them even grabbed her huge dorsal fin, but the shark didn't seem to care.

On Mini's next lap, one of the divers took one end of a tape measure and swam as fast as she could to keep even with Mini's nose. Her diving partner was also swimming like crazy. He had to duck Mini's flapping tail while reading the numbers on the other end of the tape. Mini measured over twenty-six feet long!

Back on the beach, the other scientists were faced with another big problem. If they were going to keep the shark alive, they had to find something for her to eat.

A cook on the island offered fifty pounds of shrimp. A person offered to lend the scientists a small boat to get the shrimp out to Mini. Now the question was: Would she eat?

The next morning the scientists headed out into the pond and anchored over Mini's usual path. As she passed under the boat, one person threw some shrimp in front of her. Mini sensed the food right away and did something incredible. She swam over to the boat and bumped it with her snout! The scientists almost fell overboard in surprise. Then she came straight to the surface, shoved her head out of the water, and opened her big mouth wide. "Food," Mini seemed to be saying. "Now!"

The people in the boat were so caught off guard that they just sat there for a moment. Then one person threw a handful of shrimp into Mini's wide open mouth.

Fwooosh! Out came the shrimp, along with a great blast of water. Mini sank back into the water, then bobbed up again. Once more she opened her mouth.

Food was thrown to her again and again. Each time Mini spit it back out. It seemed that she was hungry, but why wouldn't she eat?

Not knowing what else to do, one person took the rest of the bucket of shrimp and dumped it down Mini's throat. She spit it out as before, but this time she sucked the shrimp back in.

Then the scientists understood. Whale sharks are filter feeders. In order to eat, they have to take in a great deal of water along with their food. As they squish the sea water out through their gills, the food catches on rows of strainerlike gill rakers in their throats. Then they swallow it down.

Mini bumped the boat and opened her mouth again. Her message was clear: "More!" The scientists fired up the motor and headed back to the beach as fast as they could, yelling for more food. They could not believe what had happened — a wild whale shark begging for food like a pet dog!

The scientific team studied Mini for several weeks. They watched what she ate and how she acted. They even clipped a metal tag to her dorsal fin so they would be able to keep track of her in the open sea. However, getting her to go back to the sea was still a problem. Not even food could lure her back through the passage in the reef to freedom.

Then the island people had an idea. They tied many nets together to form one great big net three hundred feet long. Then they stretched it across the pond. Mini was cornered in the end nearest the reef.

On official "Free Mini Day," the whole island showed up to help and to cheer Mini on. The net was pulled toward the reef. Mini swam slowly ahead of it. Would she be free at last? Her swimming space got smaller and smaller. Soon there was just barely enough room for her to turn around.

When Mini was right in front of the opening that led to the lagoon, she stopped. She sank like a rock; then without warning she charged the net.

Splash! Into the water went many of Mini's would-be rescuers. She fled to the other end of the pond. Soon she was swimming her old route once more, quiet as a goldfish.

For four days the island people tried to free the shark, and for four days they failed. Finally everybody gave up. They were worn out. When they returned a day later, Mini was gone. She had finally taken the path to freedom.

But she hadn't gone far!

There in the big lagoon, just across the reef from her old pond, swam Mini. Back and forth, back and forth she went, only this time her route was ten miles long.

Mini stayed there for over a year. Then, as suddenly as she had appeared, she was gone. Everyone was glad for her. They knew the ocean was the only proper place for a whale shark — even a friendly one like Mini!

Author

Chris Morningforest's sons were very interested in nature as they grew up. Their interest inspired her to write nature articles for children's magazines. Chris Morningforest is also an artist, and her ability to observe closely helps her to paint accurate word pictures in her articles.

Thinking It Over

Comprehension Questions

1. How did Mini get enough food in the pond?
2. How could the scientists track Mini in the ocean?
3. What happened when people tried to guide Mini out of the pond with a net?
4. How did Mini show that she had not been scared by her stay in the pond?

Vocabulary

The words in the list below are sea creatures. Look each word up in a reference source to determine whether it is a mammal or fish. Write each word on a separate card, and separate the cards into two categories, mammals or fish. See how many other fish or mammals that live in the sea you can add to the categories.

whales	**seals**	**flounders**
minnows	**tunas**	**porpoises**
sharks	**guppies**	**otters**

Writing a Report

Look up *Sharks* in the card catalog in the library. Find a book that will give you information about whale sharks, and write a short report about them.

Summarizing

What Is Summarizing?

Do you remember the story about Ernie and the mile-long muffler? Suppose you wanted to tell someone about that story. You certainly wouldn't use all the words that the author used. You wouldn't take the time to retell the whole story.

Instead of telling everything you have read in a story or have seen in a movie or television show, you can give a **summary.** This is a short way of retelling a longer selection. You tell only the most important parts. When you tell or write a summary, you are **summarizing.**

Summarizing can help you to understand and remember what you read. It also will help you to tell other people about things you have learned.

What Is a Good Summary?

In general, when you summarize, you will tell about a whole article or story. In this lesson, however, you will begin by summarizing paragraphs.

At the top of the next page is a paragraph from "Ernie and the Mile-Long Muffler." Read it, and then read the two summaries that follow it. Decide which one is better. As you read, keep these two questions in mind:

Is the summary shorter than the part from the story?
Does it tell only the most important things?

Ernie told the class all about his Uncle Simon's being a sailor. He told them about the things Uncle Simon had eaten in his travels and the places Uncle Simon had been. He told them about Uncle Simon's terrific sweater. He told them that Uncle Simon liked best to read mysteries; next, to bake bread; and third, to knit. He told them what Uncle Simon had said about people in armies and navies having lots of time while they waited for things to happen, so soldiers and sailors for hundreds of years knitted to keep from being bored.

Summary 1

Ernie told the class about the things Uncle Simon had eaten. He told them that Uncle Simon liked best to read mysteries. He told them what Uncle Simon had said about people in armies and navies having lots of time while they waited for things to happen.

Is this a good summary? Why?

Summary 2

Ernie told the class about his Uncle Simon, who was a sailor. He told them about some of Uncle Simon's hobbies, including knitting. Uncle Simon said that soldiers and sailors had knitted for hundreds of years.

Is this a good summary? Why?

You can see that both summaries are shorter than the paragraph from the story. They have about half as many words.

Do the summaries tell only the most important things? Did you notice that the first summary is missing some important facts? The person who wrote that one did what many people do when they try to summarize. They read until they find some sentences that seem important. They copy those words. Then they read some more and copy again.

A summary that is written by just copying some words and leaving out others may not have all the important facts.

How Do You Find the Important Information?

Summary 2 is good because it covers only the most important things in the paragraph. Read the first sentence of the summary:

Ernie told the class about his Uncle Simon, who was a sailor.

That sentence tells what the paragraph is about. It gives the main idea of the paragraph.

Always try to start a summary with a sentence that gives the main idea. Sometimes the main idea will be stated in a sentence in the selection you are summarizing. At other times, you will have to write your own main idea sentence.

When you write the rest of the summary, try to use only facts that are about the main idea. To find the information that you need, read the piece again very carefully. In Summary 2, these are the sentences that follow the main idea sentence:

He told them about some of Uncle Simon's hobbies, including knitting. Uncle Simon said that soldiers and sailors had knitted for hundreds of years.

Notice that all those sentences fit together and have something to do with the main idea.

How Do You Write Short Sentences?

The author of Summary 2 copied only part of the first sentence from the story. Then short sentences were used to give important information. How do you write short sentences without losing important points?

First, leave out anything that is repeated many times. For example, in the story paragraph, the words *He told them that Uncle Simon* and *He told them about Uncle Simon* appear five times. In Summary 2, only one sentence begins with the words *He told*.

Second, use a few words to take the place of many. Read this sentence from the story again:

He told them that Uncle Simon liked best to read mysteries; next, to bake bread; and third, to knit.

This is the shorter sentence that was used in Summary 2:

He told them about some of Uncle Simon's hobbies, including knitting.

That sentence gives the name of a group (hobbies) in place of the names of things in that group (reading mysteries, baking bread, and knitting).

To be sure that your sentences have all the important facts and are as short as possible, you may need to write a rough draft first. Read it over to be sure that all the facts are there. Cross out words that you don't need. Then write your summary again in final form.

Making a Summary

Read the paragraph below from the same story about Ernie. Then give a short summary. Try to have no more than four sentences in your summary.

All the things sold at the fair were knitted by the fourth grade. Frankie was good at mittens and so was Edward. Frankie knitted all the right-hand ones and Edward all the left-hand ones. Between them, they made five pairs of mittens for the fair. Alfred made bean bags. Cynthia made pot holders. Other people made mufflers (the regular length). Mrs. Crownfeld made cat and dog sweaters. Someone else made pincushions. Everyone in the fourth grade made something. The fair was a huge success. They sold $173.42 worth of stuff, including six pairs of slipper socks in bright colors that Ernie made and delicious cookies that Frankie, Alfred, and Ernie baked and sold.

Skill Summary

Summarizing will help you to understand and remember what you read. When you make a summary, remember these points:

- Keep only the most important facts.
- Begin with a main idea sentence.
- Then add other sentences that relate to the main idea.
- To keep sentences short, leave out words that are repeated and use a few words in place of many.
- Use just a few words to stand for many words.

"Two Big Bears"

an excerpt from
Little House in the Big Woods

written by
Laura Ingalls Wilder

illustrated by Troy Howell

In 1872 Laura Ingalls and her family lived in the Big Woods of Wisconsin. Miles from any store, her family provided their own food from what they could grow and catch. Sometimes life was scary because bears and wolves roamed the woods. Then there were also wonderful, happy times when friends and relatives gathered for a sugaring off party or holiday feast. Laura Ingalls Wilder's marvelous true stories about her family's life and adventures as pioneers are part of the famous series of "Little House" books.

Little House in the
Big Woods

by Laura Ingalls Wilder

illustrated by Troy Howell

Two Big Bears

"Two Big Bears" is part of a book called Little House in the Big Woods *by Laura Ingalls Wilder. The author really is the girl Laura in the story. In the book she tells about the exciting time, many years ago, when she was growing up in a log cabin home in the Big Woods of Wisconsin.*

Once upon a time, many years ago, a little girl lived in the Big Woods of Wisconsin, in a little gray house made of logs.

The great, dark trees of the Big Woods stood all around the house, and beyond them were other trees, and beyond them were more trees. As far as a person could go to the north in a day, or a week, or a whole month, there was nothing but woods. There were no houses. There were no roads. There were no people. There were only trees and the wild animals who had their homes among them.

Wolves lived in the Big Woods, and bears, and huge wild cats.

So far as the little girl could see, there was only the one little house where she lived with her father and mother, her sister Mary, and baby sister Carrie. A wagon track ran before the house, turning and twisting out of sight in the woods where the wild animals lived, but the little girl did not know where it went, nor what might be at the end of it.

The little girl was named Laura and she called her father, Pa, and her mother, Ma.

At night, when Laura lay awake in the trundle bed, she listened and could not hear anything at all but the sound of the trees whispering together. Sometimes, far away in the night, a wolf howled. Then he came nearer and howled again.

It was a scary sound. Laura knew that wolves would eat little girls. But she was safe inside the solid log walls. Her father's gun hung over the door and good old Jack, the brindle bulldog, lay on guard before it. Her father would say, "Go to sleep, Laura. Jack won't let the wolves in." So Laura snuggled under the covers of the trundle bed, close beside Mary, and went to sleep.

Then one day Pa said that spring was coming.

Pa said he must go to town to trade the furs of the wild animals he had been trapping all winter. So one evening he made a big bundle of them. There were so many furs that when they were packed tightly and tied together they made a bundle almost as big as Pa.

Very early one morning, Pa strapped the bundle of furs on his shoulders and started to walk to town. There were so many furs to carry that he could not take his gun.

Ma was worried, but Pa said that by starting before sun-up and walking very fast all day, he could get home again before dark.

The nearest town was far away. Laura and Mary had never seen a town. They had never seen a store. They had never seen even two houses together.

373

But they knew that in a town there were many houses, and a store full of candy and calico and other wonderful things — powder and shot and salt and store sugar.

They knew that Pa would trade his furs to the storekeeper for beautiful things from town, and all day they were expecting the presents he would bring them. When the sun sank low above the treetops and no more drops fell from the tips of the icicles, they began to watch eagerly for Pa.

The sun sank out of sight, the woods grew dark, and he did not come. Ma started supper and set the table, but he did not come. It was time to do the chores, and still he had not come.

Ma said that Laura might come with her while she milked the cow. Laura could carry the lantern.

So Laura put on her coat. Then Laura put her hands into her red mittens that hung by a red yarn string around her neck, while Ma lighted the candle in the lantern.

Laura was proud to be helping Ma with the milking, and she carried the lantern very carefully. Its sides were of tin, with places cut in them for the candlelight to shine through.

When Laura walked behind Ma on the path to the barn, the little bits of candlelight from the lantern leaped all around her on the snow. The night was not yet quite dark. The woods were dark, but there was a

gray light on the snowy path, and in the sky there were a few faint stars. The stars did not look as warm and bright as the little lights that came from the lantern.

Laura was surprised to see the dark shape of Sukey, the brown cow, standing at the barnyard gate. Ma was surprised too.

It was too early in the spring for Sukey to be let out in the Big Woods to eat grass. She lived in the barn, but sometimes on warm days Pa left the door of her stall open so she could come into the barnyard. Now Ma and Laura saw her behind the bars, waiting for them.

Ma went up to the gate and pushed against it to open it. It did not open very far, because there was Sukey, standing against it. Ma said, "Sukey, get over!" She reached across the gate and slapped Sukey's shoulder.

Just then one of the dancing little bits of light from the lantern jumped between the bars of the gate, and Laura saw long, shaggy, black fur, and two little, glittering eyes.

Sukey had thin, short, brown fur. Sukey had large, gentle eyes.

Ma said, "Laura, walk back to the house."

So Laura turned around and began to walk toward the house. Ma came behind her. When they had gone part way, Ma snatched her up, lantern and all, and ran. Ma ran with her into the house and slammed the door.

Then Laura said, "Ma, was it a bear?"

"Yes, Laura," Ma said. "It was a bear."

Laura began to cry. She hung onto Ma and sobbed, "Oh, will he eat Sukey?"

"No," Ma said, hugging her. "Sukey is safe in the barn. Think, Laura — all those big, heavy logs in the barn walls. The door is heavy and solid, made to keep bears out. No, Laura, the bear cannot get in and eat Sukey."

Laura felt better then. "But it could have hurt us, couldn't it?" she asked.

"It didn't hurt us," Ma said. "You were a good girl, Laura, to do exactly as I told you, and to do it quickly, without asking why."

Ma was trembling, and she began to laugh a little. "To think," she said, "I've slapped a bear!"

Then she put supper on the table for Laura and Mary. Pa had not come yet. Laura and Mary were undressed, and they said their prayers and snuggled into the trundle bed.

Ma sat by the lamp, mending one of Pa's shirts. The house seemed cold and still and strange, without Pa.

Laura listened to the wind in the Big Woods. All around the house the wind went crying as though it were lost in the dark and the cold. The wind sounded frightened.

Ma finished mending the shirt. Laura saw her fold it slowly and carefully. She smoothed it with her hand. Then she did a thing she had never done before. She went to the door and pulled the leather latch-string through its hole in the door so that nobody could get in from outside unless she lifted the latch. She came and took Carrie, all limp and sleeping, out of the big bed.

She saw that Laura and Mary were still awake, and she said to them, "Go to sleep, girls. Everything is all right. Pa will be here in the morning."

Then she went back to her rocking chair and sat there rocking gently and holding Baby Carrie in her arms.

She was sitting up late, waiting for Pa. Laura and Mary meant to stay awake, too, till he came, but at last they went to sleep.

In the morning Pa was there. He had brought treats for Laura and Mary, and two pieces of pretty calico to make them each a dress. Mary's was a china-blue pattern on a white ground, and Laura's was dark red with little golden-brown dots on it. Ma had calico for a dress too; it was brown, with a big, feathery white pattern all over it.

They were all happy because Pa had got such good prices for his furs that he could afford to get them such beautiful presents.

The tracks of the big bear were all around the barn. There were marks of his claws on the walls, but Sukey and the horses were safe inside.

All that day the sun shone, the snow melted, and little streams of water ran from the icicles, which all the time grew thinner. Before the sun set, the bear tracks were only shapeless marks in the wet, soft snow.

After supper Pa took Laura and Mary on his knees and said he had a new story to tell them.

"When I went to town yesterday with the furs, I found it hard walking in the soft snow. It took me a long time to get to town, and other men with furs had come in earlier to do their trading. The store-keeper was busy, and I had to wait until he could look at my furs.

"Then we had to bargain about the price of each one, and then I had to pick out the things I wanted to take in trade.

"So it was nearly sundown before I could start home.

"I tried to hurry, but the walking was hard and I was tired, so I had not gone far before night came. I was alone in the Big Woods without my gun.

"There were still six miles to walk, and I came along as fast as I could. The night grew darker and darker, and I wished for my gun because I knew that some of the bears had come out of their winter dens. I had seen their tracks when I went to town in the morning.

"Bears are hungry and cross at this time of year; you know they have been sleeping in their dens all winter long with nothing to eat, and that makes them thin and angry when they wake up. I did not want to meet one.

"I hurried along as quickly as I could in the dark. By and by the stars gave a little light. It was still black as pitch where the woods were thick, but in the open places I could see, dimly. I could see the snowy road ahead a little way, and I could see the dark woods standing all around me. I was glad when I came into an open place where the stars gave me this faint light.

"All the time I was watching, as well as I could, for bears. I was listening for the sounds they make when they go carelessly through the bushes.

"Then I came again into an open place, and there, right in the middle of my road, I saw a big black bear.

"It was standing up on its hind legs, looking at me. I could see its eyes shine. I could see its pig-snout. I could even see one of its claws, in the starlight.

"My scalp prickled, and my hair stood straight up. I stopped in my tracks and stood still. The bear did not move. There it stood, looking at me.

"I knew it would do no good to try to go around it. It would follow me into the dark woods, where it could see better than I could. I did not want to fight a winter-starved bear in the dark. Oh, how I wished for my gun!

"I had to pass that bear to get home. I thought that if I could scare it, it might get out of the road and let me go by. So I took a deep breath, and suddenly I shouted with all my might and ran at it, waving my arms.

"It didn't move.

"I did not run very far toward it, I tell you! I stopped and looked at it, and it stood looking at me. Then I shouted again. There it stood. I kept on shouting and waving my arms, but it did not budge.

"Well, it would do me no good to run away. There were other bears in the woods. I might meet one any time. I might as well deal with this one as with another. Besides, I was coming home to Ma and you girls. I would never get here if I ran away from everything in the woods that scared me.

"So at last I looked around, and I got a good big club, a solid, heavy branch that had been broken from a tree by the weight of snow in the winter.

"I lifted it up in my hands, and I ran straight at that bear. I swung my club as hard as I could and brought it down, bang! on its head.

"And there it still stood, for it was nothing but a big, black, burned stump!

"I had passed it on my way to town that morning. It wasn't a bear at all. I only thought it was a bear, because I had been thinking all the time about bears and being afraid I'd meet one."

"It really wasn't a bear at all?" Mary asked.

"No, Mary, it wasn't a bear at all. There I had been yelling, and dancing, and waving my arms, all by myself in the Big Woods, trying to scare a stump!"

Laura said, "Ours was really a bear; but we were not scared because we thought it was Sukey."

Pa did not say anything, but he hugged her tighter.

"Oh-oo! That bear might have eaten Ma and me all up!" Laura said, snuggling closer to him. "But Ma walked right up to it and slapped it, and it didn't do anything at all. Why didn't it do anything?"

"I guess it was too surprised to do anything, Laura," Pa said. "I guess it was afraid when the lantern shone in its eyes. When Ma walked up to it and slapped it, it knew *she* wasn't afraid."

"Well, you were brave too," Laura said. "Even if it was only a stump, you thought it was a bear. You'd have hit it on the head with a club if it *had* been a bear, wouldn't you, Pa?"

"Yes," said Pa. "I would. You see, I had to."

385

Author

Laura Ingalls Wilder was born in 1867 in The Little House in the Big Woods of Wisconsin. She went by covered wagon to the Dakota Territory. In the "Little House" books, an award-winning series of eight books for children, she told the story of her childhood and of growing up in the early West. Mrs. Wilder wrote her first pioneer story in 1932. Her *Little House on the Prairie* was adapted for television in 1975.

Illustrator

Troy Howell, originally from California, now lives in the woods of Virginia. He has always loved to draw and paint, and his work was first published in *Cricket* magazine when he was eighteen. He has illustrated many children's books, including *Heidi* and *Pinocchio*.

Comprehension Questions

1. What were the two big bears?
2. Why was Ma pleased with Laura?
3. What did Ma do that showed she was worried when Pa didn't come home?
4. Why was Pa late coming home?

Vocabulary

Use the words below to fill in the blanks:

after   **then**   **before**
finally   **next**   **first**

_____ Ma could make a cake, she had to make butter. _____ she had milked the cow, she started. _____, she let the milk stand in a cool place until the cream rose to the top. _____, she put the cream in the churn and churned until the globs of butter separated from the cream. _____ she could take the butter out of the churn. _____ Ma had butter for her cake.

Writing a Summary

Imagine that you are Laura writing to a friend about Pa's trip to town. Summarize the first paragraph on page 380.

Magazine Wrap-up

Literary Skill: Problem

In "Two Big Bears," Pa's problem was that he had to get home even though he thought a big bear was blocking the road. How did Pa solve his problem? It was around this problem and its solution that Laura Ingalls Wilder told her story.

Often an author will describe a problem that involves one or more of the characters. The problem keeps your interest in the story. You want to read the rest of the story to find out how it is solved.

Think about each of the following stories that you read in Magazine Three. Tell what character or characters in each story had a problem, what the problem was, and how it was solved:

- "Ernie and the Mile-Long Muffler"
- "The Once-a-Year Day"
- "Paul Bunyan"

Vocabulary: Studying Fish

Use words from the list to complete the paragraphs below. Copy the paragraphs on your paper.

aquarium	net
captivity	research
diving helmet	sharks
ichthyologist	scuba gear

Imagine a visit to Eugenie Clark at her marine laboratory on the Red Sea. Eugenie is there with another _____ to do _____ on the Moses sole. That night you slip on _____ and swim out to watch the line with the Moses sole on it. The eager _____ hungrily attack the other fish on the line.

The next day you look for fish with Eugenie. Because you are not wearing a _____, you can swim in and out of caves, and you net different fish to study in _____. Your visit ends too soon, but the fish in your _____ at home are waiting for you.

Writing: First-Person Point of View

The stories you read in Magazine Three were all written as though the author was telling the story, from the third-person point of view.

Read the list of stories and the descriptions of the events. Choose one story and pretend you are that character. Write about the event from the first-person point of view. Use words such as *I, me, we,* or *us.*

- "The Once-a-Year Day": when Annie shared the piece of orange with Emma.
- "Paul Bunyan": when Paul decided on his life's work.
- "Two Big Bears": when Laura walked back to the house after Ma had touched the bear.

Books to Enjoy

Ramona Quimby, Age 8
by Beverly Cleary
Ramona, the star of several other books, has more ups and downs, both serious and funny.

Apples on a Stick
by Barbara Michels and Bettye White
These Texas playground chants and rhymes are fun to read aloud.

A Chance Wild Apple
by Marian Potter
Maureen grows up on a Missouri farm, in a lively story set in the thirties.

Blind Outlaw
by Glen Rounds
In this moving story, a boy who cannot speak tames a blind horse.

Flights
Magazine Four

Contents

Stories

The Gift

by Helen Coutant

Anna's special friend was coming home from the hospital today. What gift could Anna give her that would be worthy of their friendship?

Anna left the house early that morning. It would take her five minutes to run to Nana Marie's house. By now, Nana Marie might be back from the hospital. She had disappeared without warning more than a week ago. For two days, no one had answered when Anna knocked on the door after school. By the third day, Anna could scarcely eat, she was so worried. Had they taken Nana Marie to one of those homes for very old people? But the next afternoon the daughter-in-law, Rita, who took care of Nana Marie, had opened the door an inch. It was just enough so that Anna could hear her voice over the blare of the TV. "You here to see Nana Marie? She's in the hospital." That was all Anna found out.

Now, rounding a bend in the road, Anna could see Rita standing by the gate in front of Nana Marie's house. Rita's loud voice rang out. "She's coming home today! Home from the hospital! Nana Marie!"

Nana Marie was coming home. Anna's heart gave a joyful leap.

"We're throwing a little party," Rita went on, "just a few neighbors on the hill to welcome her back, cheer her up. Drop by. She'll be looking for you."

A party. That meant Anna would have to share Nana Marie with everyone else. Rita's voice, suddenly lower, caught Anna's attention.

"She won't really be looking for you, Nana Marie won't. Come to see her anyway, though. She'll need your company now that she's blind. . . ."

Blind? Rita's voice rattled on, but Anna heard nothing more. Her heart seemed to have stopped on the word *blind*. How could Nana Marie suddenly be blind? There had been nothing wrong with Nana Marie's eyes. In fact,

it was those extraordinary warm eyes, a cornflower blue, that had drawn Anna to Nana Marie in the first place. A small, choking noise escaped from Anna's throat.

Rita cocked her head and looked down, waiting for Anna to speak; then she resumed her monologue. "Just happened, just like that," she said, shaking her head. "It's a pity. It's terrible. But you come by this afternoon for the party. We'll cheer her up, give Nana Marie some little presents to help her forget. Can I count on you?"

Count on her! Had Anna ever missed a chance to visit Nana Marie in the last six months, ever since the two had discovered each other one balmy September afternoon?

"So you come!" Rita repeated, her voice rising.

Anna couldn't answer. She pulled back, nodding, and turned away. She walked carefully around the puddles in the road. Her whispered "good-by" floated up unheard by Rita, who was already going in the house, shivering from the cold.

When the door banged, Anna took off, propelled by anger and sorrow. Her heart was pumping "blind, blind, blind," faster and faster. Blind without any warning. How could it happen? Yet it had.

She got to the foot of the hill and headed for her favorite path, which led upward into the woods. The day was hers to do as she pleased.

There must be something she could do for Nana Marie. Rita had said something about a present. What present could ever console a person who had become blind?

Anna remembered a time she had imagined being blind. Once in the middle of the night she had opened her eyes thinking it was morning. The unexpected blackness pressed down on her. She turned her head this way and that and saw nothing, as if she had been buried. Just when she was ready to scream, her hand shot out and touched the light, nudging it on. The brightness, which then appeared so suddenly, dazzled her eyes. The patch-work quilt shone. The yellow walls glistened as if they had been freshly painted, and the air rushed out of her lungs in relief. Now she wondered how Nana Marie had felt waking up blind.

Anna broke into a trot. Ahead was a place she often came to, a small, deep spring in the woods. When she knelt to gaze into the bottomless pool, at first she saw nothing but darkness. Then as the sun came out, the water seemed to open up, reflecting the bark of silver beeches, shining like armor. The reflection of luminous silver reminded her of Nana Marie. She sat back on her heels, remembering.

Six months ago, at the end of summer, Anna and her parents moved to the house just up the hill from Rita's. A week later Anna started school. She didn't know anyone and found it hard to make friends with the other students. She was very lonely until one afternoon when she had looked up and saw Nana Marie's welcoming smile.

There was a small moving van outside Rita's house that day. From a safe distance, half concealed by bushes, Anna watched it being unloaded. There were only a half-dozen pieces of furniture, all a lovely dark wood, highly polished. Rita stood by, directing the operations. Anna could see the simple delight on Rita's face and wondered where this furniture was coming from.

As Anna watched, Rita's husband got out of his car, walked around it, and opened the door by the front seat.

Then there was a long wait. Finally a white head emerged. Haltingly, as though every movement took a great deal of thought, a very old woman rose and, holding on to her son's arm, began to walk toward the house. Halfway to the steps, she paused for breath. Then, as if she felt Anna's eyes on her, the old woman looked up. Their eyes met, and Nana Marie smiled.

The next afternoon when Anna came home from school, she saw Nana Marie sitting in a rocking chair on the front porch. Slowly Anna approached, her school shoes raising little puffs of dust. The moment Nana Marie saw her she smiled, and the next thing Anna knew she was sitting cross-legged at Nana Marie's feet. Then they began to talk as if they had known each other for years. On and on till supper time they talked, "like old friends reunited," Nana Marie said. They even found out they had birthdays the same month and only two days apart.

Every day after that, when the school bus let Anna off at the bottom of the hill, she raced up to Rita's house to keep Nana Marie company. As long as the afternoons were warm they sat on the porch until twilight. They never ran out of things to talk about. Nana Marie pointed out the fat groundhog scavenging for corn in the stubble of the field below Rita's house and the flock of wild geese whose perfect "V" cut the sky as they flew south with haunting cries. And always, if she told Anna to listen, from far away would come the hollow *clack-clack* of a woodpecker at work on a tree. Anna would linger, enchanted, until there was just enough light left for her to run home. Sometimes an autumn moon, perfectly round, lit her way.

When cold weather arrived, Anna climbed the steep stairs to Nana Marie's room. Sitting by the window, they could see the world just as well as from the porch. They watched the trees on the top of the mountain turn bare and black, while there was still a wide strip of deep yellow at the foot of the mountain. Day by day this strip shrank, until one day, after heavy rains, it was gone. Next came the snow, pure magic seen from Nana Marie's window.

Although most of Nana Marie's polished furniture was downstairs in Rita's living room, it was still cozy in Nana Marie's room. There was a bed, a table, a large chest of drawers, and a trunk. As soon as Anna arrived, she would put her books on the trunk and boil water on the hot plate in one corner. Then the two of them would have something to drink and share the events of the day. As the weeks passed, Anna learned that every object in Nana Marie's room had a meaning and a story. One by one, Anna learned the stories.

The silver hairbrush and matching hand mirror that lay on the chest of drawers had been an engagement present from Nana Marie's husband. A large *MK* with many curlicues was engraved on the back of each piece. Next to the hairbrush was a battered red and yellow tin box. When Anna opened the lid, she found a large round watch that dangled from a chain. The watch ticked once or twice when Anna moved it, then stopped. It had belonged to Nana Marie's father. On the trunk was a very shiny bright-blue clay bowl overflowing with odds and ends. One side of the bowl was crooked, and it tipped when Anna touched it. It had been a present from Nana Marie's grandson when he was seven. Boxes of letters and photographs completely covered the table. Anna loved best the teapot with its two Chinese pheasants. Its spout was stained brown from all the tea that had been poured, and Nana Marie said the teapot was six times as old as Anna.

Finally, what at first had seemed to Anna only a small, cluttered room expanded to become a history of Nana Marie's life, of her joys and sorrows and memories stretching over almost a century.

Gazing deep into the shining pool again, Anna decided that Nana Marie was like this spring. Each day of her old age she had quietly caught and held a different reflection. Stored in her depths were layers of reflections,

shining images of the world. Many of these she had shared with Anna. But now that she was blind, would these images be gone, the way water became dark when there was no light? What would her days be like?

Anna's thoughts moved to the party that Rita would hold in the afternoon. She knew what the neighbors were likely to bring: scarves, flowers. She could do the same, yet none of these gifts would express what she felt for Nana Marie. Could any of them really make Nana Marie feel better?

Lost in thought, Anna continued to follow the path up the mountain. Even though her sneakers were wet from the soft thawing soil of the woods, she decided to stay there. Maybe later she would know what to bring Nana Marie.

Slowly the world about her drew Anna in, just as if she had been with Nana Marie. The warm March sun was swallowed by a thick mist, which the mountain seemed to exhale with each gust of wind. Although the air was damp, it had an edge of warmth that had been absent in the morning. It felt almost like the beginnings of spring. As the hours passed, Anna picked up objects she thought Nana Marie would like: a striped rock, a tiny fern, a clump of moss, an empty milkweed pod. None of them, on second thought, seemed a proper gift for Nana Marie. Other days, she would have loved them. Now Anna thought they could easily make her sad, for in touching them, Nana Marie would be reminded of the things she would never see again. There had to be a way to bring the whole woods, the sky, and the fields to Nana Marie. What else would do? What else would be worthy of their friendship?

Suddenly Anna knew what her gift would be. It would be like no other gift, and a gift no one else could bring. All day long Anna had been seeing the world the way Nana Marie had shown her. Now she would bring everything she had seen to Nana Marie.

Her wet feet and her damp jeans and jacket no longer mattered. Eagerly she turned and began the long trudge back to Nana Marie's house. Her hands were empty in her pockets, but the gift she carried in her head was as big as the world.

Just as the sun went over the mountain, Anna emerged from the woods. Ahead of her was the road and Nana Marie's house. She looked at Nana Marie's room,

the window directly over the front door. A light should be on by now. But the blinds were down as they had been all week, and the window was so dark it reflected, eerily, the reddish glow of twilight. Everyone must be downstairs at the party. Probably Rita hadn't even bothered to go upstairs and raise the blinds. Yet downstairs the windows were dark too. What had happened? Where was Nana Marie?

Anna stopped to catch her breath. Her entire body was pounding. She ran around Rita's car to the kitchen door. She hesitated, biting her lip, before she rapped softly on the glass part of the door. There was no answer. She could see a light in the living room; the TV set was turned on. She knocked again, louder, then put her hand on the doorknob. It opened from the other side, and Rita stood there in her bathrobe. The kitchen table was covered with the remains of the party: tissue paper, stacked plates, and cups. So the neighbors had come and gone. Anna was too late for the party, but Nana Marie must be there!

"Well, here at last," Rita said. "I figured you went home and forgot. The party ended half an hour ago. I told Nana Marie it wasn't any use waiting up for you longer. I expect she's asleep by now. She was disappointed you didn't come, though she got lots of nice things from everybody. Why don't you come back tomorrow when she's rested."

"Please, I can't," Anna said. She bent, tearing at her wet shoelaces. "I have a present for Nana Marie. It won't take long. I'll take my shoes off and go upstairs to her room."

Rita shrugged. She seemed anxious to get back to her TV show. At the door to the living room she called back, "Don't go waking her up. I just got her settled. You can leave the present on her table. I'll tell her about it tomorrow."

Nodding, Anna headed for the stairs on tiptoe. The world of Rita dropped away as she climbed toward Nana Marie's room. The landing at the top of the stairs was dark, and the door to Nana Marie's room was closed. Anna's hand hesitated on the doorknob. Then she opened the door and shut it behind her.

Nana Marie's room was pitch black. There was no sound at all. Was the room empty? The window was straight ahead. Anna ran to it, groping for the cords. The blinds clattered up, crashing in the darkness. Rita was sure to come up. Then a faint light flowed into the room. Outside, in the winter twilight, a small frozen moon was wandering upward.

"Anna," Nana Marie was calling her name. She was not asleep after all. "Anna," Nana Marie said, and now there was surprise and joy in her voice. Nana Marie was sitting in her wooden rocking chair. Her eyes were wide open and as blue as they had always been, like the sky on a summer morning.

"Oh, Nana Marie!" Anna exclaimed. She patted the old warm skin of Nana Marie's cheek.

"You came," Nana Marie said. "I thought maybe you were getting tired of having such a very old lady for a friend."

"I brought you a present," Anna said. "I'm late because it took me all day to get it."

"Gracious," said Nana Marie. "You shouldn't have done that!"

"I brought you a last day," Anna said.

"A last day . . ." Nana Marie's voice trailed off. At the hospital someone had arranged her hair in soft waves. She put her hand up as if to touch them, but halfway there her fingers stretched out, reaching for Anna. She took Anna's hand and held it firmly.

"You didn't have a last day to look at the world," Anna said, "so I brought it to you. Everything I saw today. Just as if you saw it with me. The way you would see it. And tomorrow I'll bring you another — and the next day another. I'll bring you enough seeing to last forever. That's my present, Nana Marie."

Nana Marie was silent for a minute. Then she added softly, almost to herself, "Bless you, child, how did you ever think of that?" She leaned back in the rocking chair. One hand held on to Anna's. With the other she gestured toward a chair. "Pull it up right here, Anna," she said, "so we can look out over the valley and the moonlight together. The moon is out, isn't it, Anna? I can feel it." She closed her eyes.

Anna pulled Nana Marie's hand into her lap and held it with both of her own as she described the silver beeches reflected in the spring, the yellow mist breathing in and out, the pale sun — everything she had seen that day.

When Anna was finished, Nana Marie sat up and turned toward her. Nana Marie's blue eyes shone with contentment. "Thank you, Anna," she said. "That was beautiful." She paused briefly, and when she continued it was almost as though she was speaking to herself. "*This* is a day I'll always remember."

Anna sat holding on to Nana Marie's hand until the moon disappeared over the house. Even though she had gone blind, Nana Maria really hadn't changed. She could still marvel at the world; she could still feel the moonlight. Anna knew she was going to be all right.

Author

The Gift, which you have just read, is Helen Coutant's second book for children. Her first book was the award-winning *First Snow.* Helen Coutant is an English teacher and translator as well as an author. She and her husband have translated short stories from the Vietnamese language into English.

Comprehension Questions

1. What was the special gift that Anna brought Nana Marie?
2. What part of the year was it when Anna and Nana Marie first met?
3. How were Nana Marie's possessions part of the history of her life?
4. What did Nana Marie and Anna talk about together?
5. How did Anna know that her friend would be all right?

Vocabulary

Add either a prefix or a suffix to the words below to form words from the story. The meanings of the new words are given in quotation marks. Use the new words in sentences.

heard	"not heard"
united	"together again"
expected	"surprising"
appear	"go away"

Writing a Description

Anna loved Nana Marie's stories about the objects in her room. Write about some object in your house. Describe it and give its history.

SQRRR

When you study a textbook, you want to get as much information as you can. There is a plan for studying that will help you to understand and remember what you read. If you use the five-step plan, you will be able to learn more from your books in less time.

The letters **SQRRR** stand for those five steps. You may have already used the first three steps as you read some of the articles in this book.

Step 1 of SQRRR

Step 1, **S**, stands for **Survey**. This means "to look over." After reading the title of a chapter or article, look over each heading. Headings often are in special type, which sets them apart. *Step 1 of SQRRR* is the heading of this part of the lesson. What is the first heading in the article "Power" on pages 413-414?

When you start to study a lesson or a book, read each heading to get an idea of what you will be learning. Do not take much time to do this step.

Survey the headings in "Power." What do they tell you about what you will learn from the article?

Step 2 of SQRRR

Step 2, **Q**, stands for **Question**. In Step 2, change the first heading into a question if it is not written as one. For example, the question for the first heading in this lesson would be *What Is Step 1 of SQRRR?* What question could you make from the first heading in "Power"?

You are more likely to pick out and remember what is important information when you read to find the answer to a question. If the heading already is a question, then go on to Step 3.

Power

Every day we use power to do many different things, and we get power from many different sources. However, we are using so much power that in the near future we will need to find new sources.

Uses for Power

Almost everywhere we look, we see power being used. We use power to light our streets. We use power to run our buses, cars, and ships. We use power to cook our food and to heat our homes, schools, and factories. We also use power to build those homes, schools, and factories.

Where Power Comes From

Today, most of the power we use comes from mineral fuels — oil, coal, and natural

The lights of New York City require a great deal of power.

Hoover Dam, on the Colorado River, helps provide power for a large area of the Southwest.

gas. Water gives us some of our power, as does the wind. We also get some from nuclear power plants and the sun.

Need for New Sources

Most scientists believe that we are using up oil, coal, and natural gas too quickly. It takes millions and millions of years for Earth to make these fuels. Once our coal, oil, and natural gas are gone, there will be no more for millions of years. Some people say that we should be working hard to find new sources of power before we use up the fuels that we have.

Step 3 of SQRRR

Step 3, the first **R**, stands for **Read**. Read the paragraph under the first heading in "Power" to answer the question that you asked in Step 2. Read carefully to be sure you have answered the question completely. What answers did you find?

Step 4 of SQRRR

Step 4, the second **R**, stands for **Recite**. This means "to repeat from memory." When you have finished reading the information under a heading, tell yourself the answer to your question. Use your own words, so that you will be more likely to remember the answer. For the first heading in "Power," you might recite something like this: "Some uses for power are to light streets; to run buses, cars, and ships; to cook food; and to build and heat homes, schools, and factories."

For each heading in "Power," repeat Steps 2, 3, and 4. For each heading, ask a *question, read* to answer that question, and then *recite* the answer to yourself.

Step 5 of SQRRR

Step 5, the last **R**, stands for **Review**. To review means "to go back over." Go back over each heading in "Power," and again tell yourself the answer to the question that came from the heading.

It also is a good idea to review the information the day after you first study it. This will help you to remember it longer. If you are going to be tested on what you have read, then review the lesson again before the test.

Using SQRRR

Study the following article using each of the five steps in SQRRR: Survey, Question, Read, Recite, Review. Make a question from each heading. Be prepared to give, in your own words, the answers to those questions.

Rice

Rice is the major food for at least half of the people in the world. Millions of farm families spend their lives growing this important food crop.

Where Rice Is Grown

Rice is grown where there is plenty of water and a long, warm growing season. Over ninety percent of the world's rice is grown in Asia: The People's Republic of China grows the most rice, followed by India and Japan. In the United States, rice is grown mostly in

Texas, California, Louisiana, and Arkansas. In Europe, Italy is where the most rice is grown. In Africa, it is grown mostly along the Nile River in Egypt.

The Major Kinds of Rice

There are two major kinds of rice: upland rice and lowland rice. Upland rice, which is also called dry rice, is grown in places where there is plenty of rain. Lowland rice, or wet rice, is grown in fields that have been flooded with water. Most farmers grow this second kind of rice.

How Lowland Rice Is Grown

First, rice is planted in a muddy field. After about four weeks, the young rice plants are ready to be moved to a plowed and flooded field. This field is called the rice paddy. When the leaves on the plants begin to turn from green to yellow, the field is drained. The rice becomes ripe in the sun; then the rice is harvested.

Brown, White, and Wild Rice

Brown rice has more food value than white rice. When brown rice is polished to make it white, most of the vitamins and minerals and part of the fat in the rice are destroyed.

Wild rice is called "wild" because it grows that way. It is a different plant from upland and lowland rices. It is used the same way, but it is not a true rice.

Skill Summary

Use the five steps of SQRRR to understand and remember what you read. The five steps of SQRRR are **S**urvey, **Q**uestion, **R**ead, **R**ecite, and **R**eview.

Social Studies

How is reading a social studies lesson different from reading a story for fun? Your purpose for reading the lesson, the way it is put together, and the words that are used are different.

Before you begin to read a social studies lesson, think about *how* you are going to read it and *why* you are reading it. This helps you get more from it.

Importance of SQRRR

A lesson often has parts with a heading over each part. Because of the way a lesson is put together and because you want to remember the facts, SQRRR is a good way to study a lesson.

When you survey the lesson, you get an idea of what the lesson is about. The questions you make from the headings in the second step of SQRRR give you a purpose for reading. By reciting the answers to the questions, you form a summary in your mind of what is in the lesson.

After you are through reading, the review step helps you remember what you have just learned. This step will also help you answer questions about the lesson.

Reading a Social Studies Lesson

It is a good idea to read a social studies lesson carefully and slowly. You want to understand all the important details. You may find it helpful to keep paper and pencil handy to write down what is important. As you read, be sure you really understand. If you don't, you should first reread, and then if you still don't understand, ask someone to explain it to you.

Noticing Clue Words

In social studies, there are certain words that help you understand when things happened. Look for words such as *first, before, later,* and *after,* which help you figure out when things happened in relationship to each other. If you write down dates when important things happened, you can help yourself remember the order in which these things took place.

There are also words in social studies that give you clues to why things happened. Look for words such as *because, since, as a result, so,* and *therefore.*

Learning Social Studies Terms

Important social studies words are usually in boldface so that you won't miss them. Often you can find the meaning of the word right in the same sentence or in a footnote at the bottom of the page. If you can't find the meaning on the page and you can't figure it out from the sense of the words in the sentences around it, look up the word in either the glossary or a dictionary.

Learning the important terms will help you understand the lesson. You may find it useful to write down each new word and its meaning in a list.

Using Pictures

In social studies lessons, pictures are a big help to understanding. They can show easily what might be hard to put into words. To learn the most from the pictures, look at them carefully and read the captions. Read the legends on the maps, and find the places in the lesson that go with the pictures.

Skill Summary

When you read a social studies lesson, remember these points:
- Think ahead about the purpose of the lesson.
- Use SQRRR.
- Look for words that tell when and why things happened.
- Look at the pictures and read the captions.

Preview

"The Adobe Way," the next selection, is written like a social studies lesson. When you have finished reading "The Adobe Way," be able to tell how you used what you learned in this lesson.

THE ADOBE WAY

Soil, straw, and water . . . these are materials you might once have used to make mud pies, but would you use them to build a house? The Pueblo Indians and the early Spanish settlers who lived in the American Southwest did. Many people still do. Soil, straw, and water are easy to find. They are usually free, and when mixed together in the right amounts, they make a strong building brick called **adobe** (ə **dō′**bē).

Part of a wall made from adobe bricks.

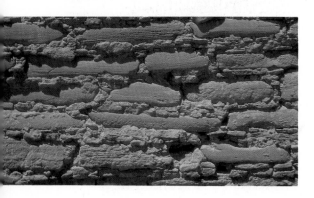

Advantages of Adobe

Adobe is the Spanish word for sun-dried bricks that are made from a special soil, which has just the right amount of clay. Buildings made from adobe are called adobes. Today, builders use adobe for several reasons. First, it does not cost much. Second, it is easy to use. It also saves heat energy. Finally, homes built with adobe are pleasing to look at.

First Adobes

About two thousand years ago, the Pueblo Indians began building with adobe. If you visit the southwestern part of the United States today, you can still see very old Pueblo adobes, as well as new, modern ones.

An early Spanish ranch house.

The apartment-like buildings of the early Pueblos stood three to four stories high. Each level was built on top of the other in tiers, which were like giant steps. The flat roof of the ground floor made a front porch for the families living on the second floor, and so on up to the top.

The living spaces inside the apartments were small, and each family lived in one room. Narrow, T-shaped doors connected the rooms on each apartment level. The walls were painted with a fresh whitewash made from a chalk found in the desert. The whitewash gave the room a clean, fresh look and reflected firelight.

Early Spanish Ranch Houses

When Spanish settlers first came to the Southwest from Mexico about four hundred years ago, they were not surprised to see that the Pueblos built with adobe. The Spanish had been using it for hundreds of years in their own country. But Spanish adobes were built in a different way.

The home pictured above was built in 1705. It gives you a good idea of how an old Spanish ranch house, or **hacienda** (hä′sē ĕn′də), looked. The house has several long rooms arranged around a court in the center. Do you see the beehive-shaped oven? It was used for baking bread.

Present-Day Adobes

Today you will find new adobes all through the Southwest and in some other parts of the country. Many of them look like the ones that were built in the past.

Some new adobes look like old Pueblo apartments, but they have modern features such as large windows and front doors.

Energy-Saving Adobe

All adobe homes, both past and present, are alike in one way. Their thick adobe walls help to save energy because adobe bricks slowly soak up heat, then release it over hours of time. That is why people often use adobe to build sun-heated homes, like the one in the picture on the next page.

In the winter, the sun enters the house through the large windows. Its heat is trapped in an extra thick wall built across from the windows. During the warm hours of the day, the thick wall soaks up the sunshine. At night, when the air starts to cool, the heat in the wall warms the room.

In the summer, when the sun climbs higher in the sky, the ledge above the window stops the heat from entering the house so the house stays cool.

The inside of this house looks like an old Spanish ranch house. Its fireplace is like those in old Pueblo apartments. The white walls help make the room lighter.

Because of its advantages, adobe will be important to tomorrow's builders. It comes from the earth, so there is plenty of it, and it is not expensive. Adobe saves heat, which makes it a good choice for tomorrow's homes. The adobes of tomorrow may look different, but they will always be popular.

A sun-heated adobe house.

Comprehension Questions

1. What is adobe made from?
2. Who were the first people to build with adobe in the United States, and when did they start using it?
3. How were the Spanish ranch homes different from the Indian adobes?
4. Why will adobe buildings continue to be popular?

Activity

Find out more about the homes of the Pueblo Indians, or Cliff Dwellers, by looking them up in an encyclopedia. Make a model of an early Pueblo adobe. Cardboard boxes of different sizes can be covered with paper or painted to look like adobe. Toothpicks glued together could make a ladder like the ones the Indians used to enter their homes. When you are through, label your model with the name of one of the famous cliff dwellings in the Southwest.

Sensory Images

How do you like my new TV? I got it for half price.

The picture is great, but I can't hear the sound.

Oh, there isn't any sound. That's why I got it for only half price!

As you can see, pictures without sound tell only half the story. When you want to describe something, you can tell the whole story by using both picture and sound words.

Picture words tell how something looks. They help you to "see" the picture. Read the sentence at the top of the next column.

The speeding roller coaster whipped around the track.

Speeding and *whipped* are picture words that tell how the roller coaster looked.

Now read this next sentence:

Screams and laughter filled the air as the speeding roller coaster whipped around the track.

424

Screams and *laughter* are sound words that help you to "hear" the roller coaster ride. Which of the two sentences do you think is the more interesting?

Read the following paragraph. Find the picture words that help you see the roller coaster ride. Then find the sound words that help you hear the ride.

I stare down the winding thread of track. My heart is pounding like a drum. Whump! With a jerk, the train begins. Clickity-clack, clickity-clack. I see the giant circle ahead. It waits patiently. I grab the safety bar of my car as it picks up speed. Faster and faster. The rattle of rails grows louder as the crowds below change into a whirlwind of bright colors. All too soon, I'm spinning in the loop. I scream, but the sound is lost in the roar of rushing air. First up, then down; then up-side down! Around and around. The world spins into a blur of blue. Swoosh-sh! I sail into empty sky. Whoosh-sh-sh! Into the last loop.

Right side up again, I can hear high-pitched shrieks. As wheels screech to a halt, the screams turn into shouts of laughter. I can hardly wait for the car to stop. Then I will jump out, run as fast as I can, and buy another ticket.

Look at the picture above. Imagine that you are standing inside the park. What picture words would you use to tell about the park? What sound words would you use?

The Pinto

by Stephen Tracy
with Patricia Olivérez

When Antonio's pinto pony ran away to join wild
horses, Antonio and his brother went after it. The
two boys had their courage tested in an unexpected
way.

It was a clear morning in 1842, when Monterey was still the capital of California and California still belonged to Mexico. The excitement of the upcoming rodeo stirred the air as groups of cowhands gathered at the Custom House. They joked and boasted about their horses, tied in a long line. Some of the cowhands looked at the new goods that had just arrived by ship. Some of the others bought cloth, sugar, and coffee to take back to the ranches where they worked.

The *vaqueros*[1], or cowhands, wore shiny leather boots or deerskin shoes embroidered with silver. They were dressed in velvet pants with gold braid and silver buttons and wore their wide, flat-topped hats. These people lived in the saddle. They roped cattle at full gallop. It was easy for them to pick up a coin, a handkerchief, or a trailing lasso from their galloping horses.

As Hernando, a cowhand, stepped out of the Custom House, he nearly bumped into his younger brother Antonio.

"Azul is gone!" Antonio cried. Anger and pain mixed in his voice.

Hernando circled his brother's shoulders with one arm. "I'm sorry, Antonio," he said, "but horses are easy to come by. You know that."

Then Hernando held out the silver that had just arrived for him at the Custom House. "Look at this silver! It came all the way by ship from Mexico. I can use it to make a beautiful bridle. It will be something truly special."

"Azul was special!" Antonio insisted.

---

[1]**vaqueros** (vä kâr′ōs)

Antonio loved the large brown spots on his pony's shiny white coat. He loved the flecks of blue in the pony's eyes. That was why he called his pony Azul — the Spanish word for blue. His pony was also exactly the right size, and no full-sized horse could stop or turn or follow a calf any better. For Antonio, Azul was truly special.

"Without Azul, I can't ride in the rodeo," Antonio said. "I must find him!"

"I see," Hernando said, "but he might have joined a wild herd. He will not be easy to find. The herd may be in the valley by now, and that's a day's journey."

"I'll track them," Antonio said. "I'll get Azul back."

"If they have gone as far as the valley," Hernando said, "you will need two days. You will have to camp. That is too much for a ten-year-old. Besides, how will you catch him? Do you think this pony who has run off will now come when you call him?"

Antonio had not thought of this. He was not thinking clearly.

"There will be other ponies and other rodeos," Hernando said, trying to comfort Antonio.

"There is no pony like Azul!" Antonio said. "With Azul, I was ready for the rodeo. I have worked with him all year. We were partners. We *are* partners!"

After this, Antonio stared at his feet. Hernando carefully placed his new silver in his saddle bag. Suddenly Antonio had an idea.

"Will you help me track Azul, Hernando?" he asked.

"I can't," Hernando said. "I have traded a saddle for this silver. Now I'm ready to finish the most beautiful bridle I have ever made. I have only two days before the rodeo. Just think of this silver on the headband!"

"How can you worry about that?" Antonio said with a sigh. "I won't even have a horse."

Hernando gave his younger brother a long look. He had watched Antonio and Azul practice turns and roping day after day. For a year now, hardly a day had passed without Antonio riding out into the pasture to work on his roping. Hernando tightened his saddle with a quick tug. He slapped down the leather flap.

"All right, Antonio. We will look for this little pinto of yours. Tomorrow morning we will leave before sunrise. Now I have work to do."

Hernando gave his horse, Pepe, a kick. The horse broke into a jog, and a cloud of thick dust rose around them.

Before the sun rose the next morning, Hernando and Antonio had already started out of Monterey. Hernando rode Pepe. Antonio rode a burro he had saddled with Azul's saddle and bridle. Their ropes were tied to their saddles.

As the boys rode, their long shadows stretched back in the cold gray morning. The herd had headed south, past the old church. Hours later the boys reached the river. Here they turned east and followed the river back into the valley.

Kingfishers dove from willows into the cold rushing water. The fish flashed silver in their beaks and then disappeared. Quail rushed wildly for cover as the boys rode. Hernando and Antonio watched for signs of the horses.

"This is quite a herd," Hernando said, waving with one arm. "Look at the grass they've stamped down here."

"It has made them easy to follow," Antonio said. He pulled a bit of horse hair from the bark of an oak tree as he passed.

"Yes," Hernando agreed. "The hard part will be finding Azul among the others."

Antonio rocked back and forth as the burro followed along the riverbank behind Hernando. The sun was hotter here in the valley where the sea breeze didn't often reach. They followed a track made by cattle and deer and other wilder animals. In the middle of the afternoon, they found a wide crossing on the riverbank. There they got off their mounts.

"Look at these tracks," Hernando said. "There is a mountain lion's print. Those little prints belong to bobcats, and these are coyotes'."

Then they spotted a paw print much bigger than the rest. The print had filled with water. A water bug skimmed the pools that had formed.

"That's a grizzly bear's print," Hernando said, "and look at that tree." Above them the bark of a pine tree was ripped. "That's where the bears sharpened their claws," Hernando explained.

Antonio had heard stories about these bears from the cowhands. They could stand over six feet tall. He knew they could weigh up to a ton and could outrun people. Sometimes the bears stole cattle, and the cowhands had to rope the bears. Antonio knew it would be a long time before he tried to rope a grizzly.

"I guess a lot goes on here," Antonio said.

"It's not as safe as home is," Hernando said and got back on Pepe. Then he and Antonio crossed the river, stirring up the mud in the water.

The trail climbed up the hill from the river and through a line of birch trees. Beyond this a meadow stretched. Hernando pulled his horse to a stop. There was the herd, peacefully nibbling at the knee-high meadow grass.

"There must be two hundred horses," Antonio whispered to his brother.

"Are you going to call for your Azul now?" Hernando asked, smiling.

Antonio didn't take time to answer. He was too busy searching the meadow for the spotted pony.

"I see him!" he said suddenly. "There! Right at the edge, next to that cream-colored horse."

"You have good eyes," Hernando teased, "to see such a small horse."

Hernando took his rope from his saddle horn and recoiled it again on his thigh. He brushed back his black hair from his forehead and pulled the strap of his hat tight.

"Watch," he said and moved his horse slowly forward. Pepe stepped carefully like a cat after a bird. Neither horse nor rider made a sound. Hernando did not want to scare the herd into a stampede.

It was not easy to come near the wild horses without frightening the herd. A few horses raised their heads as Hernando moved toward them. Somewhere in the herd a horse gave a warning snort. Then, as suddenly as a flock of birds, the horses took flight, but it was not a fluttering sound. The meadow shook with the wild pounding.

Yellow dust rose up in clouds under the thundering hooves.

Pepe lowered his head. Hernando guided him toward the little spotted pony. The pinto pony turned. Pepe turned. The pony turned the other way. Pepe followed, closing in like a shrinking shadow.

Suddenly the little pinto turned and twisted. Then it raced in a different direction, startling Pepe.

Hernando tried again, racing after the pony. At just the right time, he whipped his rope twice over his head and then sent it sailing out over Azul's straining neck.

Pepe dug his back heels into the ground, and the pony jerked back, but Azul did not fight. It was as if he sensed that his holiday was over.

Antonio moved forward on his burro, urging the burro to run. He jumped from the saddle and calmed the panting pony. He slipped the bridle from the burro to Azul and threw his arms around the pinto's neck.

"Thank you, Hernando," Antonio said. "Thank you." Antonio took the rope from Azul's neck and handed it up to his brother. The figure of Hernando blurred in the sun as tears suddenly filled Antonio's eyes. They were tears of relief and joy. Azul was his again!

Antonio and Hernando found a place to camp next to the river. In a small, dead-end canyon, they built a rough corral for their horses and the burro. After they ate, Antonio and Hernando pulled their blankets around them and listened to a chorus of coyote, cricket, frog, and owl sounds. The last thought Antonio had before falling asleep was about Azul. Even with his eyes closed, Antonio could see himself throwing a rope as Azul ran. Then in his mind's eye Azul pulled to a sudden stop as the rope stretched tight around a hoof of a calf — just the way they had practiced a thousand times.

In the early morning, the sky was barely turning purplish gray as Hernando quickly brushed and saddled his horse. He told Antonio that they would skip breakfast. Antonio knew that Hernando was in a hurry to get back to Monterey to work on his bridle.

Antonio had just tightened the cinch of his saddle when the burro squealed from the still dark corner of the corral.

"Now what?" Hernando demanded. "Don't I have anything better to do than look after a noisy burro?"

Hernando climbed into his saddle. Antonio tried to see into the shadows where the noise had come from. A huge shadow loomed above the burro. Was it only a shadow? A deep growl suddenly filled the canyon. Nothing could make a noise like that — nothing except a grizzly.

Hernando's horse, Pepe, jumped sideways at the sound, but Hernando was in no mood for a shy horse. He gave his horse a kick and charged forward. In an instant, he had tossed his lasso and pulled it tightly around one of the grizzly's huge front paws. In the first glint of morning sun, Antonio saw the bear standing on his hind legs. He also saw that Hernando had made a mistake.

Still standing, the grizzly struck at the rope, like a giant pulling in a kite, paw over paw. Now Hernando was cornered. The grizzly had turned away from the burro and was pulling Hernando and Pepe closer. The frightened burro had the good sense to escape. It galloped out of the campsite and across the river, as far and as fast as it could go.

Antonio took several steps in the same direction, terrified, but then he turned quickly, leaped into his saddle, and loosened his own rope. Now was no time to run! He spun Azul around to face the snarling bear. Antonio knew he didn't have a moment to lose. He screamed — partly to attract the grizzly's attention, but mostly because he couldn't help screaming. A whirlwind of fear had risen in his chest. The bear dropped to all fours. Antonio nudged Azul, and as the animal stepped closer to Hernando, he dropped his rope under the bear's back foot. It was a toss Antonio had worked at hundreds of times. The whole motion seemed to live in his arms, separate from his head and its cloud of fear. For a moment, everything slowed down, and the rope and the

bear seemed to move in slow motion. The loop circled the bear's hind paw.

Then Antonio turned Azul and charged away, wrapping the end of the rope around his saddle horn. The rope snapped tight. Hernando and Pepe had one paw. Antonio and Azul had another. Both teams pulled, and the bear hung between them like a huge fur coat on a sagging clothesline. The horses had been trained to keep the ropes tight because a loose rope meant that a cow might escape. Now a grizzly raged, struggling to escape. The horses and riders kept the bear off balance and strung between them.

"Well, Antonio, I think we've caught something on our line!" Hernando tried to catch his breath and make a joke at the same time.

Antonio could hardly talk over the sound of his pounding heart. "What now?" he got out.

"This is a little bit tricky," Hernando said, "but I would like to get out of this corner. Pull our friend a little your way, and I will follow. Don't let him stand up, or he will have us for breakfast."

Slowly and carefully the two brothers dragged the struggling beast out of the corner.

"Unless we want to drag this bear back to Monterey," Hernando said, "we will have to give him our ropes to play with."

"Yes," Antonio agreed. He wanted very much to let go of his end and run.

"When I count to three, we will both let go," Hernando directed, "and then we run. All right?"

"Yes."

"Ready, Antonio? One . . . Two . . . THREE!"

With that, Pepe and Azul spun away from the bear, which was now tangled in rope. The horses dashed with their riders across the river and scrambled up the muddy bank. Then they raced along the opposite side. The horses ran until foam flew from their mouths and gathered like soap suds on the horses' chests. When they reached a wide clearing at the side of the trail, the brothers pulled their horses to a walk. The burro came up behind them.

"We are all safe," Hernando said, "thanks to my very brave brother and his pony. You did well, you two, very well indeed."

"We lost our lassos," Antonio said.

"Don't worry," Hernando answered. "I will make you another one. In fact, you and Azul have earned more of a reward than that. I am about to finish a bridle, one with a silver headband. That will do nicely."

At just that moment, the sun slipped up over the mountains in the east. For Antonio, swaying gently back and forth on his spotted pony, the world seemed to be made of gold.

Authors

Patricia Olivérez, a librarian in Salinas, California, edits the young adults' newsletter at the John Steinbeck Library. She has been a teacher and has a particular interest in reading.

Stephen Tracy has worked at shoeing horses and at teaching creative writing. His stories have appeared in *The New Yorker* magazine, and in 1976 he won the Joseph Henry Jackson Award for fiction.

Comprehension Questions

1. How was Antonio's and Hernando's courage tested?
2. How did Antonio feel when Azul ran away?
3. Why didn't Hernando want to go look for Azul?
4. At the end, why did Antonio think that the world seemed to be made of gold?

Vocabulary

These opposites, or antonyms, appear in "The Pinto":

older/_younger_   **_easy_/_hard_**   **_back_/_forth_**

Think of antonyms for the words below and add six other words and their antonyms. Put each word and each antonym on a separate card, and play a card game with your classmates to see who gets the most pairs first.

wild   **large**   **quick**   **sharp**

Writing a Report

Look up the main topic _Horses_ or the main topic _Cowhands_ in a reference book. Read about how horses came to the United States or about a cowhand's life. Write a short report on one of these topics.

Reading Diagrams

When you are reading something that gives facts, you may find that there is a certain kind of drawing that goes along with what you are reading. This drawing may show how something is put together and how its parts connect to one another. The drawing also may show how something works. Sometimes the drawing may give you an overview of what you are reading. Such drawings are called **diagrams**. By studying them, you can understand better what you are reading.

Parts of a Diagram

Most diagrams have captions, or titles, that explain them. If there is no title, use sentences in what you are reading to learn what the diagram is about. Look at the diagram on page 441. Read the caption below it. The caption tells you that this is a drawing of an old-fashioned sled. The drawing shows how an old-fashioned wooden sled was put together.

The important parts of diagrams have labels. Sometimes lines are drawn from the labels to the parts they name. Look at the labels on the sled. The words *seat, brace,* and *runners* name the parts. The sizes of the different pieces also are given.

Sometimes more than one diagram is shown. When this happens, each drawing is numbered *Figure 1, Figure 2,* and so on. The diagrams in this lesson are numbered in that way.

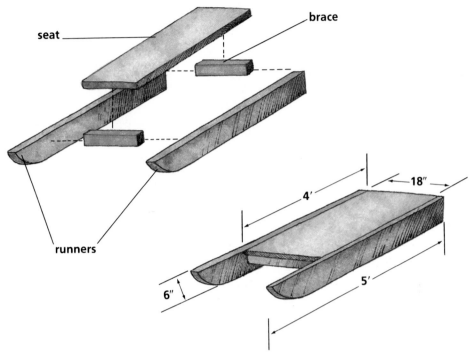

Figure 1.   An Old-Fashioned Sled.

How Diagrams Are Useful

When you are reading something that has diagrams, be sure to study them. Sometimes the diagrams will make something clear that is hard to explain in words. They may help you to see how the parts of something, like the sled, fit together. They may give you an overview of the whole piece of writing. Sentences in the piece of writing may further explain the diagrams. Also study the caption and labels of a diagram. They may tell about things that are not told about in the piece.

Read the following short piece about bicycles, and look at the diagram.

How a Bicycle Moves

As shown in Figure 2, the chain wheel is a large sprocket. This is a wheel with teeth. When a rider pushes the bicycle pedals, the chain wheel is turned. A chain connects the chain wheel to a smaller sprocket. This is on the rear wheel of the bicycle. The chain wheel moves the chain as it turns. The chain then turns the smaller sprocket, which moves the rear wheel.

To stop some bicycles, the rider pushes the pedals backward. When this happens, the bicycle is stopped by the brake, which is inside the hub attached to the rear sprocket.

Figure 2.   Parts of a Bicycle.

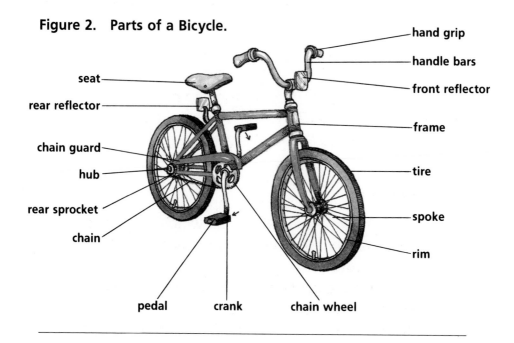

If you did not know what the parts of a bicycle looked like, this piece would be hard to follow without the diagram. The author used the diagram to show you what the parts of a bicycle look like and to explain clearly how a bicycle moves. You can see the large and small sprockets and the chain that connects them. The arrow shows the direction in which the pedals and chain move.

You also can use the diagram to learn about many other parts of a bicycle. The article names only parts that make the bicycle move, but the drawing shows all the important parts. Can you find some parts that are named in the diagram of the bicycle but not in the piece of writing?

Reading a Diagram

Read the article about bicycles again and look at Figure 2 as you read it. Then answer the questions below.

1. What parts make up the wheel of a bicycle?
2. How many reflectors are on the bicycle?
3. What connects the pedal to the chain wheel?
4. What covers the upper part of the chain?
5. What is one way of braking a bicycle?

Skill Summary

- A diagram is a certain kind of drawing that shows how something is put together, how its parts are connected, or how it works.
- A diagram has a caption that tells what the diagram shows and labels for the important parts.
- Diagrams are often used to explain something that is hard to put into words.
- Diagrams are also used to give an overview of the piece of writing or to give facts that are not in the written piece.

Bicycle Rider

by Mary Scioscia

Marshall Taylor's expert tricks on his bicycle got him his first job, but what helped him to become famous?

"Out of the way! Here I come! I'm winning!" shouted Marshall, pedaling his bicycle as fast as he could.

Walter laughed. "But I just won! That line back there in the sidewalk is the finish line."

"I almost won," said Marshall, pulling up beside his big brother.

As they entered the kitchen, Mama said, "I'm glad you're home, boys. Walter, we need more wood for the stove. Marshall, please get me a bucket of water from the well. Supper is nearly ready."

Big sister Pearl stirred a huge pot of stew on the iron cookstove. Geneva popped a pan of biscuits into the oven. Carlton carried the eighth chair to the table. Ruth cuddled the baby in her arms as they went back and forth in the rocking chair. Papa stood in the hallway, brushing his red coachman's jacket. Walter set down an armload of wood beside the stove. Marshall brought Mama a bucket of water.

"Supper is ready," said Mama.

The Taylor family sat down together. They all bowed their heads; Papa said grace. Gaslights flickered above the table, making dancing shadows on everyone's face.

"Papa, I almost beat Walter today when we raced home from his job," said Marshall.

"It's true," Walter said as he passed the biscuits. "I'm glad I gave him my old bike."

"I declare," said Mama, "if that boy isn't faster than any horse and carriage in Indiana."

"I'm going to be just like you, Marshall, when I get big," whispered Carlton.

"Papa," said Marshall. "I want a job."

"You're too little to have a job," said Ruth. "You're one of the younger children."

"I'm the oldest of the younger children," said Marshall. "I can't be a carpenter yet, like Walter, or a coachman, like Papa, but I have my bike, and I'm a fast rider. I can deliver packages for the store."

"Maybe," said Papa.

"Can I try this Saturday?"

Papa looked at Mama. "What do you think?" he asked.

Mama nodded. "Well," she said, "he's a good bicycle rider and dependable."

"Yes. You may try to find a job, son," said Papa.

"Not this Saturday," said Carlton. "You promised to take me to the bicycle store, Marshall, and to teach me the bicycle tricks you made up."

"Those tricks? They don't amount to a hill of beans, Carlton."

"Marshall, you promised," complained Carlton.

"All right. We'll go to the bicycle store *after* I look for a job. Then I'll teach you the bicycle tricks."

On Saturday morning Marshall biked downtown. Mercer's dry goods store was the biggest store on Main Street. Rolls of brown wool and pink and yellow flowered calico were arranged behind gleaming scissors and brightly colored spools of thread in the store window. Inside the store, Mrs. Mercer stood behind the counter.

"May I help you?" she asked Marshall.

"Yes, ma'am. I want a job. I have my own bicycle. Do you need someone to deliver packages?"

"Dear me, no," she said briskly. "We do everything ourselves. My husband delivers packages on his way home every night."

Next Marshall tried Caldwell's grocery store.

"Mr. Caldwell, sir," said Marshall, "I want a job as an errand boy. I have a bicycle. I'm a fast rider, and I can deliver groceries."

Mr. Caldwell was arranging a pyramid of oranges. Slowly, he placed each orange in the design. When he put the last orange carefully at the top of the pyramid, he stepped back to admire the arrangement. He patted his stomach.

"Well, young fellow," he finally drawled, "Caldwell's has its own delivery wagon drawn by two fine brown horses. Grocery orders are too big to go out on a bicycle. Come back another year, when you're older. We might be able to use you somewhere else in the business."

"Thank you, sir," said Marshall.

Grocery orders might be too big to go on a bicycle, but medicines were always in small boxes. Marshall went to Smith's drugstore. Mr. Smith was making a soda drink for a woman and her little girl. Marshall stood waiting politely till he finished.

"What would you like?" asked Mr. Smith after he had served the woman and girl.

"I want a job, sir. Could I deliver medicines for you? I have my own bicycle, and I ride fast."

"Right now a high school boy named Roger does that for me. Come back next year when Roger goes to college," said Mr. Smith.

At home for his midday meal, Marshall was downcast. "Job hunting is hard. Everyone thinks I'm too young."

"Don't worry. Next year, when you're bigger, you'll get a job," Mama answered him.

In the afternoon, Carlton got up behind Marshall on the bicycle. They rode down Main Street to Hay and Willit's bicycle store.

"That's my favorite," said Marshall, pointing at a shiny red racing bicycle in the center of the window.

Carlton liked the funny one beside it with a big front wheel and a tiny back wheel. They both admired the sparkling gold medal pinned to a black velvet stand.

"Read me that sign," Carlton said.

"'Hay and Willit's bicycle store. Best in Indianapolis. This gold medal will go to the winner of the ten-mile race. May 10, 1892,'" Marshall read.

"I'll bet you could win that race," said Carlton.

"Not me," said Marshall. "I'm not that fast, even though I am almost as fast as Walter. Hey, Carlton, look how wide the sidewalk is here in front of the store. Want me to show you some of the bike tricks now?"

Carlton clapped his hands. "Yes. Show me, Marshall."

Marshall lay on the bicycle seat and pushed the pedals with his hands. He helped Carlton do the same trick. People walking past the store stopped to look.

Marshall squatted on the bicycle seat and juggled three pennies. Carlton tried squatting on the seat too. He couldn't do it. Marshall did the trick again.

More people stopped to watch.

A tall thin boy said, "That's a stupid trick. I'll bet you fall on your head."

A small girl said, "George Pepper, you mind your manners."

More people stopped to watch. A coachman pulled his carriage over to the curb to watch Marshall do his amazing tricks.

Marshall did a headstand on his bicycle seat. Then he rode his bicycle backward. Suddenly, the bicycle-shop door opened, and Mr. Hay stood in the doorway.

"Now you're in for it," jeered George Pepper. "You're in real trouble now!"

"Young man," called Mr. Hay, "I want to speak to you."

Marshall walked the bicycle over to Mr. Hay.

"Yes, sir?" said Marshall.

"Where did you learn those tricks?" asked Mr. Hay.

"I made them up, sir. I was just showing my little brother. He likes to see them."

"I don't wonder," said Mr. Hay.

"I'm sorry, sir, if we disturbed you."

"Disturbed us! Not at all! Those are the best bicycle tricks I've ever seen. My partner and I could use a boy like you. How would you like a job? We need someone to dust and sweep the store every day and to put coal in the potbellied stove. You could come here after school and on Saturdays to do these jobs. Then, if there is time, you could do your bicycle tricks in front of our store. It will make people want to come to this bicycle shop."

"Yes, sir!" cried Marshall.

"Start Monday after school," said Mr. Hay.

"I'll be here!" said Marshall.

Carlton climbed up behind Marshall on his bicycle.

As Marshall pedaled home, Carlton said, "It's funny. When you looked for a job, you didn't get one. When you didn't look for a job, you got one!"

Marshall liked his job. He didn't even mind the dusting. Every day he took the medal out and polished it carefully. Once, when he was alone in the store, Marshall

451

unpinned the gold medal and stuck it onto his shirt. He looked at his reflection in the glass case. He turned a little so the light glinted on the gold.

It was fun to pretend that Mr. Hay had given him the medal because he could ride faster than anybody else.

"But what if Mr. Hay sees me wearing this medal?" Marshall thought. "He might get angry."

Marshall put the medal back into the case.

One Saturday Mr. Hay said, "Today you and I are going to spend the day at the bicycle racetrack. I need your help taking bicycles, extra wheels, and riding clothes out to the track. We usually sell quite a few items on racing days. Mr. Willit and I thought you'd enjoy working there with me. You'll be able to see the big ten-mile race too."

Hundreds of people were in the grandstand. Children stood by the fence at the edge of the track and looked through the metal crisscrosses. Mr. Hay gave his tickets to the gateman, and he and Marshall walked inside to a booth near the edge of the track. They set out the wheels and shirts and shorts on the counter. Mr. Hay leaned the bicycles against the side of the booth.

More than a hundred racers in bright jersey tops and black shorts stood near the starting line. Beside every racer there was someone holding the bicycle.

"Each rider needs someone to push him off," said Mr. Hay.

"Can't they push off with one of their own feet?" Marshall asked.

Mr. Hay shook his head. "Racers' feet have to be fastened to the pedals."

At the judges' stand, a man stood up and shouted through a huge megaphone, "Attention, everyone! All those entering the one-mile race, line up at the starting line."

"One-mile race?" said Marshall. "Isn't it ten miles?"

"There will be several short races before the main event," said Mr. Hay.

"I see a lot of our customers lining up to be in the race," said Marshall.

"Land's sakes, Marshall! You just gave me an idea. You should ride in one of the short races. It would remind people of our store."

"Would they let me?"

"I'll ask the judges," said Mr. Hay.

When Mr. Hay came back, he said, "You can ride in the next one-mile race. Come with me to the dressing

room and put on these shorts and this yellow shirt. Choose any one of the bikes we brought."

At the starting line, Mr. Hay said, "Each time around the track is one lap. Five laps make a mile. Don't worry if you forget how many laps you've gone. When you hear the bell ring, you will know it is the bell lap. That means one left to go."

Marshall got on the bicycle. Mr. Hay held it steady while Marshall clipped his feet onto the pedals. A tall thin boy in a red shirt got in line next to Marshall.

"George Pepper!" thought Marshall, wishing George wasn't right next to him.

"What are you doing in this race, runt?" said George. "You won't last one lap."

"Come on, George, leave him alone," said another racer. "That's the boy who does those good tricks at the bicycle shop."

"You mean those stupid tricks," said George.

The man in charge blew a whistle. All the racers leaned over their handlebars. Their helpers held the bicycles steady. The man raised his pistol in the air.

"One! Two! Three!" the starter shouted.

Bang! went the pistol.

Mr. Hay gave Marshall a strong push. He shot ahead of George Pepper. A tall boy got ahead of Marshall. Four more people got ahead. Marshall rode past one of them. George came up even with Marshall.

"I'm warning you, runt. You better stay behind me if you don't want your head busted in."

Marshall pushed his legs as hard as he could, but George got ahead.

Around and around the racers went. Now there were seven people ahead of Marshall.

Ding, ding, ding, the bell rang.

One more lap to go for the mile. Marshall speeded up. A racer crossed the finish line. Two more. Another. Next was George Pepper in the red shirt. Right after George came the tall boy.

Then Marshall crossed the line. Mr. Hay hurried over to help Marshall stop.

"You came in number seven. That's great!" said Mr. Hay.

"It wasn't very good," said Marshall. "Six people beat me."

"But you beat over forty people. And you've never even been in a race before. You're good enough to try the ten-mile race."

"Oh, no," said Marshall. "I could never win that."

"No," agreed Mr. Hay. "You couldn't win. But I think you could finish. Try it, Marshall. If you get too tired, you just stop. Many racers will drop out before the fifty laps are done."

During the next race, Mr. Hay spoke to the judges again. Marshall rested with the other riders in the grassy center of the track.

"Good news," said Mr. Hay, joining Marshall. "You can try the ten-mile race."

Marshall wheeled his bicycle over to the starting line.

"Don't try to go too fast at first," said Mr. Hay. "Just keep up with the others, if you can. Save your energy for the sprints."

"What is a sprint?" asked Marshall.

"A sprint means going extra fast for one lap. Whoever passes the finish line first gets points toward winning."

"How will I know when it's time to sprint?"

"The bell rings at the start of the fifth lap. Each mile there will be a sprint race on the fifth lap."

Marshall looked at the riders lining up. "Whew!" he said. "It looks as if all the racers entered this race."

Mr. Hay nodded. "A hundred and seventeen bike racers are in the ten-mile race."

Marshall's bicycle wobbled a little as Marshall bent down to clip his feet onto the pedals. Mr. Hay steadied it.

Marshall could feel his heart thumping hard. His hands felt slippery on the bicycle handles.

"Here," said Mr. Hay. "Use my handkerchief to dry your hands."

458

The whistle blew. Marshall's legs felt shaky.

"One!" shouted the man. "Two! Three!"

Bang!

Mr. Hay shoved Marshall's bicycle so hard, Marshall could smell the dust that flew up. Marshall pushed his legs down. Around and around went the wheels.

The riders rode in a close pack. Two bicycles bumped and one fell. Marshall swerved around the fallen bicycle and rider. He almost hit another bicycle. Marshall swerved again. It was George Pepper's bicycle.

"Hey, runt," shouted George. "Out of my way."

Ding, ding, ding! The bell lap!

Marshall pulled ahead of the pack for the sprint. George Pepper passed him. Three more riders passed him. Then two more. Marshall pushed his legs hard. He passed one rider, then another. He crossed the finish line.

The first sprint was over. He could hear the crowd cheering. Nine more miles to go! Marshall wondered who had won that sprint. It was hard to know who was ahead, because the riders kept going around and around the track. When Marshall passed someone, he wondered if that person had already done more laps than he had.

Around and around they all went. Marshall's legs ached. His chest felt tight.

"I hope I can finish the first half of the race," he said to himself.

Ding, ding, ding! Another bell lap. Everyone pushed harder. Marshall shot forward. Then he passed George Pepper.

George caught up with Marshall and passed him. George crossed the finish line just ahead of Marshall, but it was impossible for Marshall to know who had won the sprint. The racers were no longer riding in a close pack. They were strung out along the whole track. A few riders had dropped out.

Around and around. Around and around.

When the bell rang, Marshall couldn't remember which sprint it was. His breath came in noisy puffs. More riders dropped out of the race.

Marshall's throat felt dry. His mouth tasted dusty. His legs hurt.

"I want to drop out," Marshall thought. "I can't make the halfway mark."

Someone shouted, "Hurray, Marshall Taylor!"

It made Marshall feel glad. He felt stronger. "Maybe I can finish a few more laps," he thought.

His bicycle went faster. Around the track. Around and around. There were more bell laps and more sprints. Marshall lost count. Around and around. His damp shirt stuck to his back. His legs ached. His back was sore from being bent over the handlebars.

The people in the grandstand stamped their feet and cheered. He heard Mr. Hay, standing at the edge of the track, shout, "Last lap coming up next!"

Ding, ding, ding!

Marshall pushed with all his strength. The wheels seemed to say, "Got to finish. Got to finish."

Scrunch.

He heard the sound of clashing metal and felt his rear wheel being pushed.

"Out of my way," shouted George, trying to knock him down.

A man at the edge of the track blew his whistle.

"Foul!" he shouted. "George Pepper. Over to the side!"

George pretended he didn't hear. He tried to get ahead of Marshall. The man blew his whistle again. Marshall stayed in front of George. Several riders seemed to be riding exactly even with one another. Marshall speeded over the finish line. Everyone was so close, he couldn't tell who was ahead or behind. His bicycle was going so fast he couldn't stop. He went around another lap to slow down.

Marshall heard the crowd shout something that sounded like "Marshall Taylor! Marshall Taylor!" Hats and programs flew into the air.

Mr. Hay hurried over to Marshall to hold his bicycle. He hugged him.

"You won, Marshall. You won!"

"Who? Me?" said Marshall.

The judges held up their hands to quiet the crowd. Then a man with a megaphone shouted, "Marshall Taylor, the winner by sixteen seconds! Marshall Taylor has won the annual Indianapolis ten-mile bicycle race!"

The crowd cheered and clapped and stamped their feet.

Mr. Hay and Marshall walked to the judges' platform. A judge gave Marshall the gold medal.

A thunder of applause came from the audience.

Marshall felt as if he were in the middle of a dream.

At supper that night, Marshall's legs ached so much it hurt to sit on his chair.

"What's the matter with you?" Carlton asked. "You're sitting in a funny way."

Marshall shrugged and gave no answer. He waited until the whole family was seated for supper and had finished saying grace. Then he held up the gold medal.

"What's that, son?" asked Papa.

"It's the medal for the ten-mile race," said Marshall.

"Did Mr. Hay say you could take it out of the store window?" asked Carlton.

"Out of the store window!" cried Mama. "Son, what have you done?"

Everybody stopped eating. Papa frowned.

"Marshall Taylor! Have you brought home something that does not belong to you?"

Marshall grinned. "I won it," he said.

Mama sucked in her breath. "Marshall, are you telling a story?"

"No. Honest, Mama. I won it."

Papa said sternly, "Explain what you mean, Marshall Taylor."

"I rode in the bicycle race today. Mr. Hay took me to help sell bicycle equipment at the track. Then he said, why didn't I enter too. He said I could drop out if I got tired."

"Are you talking about the *big* ten-mile race? Fifty times around the track?" asked Walter.

Marshall nodded.

"You've never raced before. How could you go fifty laps without stopping?" Pearl asked.

"It was Mr. Hay's idea," Marshall explained. "I didn't think I could even finish the race. Over a hundred started. Lots dropped out before the end. But I kept going. And I won!"

Carlton touched the bright medal. "Can you keep it always?"

Marshall grinned and nodded. "I can keep it forever."

Mama jumped up and ran to hug Marshall. "Son, you are really something."

Everyone else jumped up too. Walter shook his hand. Pearl and Ruth hugged him. Papa clapped him on the back.

"Congratulations, son!"

"I knew you wouldn't lie," said Carlton. "And I knew all along that you were the best bicycle rider in Indiana."

Epilogue

Marshall Taylor became the fastest bicycle rider in the world. Nicknamed Major Taylor because he stood so straight, he was the first black person to participate in national bicycle races that were integrated. His first professional race in 1896 was at Madison Square Garden in New York City. During the years from 1896 to 1910 he raced in the United States, Europe, and Australia. Several times he won both the American and the World Championships.

Bicycle racing was a major sport in the late 1800's and early 1900's. Huge crowds would go to see Major Taylor. All the newspapers would cover the event. Taylor was especially loved by his fans for his remarkable riding skills and for his fairness and good sportsmanship.

Author

Bicycle Rider is Mary Scioscia's first book for children. Mrs. Scioscia was born in Canada and has lived in California, where her sons were in amateur bicycle races. Because of their racing, she became interested in Marshall Taylor and his exciting achievements.

Thinking It Over

Comprehension Questions

1. What helped Marshall win his first race?
2. What did Marshall do to get his job?
3. Why did Marshall wait until his family was eating before showing them the medal?
4. The epilogue says that Marshall Taylor became the world's fastest bicycle rider. Is this an opinion or a statement given as fact?

Vocabulary

The word **_for_** can be confusing because of its different meanings. Read the meanings and the sentences below. Then make up your own sentence for each meaning.

''in place of''	The boys used logs **for** stools.
''in honor of''	They had a party **for** the winner.
''because''	Marshall went home, **for** it was dark.
''suited to''	She couldn't find any shoes **for** babies.

Making a Diagram

Look at the picture on page 458, and make a diagram of a bicycle like the one Marshall is riding in the picture. You may need to look in a reference book for more information. When you have finished labeling the diagram, write a caption.

The Bicycle

by John Travers Moore

Pedal a bicycle
    Off to a race,
Feet all around
    And wind in my face.
Pedal it fast,
    Or pedal it slow,
And stop, at last,
    Where no winds blow.

467

Idioms

After winning the prize, Margie felt ten feet tall.

Below the picture, it says that Margie "felt ten feet tall." But do you think Margie really felt that tall? Probably not. The words *felt ten feet tall* are another way of saying Margie *felt very proud.* An expression like that is called an **idiom.** An idiom is a group of words that has a special meaning that is different from the meanings the words usually have.

You cannot always understand an idiom just by looking at the meaning of each word in it. Sometimes you need to use the other words and sentences around it. What do you think the idiom in this sentence means?

When all the guests left, Fran said to her friends, "Let's pitch in."

468

Does Fran mean that her friends should throw things in a hole? Perhaps the meaning will become clearer if you read on.

"Let's pitch in. If we all work together, this job will be done in no time," Fran repeated.

Can you tell now what the idiom means? *Let's pitch in* means "Let's all get to work." The other words around it help make the meaning clear.

Choose the meaning for each of the idioms below.

1. Gary didn't *let it go to his head* when he got the first-place prize.
   a. put it on his head
   b. act stuck-up
2. The team knew it would be very difficult to beat the Wildcats, but they *gave it everything they had.*
   a. tried very hard
   b. gave away the things they had
3. The coach told the players to *watch their step* at the dance after the game.
   a. try to dance their best
   b. be on their best behavior

4. The students played a game at the party that *broke the ice.*
   a. wrecked the ice for skating
   b. made everyone feel more at home

Something Extra

Prepare a large chart to hang in your classroom. Write this heading on the chart "Idioms We Use." Then "keep an ear out" for idioms. Write down each idiom you hear someone say. Copy it later on the class chart. "Get in the groove" and listen!

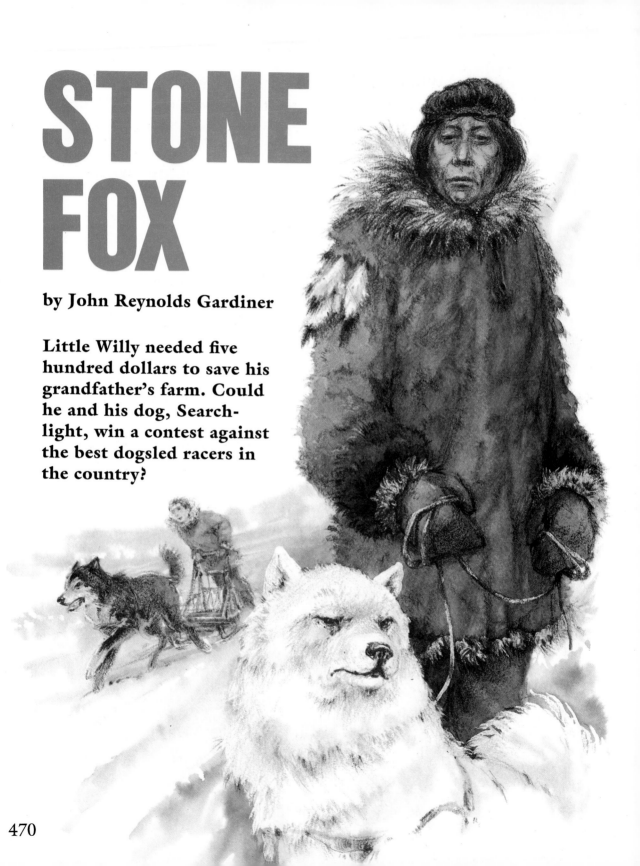

STONE FOX

by John Reynolds Gardiner

Little Willy needed five hundred dollars to save his grandfather's farm. Could he and his dog, Search-light, win a contest against the best dogsled racers in the country?

Little Willy went to see Mayor Smiley at the city hall building in town to sign up for the dogsled race.

The mayor's office was large and smelled like hair tonic. The mayor sat in a bright red chair with his feet on his desk. There was nothing on the desk except the mayor's feet.

"We have a race for you youngsters one hour before," said Mayor Smiley.

"I wanna enter the real race, Mr. Mayor."

"You must be funning," the mayor laughed. "Anyway, there's an entrance fee."

"How much?"

"Fifty dollars."

Little Willy was stunned. That was a lot of money just to enter a race, but he was determined. He ran across the street to the bank.

"Don't be stupid," Mr. Foster told little Willy. "This is not a race for amateurs. Some of the best dog teams in the Northwest will be entering."

"I have Searchlight! We go as fast as lightning. Really, Mr. Foster, we do."

Mr. Foster shook his head. "You don't stand a chance of winning."

"Yes, we do!"

"Willy . . . the money in your savings account is for your college education. You know I can't give it to you."

"You have to."

"I do?"

"It's my money!"

Little Willy left the bank with a stack of ten-dollar gold pieces — five of them, to be exact.

He walked into the mayor's office and plopped the coins down on the mayor's desk. "Searchlight and I are gonna win that five hundred dollars, Mr. Mayor. You'll see. Everybody'll see."

Mayor Smiley counted the money, wiped his neck, and entered little Willy in the race.

When little Willy stepped out of the city hall building, he felt ten feet tall. He looked up and down the snow-covered street. He was grinning from ear to ear. Searchlight walked over and stood in front of the sled, waiting to be hitched up, but little Willy wasn't ready to go yet. He put his thumbs in his belt loops and let the sun warm his face.

He felt great. In his pocket was a map Mayor Smiley had given him showing the ten miles the race covered. Down Main Street, right on North Road — little Willy could hardly hold back his excitement.

Five miles of the race he traveled every day and knew with his eyes closed. The last five miles were back into town along South Road, which was mostly straight and flat. It was speed that would count here, and with the lead he knew he could get in the first five miles, little Willy was sure he could win.

As little Willy hitched Searchlight to the sled, something down at the end of the street — some moving objects — caught his eye. They were difficult to see because they were all white. There were five of them, and they were beautiful. In fact, they were the most beautiful Samoyeds little Willy had ever seen.

The dogs held their heads up proudly and strutted in unison. They pulled a large but lightly constructed sled. They also pulled a large — but by no means lightly

473

constructed — man. Way down at the end of the street the man looked normal, but as the sled got closer, the man got bigger and bigger.

The man was an American Indian — dressed in furs and leather, with moccasins that came all the way up to his knees. His skin was dark, his hair was dark, and he wore a dark-colored headband. His eyes sparkled in the sunlight, but the rest of his face was as hard as stone.

The sled came to a stop right next to little Willy. The boy's mouth hung open as he tilted his head way back to look up at the man. Little Willy had never seen a giant before.

"Wow," little Willy gasped.

The Indian looked at little Willy. His face was solid granite, but his eyes were alive.

"Howdy," little Willy blurted out.

The Indian said nothing. His eyes shifted to Searchlight, who let out a soft moan but did not bark.

The giant walked into the city hall building.

Word that Stone Fox had entered the race spread throughout the town of Jackson within the hour, and throughout the state of Wyoming within the day.

Stories and legends about the awesome mountain man followed shortly. Little Willy heard many of them at Lester's General Store.

Little Willy learned that no white person had ever heard Stone Fox talk. Stone Fox refused to speak with a white person because of the treatment his people had received. His people, the Shoshone, who were peaceful seed gatherers, had been forced to leave Utah and settle on a reservation in Wyoming with another group of American Indians called the Arapaho.

Stone Fox's dream was for his people to return to their homeland. Stone Fox was using the money he won from racing to simply buy the land back. He had already purchased four farms and over two hundred acres.

That Stone Fox was smart, all right.

In the next week little Willy and Searchlight went over the ten-mile track every day, until they knew every inch of it by heart.

Stone Fox hardly practiced at all. In fact, little Willy saw Stone Fox do the course only once, and then he wasn't going very fast.

The race was scheduled for Saturday morning at ten o'clock. Only nine sleds were entered. Mayor Smiley had hoped for more contestants, but after Stone Fox had entered, well . . . you couldn't blame people for wanting to save their money.

It was true Stone Fox had never lost a race, but little Willy wasn't worried. He had made up his mind to win, and nothing was going to stop him — not even Stone Fox.

It was Friday night, the night before the race.

Grandfather was out of medicine. Little Willy went to see Doc Smith.

"Here." Doc Smith handed little Willy a piece of paper with some scribbling on it. "Take this to Lester at the drugstore right away."

"But it's nighttime. The store's closed."

"Just knock on the back door. He'll hear you."

"But . . . are you sure it's all right?"

"Yes. Lester knows I may have to call on him any time — day or night. People don't always get sick just during working hours, now, do they?"

"No, I guess they don't." Little Willy headed for the door.

"One other thing, Willy," Doc Smith said.

"Yes, ma'am?"

"I might as well say this now as later. It's about the race tomorrow."

"Yes, ma'am?"

"First, I want you to know that I think you're a fool for using your college money to enter that race."

Little Willy's eyes looked to the floor. "Yes, ma'am."

"But, since it's already been done, I also want you to know that I'll be rooting for you."

Little Willy looked up. "You will?"

"Win, Willy. Win that race tomorrow."

Little Willy beamed. He tried to speak but couldn't find the words. Embarrassed, he backed over to the door — gave a little wave, then turned quickly to leave.

Later, on his way to town, little Willy sang at the top of his lungs. The runners of the sled cut through the snow with a swish. This was a treacherous road at night, but the moon was out and Searchlight could see well. Anyway, they knew this road by heart. Nothing was going to happen.

Lester gave little Willy a big bottle of what looked like dirty milk.

"How's your grandfather doing?" Lester asked.

"Not so good. But after I win the race tomorrow, he'll get better. Doc Smith thinks so too."

Lester smiled. "I admire you, Willy. You got a heap of courage, going up against the likes of Stone Fox. You know he's never lost, don't you?"

"Yes, I know. Thank you for the medicine."

Little Willy waved good-by as Searchlight started off down Main Street.

Lester watched the departing sled for a long time before he yelled, "Good luck, son!"

On his way out of town, along North Road, little Willy heard dogs barking. The sounds came from the old deserted barn near the schoolhouse.

Little Willy decided to investigate.

He squeaked open the barn door and peeked in. It was dark inside, and he couldn't see anything. He couldn't hear anything either. The dogs had stopped barking.

He went inside the barn.

Little Willy's eyes took a while to get used to the dark, and then he saw them — the five Samoyeds. They were in the corner of the barn on a bed of straw. They were looking at him. They were so beautiful that little Willy couldn't keep from smiling.

Little Willy loved dogs. He had to see the Samoyeds up close. They showed no alarm as he approached, or as he held out his hand to pet them.

There was a movement through the darkness to little Willy's right. A sweeping motion, fast at first; then it appeared to slow and stop. But it didn't stop. A hand sent little Willy over backward.

"I didn't mean any harm, Mr. Stone Fox," little Willy said as he picked himself up off the ground.

Stone Fox stood tall in the darkness and said nothing. Searchlight barked outside. The Samoyeds barked in return.

Little Willy continued, "I'm going to race against you tomorrow. I know how you wanna win, but . . . I wanna win too. I gotta win. If I don't, they're gonna take away our farm. They have the right. Grandfather says that those that want to bad enough, will. So I will. I'll win. I'm gonna beat you."

Stone Fox remained motionless and silent.

Little Willy backed over to the barn door. "I'm sorry we both can't win," he said. Then he pushed open the door and left, closing it behind him.

In the barn, Stone Fox stood unmoving for another moment; then he reached out with one massive hand and gently petted one of the Samoyeds.

That night little Willy couldn't sleep, and when little Willy couldn't sleep, Searchlight couldn't sleep. Both tossed and turned for hours, and whenever little Willy looked over to see if Searchlight was asleep, she'd just be lying there with her eyes wide open, staring back at him.

Little Willy needed his rest. So did Searchlight. Tomorrow was going to be a big day. The biggest day of their lives.

The day of the race arrived. Little Willy got up early and fed Grandfather his oatmeal.

After adding more wood to the fire, little Willy kissed Grandfather, hitched up Searchlight, and started off for town.

At the edge of their property he stopped the sled for a moment and looked back at the farmhouse. The roof was covered with freshly fallen snow. A trail of smoke escaped

from the stone chimney. The jagged peaks of the Teton Mountains shot up in the background toward the clear blue sky overhead. "Yes, sir," he remembered Grandfather saying. "There are some things in this world worth dying for."

Little Willy loved this country. He loved to hike and to fish and to camp out by a lake. But he did not like to hunt.

He had killed a bird once with a slingshot, but that had been when he was only six years old, and that had been enough. In fact, to this day, he still remembered the spot where the poor thing was buried.

Lost in his thoughts, little Willy got to town before he knew it. As he turned onto Main Street, he brought the sled to an abrupt halt.

He couldn't believe what he saw.

Main Street was jammed with people, lined on both sides of the street. There were people on rooftops and people hanging out of windows. Little Willy hadn't expected such a big turnout. They must have all come to see Stone Fox.

Searchlight pulled the sled down Main Street past the crowds. Little Willy saw Miss Williams, his teacher, and Mr. Foster from the bank, and Hank from the post office, and Doc Smith, and Mayor Smiley. The city slickers were there, and even Clifford Snyder, the tax man, was there. Everybody.

Lester, the druggist, came out of the crowd and walked alongside little Willy for a while. It was one of the few times little Willy had ever seen Lester without his white apron.

"You can do it, Willy. You can beat him," Lester kept saying over and over again.

They had a race for the youngsters first, and the crowd cheered and rooted for their favorites. It was a short race. The children raced their sleds just down to the end of Main Street and back. Little Willy didn't see who won. It didn't matter.

And then it was time.

The old church clock showed a few minutes before ten as the contestants positioned themselves directly beneath the long banner that stretched across the street. They stood nine abreast. Stone Fox in the middle. Little Willy right next to him.

Little Willy had read all about the other contestants in the newspaper. They were all well-known mountain men with good racing records and excellent dog teams. But, even so, all bets were on Stone Fox. The odds were as high as a hundred to one that he'd win.

Not one cent had been bet on little Willy and his dog Searchlight.

Little Willie still felt like a winner. He was smiling. Searchlight knew the route as well as he did. They were going to win today, and that was final. Both of them knew it.

Stone Fox looked bigger than ever standing next to little Willy. In fact, the top of little Willy's head was dead even with Stone Fox's waist.

"Morning, Mr. Stone Fox," little Willy said, looking practically straight up at the tall Indian. "Sure's a nice day for a race."

Stone Fox must have heard little Willy, but he did not look at him. His face was frozen like ice, and his eyes seemed to lack that sparkle little Willy remembered seeing before.

The crowd became silent as Mayor Smiley stepped out into the street.

Miss Williams clenched her hands together until her knuckles turned white. Lester's mouth hung open, his lips wet. Hank stared without blinking. Doc Smith held

her head up proudly. Clifford Snyder removed a gold watch from his vest pocket and checked the time.

Tension filled the air.

Little Willy's throat became dry. His hands started to sweat. He could feel his heart thumping.

Mayor Smiley raised a pistol to the sky and fired.

The race had begun!

Searchlight sprang forward with such force that little Willy couldn't hang on. If it weren't for a lucky grab, he would have fallen off the sled for sure.

In what seemed only seconds, little Willy and Searchlight had traveled down Main Street, turned onto North Road, and were gone — far, far ahead of the others. They were winning, at least for the moment.

Stone Fox started off dead last. He went so slowly down Main Street that everyone was sure something must be wrong.

Swish! Little Willy's sled flew by the schoolhouse on the outskirts of town, and then by the old deserted barn.

Swish! Swish! Swish! Other racers followed in hot pursuit.

"Go, Searchlight! Go!" little Willy sang out. The cold wind pressed against his face. The snow was well packed. It was going to be a fast race today. The fastest they had ever run.

The road was full of dangerous twists and turns, but little Willy did not have to slow down as the other racers did. With only one dog and a small sled, he was able to take the sharp turns at full speed without risk of sliding off the road or losing control.

Therefore, with each turn, little Willy pulled farther and farther ahead.

Swish! The sled rounded a corner, sending snow flying. Little Willy was smiling. This was fun!

About three miles out of town the road made a half circle around a frozen lake. Instead of following the turn, little Willy took a shortcut right across the lake. This was tricky going, but Searchlight had done it many times before.

Little Willy had asked Mayor Smiley if he was permitted to go across the lake, not wanting to be disqualified. "As long as you leave town heading north and come back on South Road," the mayor had said, "anything goes!"

None of the other racers attempted to cross the lake, not even Stone Fox. The risk of falling through the ice was just too great.

Little Willy's lead increased.

Stone Fox was still running in last place, but he was picking up speed.

At the end of five miles, little Willy was so far out in front that he couldn't see anybody behind him when he looked back.

He knew, however, that the return five miles going back into town would not be this easy. The trail along South Road was practically straight and very smooth, and Stone Fox was sure to close the gap. But by how much? Little Willy didn't know.

Doc Smith's house flew by on the right. The tall trees surrounding her cabin seemed like one solid wall.

Grandfather's farm was coming up next.

When Searchlight saw the farmhouse, she started to pick up speed. "No, girl," little Willy yelled. "Not yet."

As they approached the farmhouse, little Willy thought he saw someone in Grandfather's bedroom window. The someone was a man, with a full beard.

It couldn't be. But it was! It was Grandfather!

Grandfather was sitting up in bed. He was looking out the window.

Little Willy was so excited he couldn't think straight. He started to stop the sled, but Grandfather indicated no, waving him on. "Of course," little Willy said to himself. "I must finish the race. I haven't won yet."

"Go, Searchlight!" little Willy shrieked. "Go, girl!"

Grandfather was better. Tears of joy rolled down little Willy's smiling face. Everything was going to be all right.

Then Stone Fox made his move.

One by one he began to pass the other racers. He went from last place to eighth. Then from eighth place to seventh. Then from seventh to sixth. Sixth to fifth.

He passed the others as if they were standing still.

He went from fifth place to fourth. Then to third. Then to second.

Until only little Willy remained.

But little Willy still had a good lead. In fact, it was not until the last two miles of the race that Stone Fox got his first glimpse of little Willy since the race had begun.

The five Samoyeds looked magnificent as they moved effortlessly across the snow. Stone Fox was gaining, and he was gaining fast. Little Willy wasn't aware of it.

Look back, little Willy! Look back!

But little Willy didn't look back. He was busy thinking about Grandfather. He could hear him laughing . . . and playing his harmonica . . .

Finally little Willy glanced back over his shoulder. He couldn't believe what he saw! Stone Fox was nearly on top of him!

This made little Willy mad, mad at himself. Why hadn't he looked back more often? What was he doing? He hadn't won yet. Well, no time to think of that now. He had a race to win.

"Go, Searchlight! Go, girl!"

Stone Fox kept gaining. Silently. Steadily.

"Go, Searchlight! Go!"

The lead Samoyed passed little Willy and pulled up even with Searchlight. Then it was a nose ahead. But that was all. Searchlight moved forward, inching her nose ahead. Then the Samoyed regained the lead. Then Searchlight . . .

When you enter the town of Jackson on South Road, the first buildings come into view about a half a mile

away. Whether Searchlight took those buildings to be Grandfather's farmhouse again, no one can be sure, but it was at this time that she poured on the steam.

Little Willy's sled seemed to lift up off the ground and fly. Stone Fox was left behind.

But not that far behind.

The crowd cheered madly when they saw little Willy come into view at the far end of Main Street, and even more madly when they saw that Stone Fox was right on his tail.

"Go, Searchlight! Go!"

Searchlight forged ahead. But Stone Fox was gaining!

"Go, Searchlight! Go!" little Willy cried out.

Searchlight gave it everything she had.

She was a hundred feet from the finish line when her heart burst. She died instantly. There was no suffering.

The sled and little Willy tumbled over her, slid along the snow for a while, then came to a stop about ten feet from the finish line. It had started to snow — white snowflakes landed on Searchlight's dark fur as she lay motionless on the ground.

The crowd became deathly silent.

Lester's eyes looked to the ground. Miss Williams had her hands over her mouth. Doc Smith started to run out to little Willy but stopped. Mayor Smiley looked shocked and helpless. And so did Hank, and so did the city slickers, and so did Clifford Snyder, the tax man.

Stone Fox brought his sled to a stop alongside little Willy. He stood tall in the icy wind and looked down at the young challenger, and at the dog that lay limp in his arms.

"Is she dead, Mr. Stone Fox? Is she dead?" little Willy asked, looking up at Stone Fox.

Stone Fox knelt down and put one massive hand on Searchlight's chest. He felt no heartbeat. He looked at little Willy, and the boy understood.

Little Willy squeezed Searchlight with all his might. "You did real good, girl. Real good. I'm real proud of you. You rest now. Just rest." Little Willy began to brush the snow off Searchlight's back.

Stone Fox stood up slowly.

No one spoke. No one moved. All eyes were on the Indian, the one called Stone Fox, the one who had never lost a race, and who now had another victory within his grasp.

But Stone Fox did nothing.

He just stood there, like a mountain.

His eyes shifted to his own dogs, then to the finish line, then back to little Willy, holding Searchlight.

With the heel of his moccasin Stone Fox drew a long line in the snow. Then he walked back over to his sled and pulled out his rifle.

Down at the end of Main Street, the other racers began to appear. As they approached, Stone Fox fired his rifle into the air. They came to a stop.

Stone Fox spoke.

"Anyone crosses this line — I shoot."

There wasn't anybody who didn't believe him.

Stone Fox nodded to the boy.

The town looked on in silence as little Willy, carrying Searchlight, walked the last ten feet and across the finish line.

Author

John Reynolds Gardiner is an engineer. *Stone Fox*, his first book for children, was based on a Rocky Mountain legend to which the author added imaginary characters.

Thinking It Over

Comprehension Questions

1. How did little Willy win the race?
2. What did Stone Fox do with his winnings from races?
3. Why did little Willy think he might beat Stone Fox?

Vocabulary

In "Stone Fox" little Willy **gasped**, **blurted** out, **sang** out, **yelled**, **shrieked**, and **cried** out. Notice how much stronger these words are than little Willy **said**. Use the words in six sentences of your own.

Making a Table

Make a table of your classmates' pets. Include the type of pet, the place it probably came from, the weight, and its age. Be sure to have a caption and headings.

Swift Things Are Beautiful

by Elizabeth Coatsworth

Swift things are beautiful:
Swallows and deer,
And lightning that falls
Bright-veined and clear,
Rivers and meteors,
Wind in the wheat,
The strong-withered horse,
The runner's sure feet.

And slow things are beautiful:
The closing of day,
The pause of the wave
That curves downward to spray,
The ember that crumbles,
The opening flower,
And the ox that moves on
In the quiet of power.

Magazine Wrap-up

Literary Skill: Setting

Every story happens in some place at some time. The time and place of a story is called the setting. Sometimes an author tells you directly when a story takes place. At other times, you have to use the clues an author gives to figure out the setting.

The setting for "The Gift" is a town near a mountain from September to March.

When and where did each of these stories take place? If the author has not directly told you the setting, use the clues in the story to figure it out.

- "The Pinto"
- "Bicycle Rider"
- "Stone Fox"

Vocabulary: Sensory Images

Authors often use words to describe something so that you can hear and see what is happening. These words make a story much more interesting.

Number a paper from 1 to 5, and rewrite the following sentences so that they are more interesting. Use your own words or words from the box to fill in the blanks.

black	pounding
bright	red
clammy	spun
green	thumping
growling	thundering
ice-cold	whipped
orange	yellow

1. Little Willy's hands became _____, and he could feel his heart _____.
2. More than a hundred racers in _____ jersey tops and _____ shorts stood near the finish line.
3. Anna and Nana Marie watched as the trees on the mountain turned from _____ to _____.
4. Antonio _____ Azul around to face the _____ bear.

5. _____ dust rose up in clouds under the _____ hooves.

Writing: Summarizing

Imagine that your job is to write summaries of new books for the book section of the newspaper. Write a short summary of one of the stories below:

- "The Gift"
- "Stone Fox"
- "Bicycle Rider"

Books to Enjoy

Martin Luther King, Jr., The Story of a Dream
by June Behrens

This play presents the many fine deeds of the famous leader.

Beat the Story-Drum, Pum-Pum
by Ashley Bryan

Here are five clever African folk tales, mostly about animals, with pictures by the author.

A Gift for Mama
by Esther Hautzig

In Poland, Sara, the daughter of a loving Jewish family, wants a store-bought present for Mama, not a homemade one.

Howliday Inn
by James Howe

Chester the cat and Harold the dog play major parts in some unusual mysteries.

"Wilbur's Escape"

an excerpt from
Charlotte's Web

written by E. B. White

**illustrated by
Garth Williams**

Wilbur, the new, lonely little pig who has come to live in Mr. Zuckerman's barn, often finds it hard to adjust to barnyard life. Just when it seems unbearable, he meets Charlotte. This is the heartwarming story of Wilbur's special friendship with hardworking, faithful Charlotte, who promises to save him from becoming a pork roast. How Charlotte does this and how Wilbur becomes famous make an enchanting tale that has delighted generations of readers.

Charlotte's Web was a 1953 Newbery Honor Book.

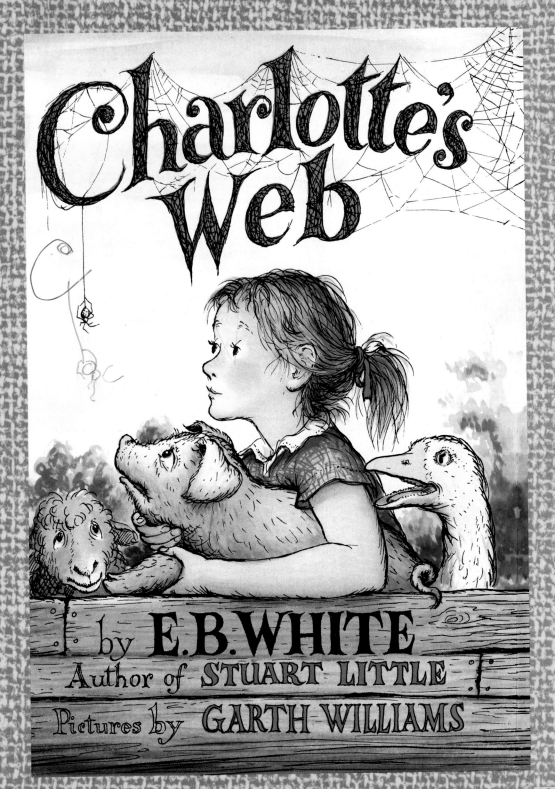

Charlotte's
Web

by E.B.WHITE
Author of STUART LITTLE
Pictures by GARTH WILLIAMS

Wilbur's Escape

Fern has sold her pig, Wilbur, to her Uncle Homer. Wilbur has gone to live in Uncle Homer's barn.

The barn was very large. It was very old. It smelled of hay. It smelled of the perspiration of tired horses and the wonderful sweet breath of patient cows. It often had a sort of peaceful smell — as though nothing bad could happen ever again in the world. It smelled of grain and of harness dressing and of axle grease and of rubber boots and of new rope. And whenever the cat was given a fish-head to eat, the barn would smell of fish. But mostly it smelled of hay, for there was always hay in the great loft up overhead. And there was always hay being pitched down to the cows and the horses and the sheep.

The barn was pleasantly warm in winter when the animals spent most of their time indoors, and it was pleasantly cool in summer when the big doors stood wide open to the breeze. The barn had stalls on the main floor for the work horses, tie-ups on the main floor for the cows, a sheepfold down below for the sheep, a pigpen down below for Wilbur, and it was full of all sorts of things that you find in barns: ladders, grindstones, pitch forks, monkey wrenches, scythes, lawn mowers, snow shovels, ax handles, milk pails, water buckets, empty grain sacks, and rusty rat traps. It was the kind of barn that swallows like to build their nests in. It was the kind of barn that children like to play in. And the whole thing was owned by Fern's uncle, Mr. Homer L. Zuckerman.

Wilbur's new home was in the lower part of the barn, directly underneath the cows. Mr. Zuckerman knew that pigs need warmth, and it was warm and comfortable down there in the barn cellar on the south side.

Fern came almost every day to visit him. She found an old milking stool that had been discarded, and she placed the stool in the sheepfold next to

Wilbur's pen. Here she sat quietly during the long afternoons, thinking and listening and watching Wilbur. The sheep soon got to know her and trust her. So did the geese, who lived with the sheep. All the animals trusted her, she was so quiet and friendly. Mr. Zuckerman did not allow her to take Wilbur out, and he did not allow her to get into the pigpen. But he told Fern that she could sit on the stool and watch Wilbur as long as she wanted to. It made her happy

just to be near the pig, and it made Wilbur happy to know that she was sitting there, right outside his pen. But he never had any fun — no walks, no rides, no swims.

One afternoon in June, when Wilbur was almost two months old, he wandered out into his small yard outside the barn. Fern had not arrived for her usual visit. Wilbur stood in the sun feeling lonely and bored.

"There's never anything to do around here," he thought. He walked slowly to his food trough and sniffed to see if anything had been overlooked at lunch. He found a small strip of potato skin and ate it. His back itched, so he leaned against the fence and rubbed against the boards. When he tired of this, he walked indoors and sat down. He didn't feel like going to sleep, he didn't feel like digging, he was tired of standing still, tired of lying down. "I'm less than two months old, and I'm tired of living," he said. He walked out to the yard again.

"When I'm out here," he said, "there's no place to go but in. When I'm indoors, there's no place to go but out in the yard."

"That's where you're wrong, my friend, my friend," said a voice.

Wilbur looked through the fence and saw the goose standing there.

"You don't have to stay in that dirty-little dirty-little dirty-little yard," said the goose, who talked rather fast. "One of the boards is loose. Push on it, push-push-push on it, and come on out!"

"What?" said Wilbur. "Say it slower!"

504

"At-at-at, at the risk of repeating myself," said the goose, "I suggest that you come on out. It's wonderful out here."

"Did you say a board was loose?"

"That I did, that I did," said the goose.

Wilbur walked up to the fence and saw that the goose was right — one board was loose. He put his head down, shut his eyes, and pushed. The board gave way. In a minute he had squeezed through the fence and was standing in the long grass outside his yard. The goose chuckled.

"How does it feel to be free?" she asked.

"I like it," said Wilbur. "That is, I *guess* I like it." Actually, Wilbur felt queer to be outside his fence, with nothing between him and the big world.

"Where do you think I'd better go?"

"Anywhere you like, anywhere you like," said the goose. "Go down through the orchard, root up the sod! Go down through the garden, dig up the radishes! Root up everything! Eat grass! Look for corn! Look for oats! Run all over! Skip and dance, jump and prance! Go down through the orchard and stroll in the woods! The world is a wonderful place when you're young."

"I can see that," replied Wilbur. He gave a jump in the air, twirled, ran a few steps, stopped, looked all around, sniffed the smells of afternoon, and then set off walking down through the orchard. Pausing in the shade of an apple tree, he put his strong snout into the ground and began pushing, digging, and rooting. He felt very happy. He had plowed up quite a piece of ground before anyone noticed him. Mrs. Zuckerman was the first to see him. She saw him from the kitchen window, and she immediately shouted for the men.

"Ho-*mer!*" she cried. "Pig's out! Lurvy! Pig's out! Homer! Lurvy! Pig's out. He's down there under that apple tree."

"Now the trouble starts," thought Wilbur. "Now I'll catch it."

The goose heard the racket and she, too, started hollering. "Run-run-run downhill, make for the woods, the woods!" she shouted to Wilbur. "They'll never-never-never catch you in the woods."

The cocker spaniel heard the commotion, and he ran out from the barn to join the chase. Mr. Zuckerman heard, and he came out of the machine shed where he was mending a tool. Lurvy, the hired man, heard the noise and came up from the asparagus patch where he was pulling weeds. Everybody walked toward Wilbur, and Wilbur didn't know what to do. The woods seemed a long way off, and anyway he had never been down there in the woods and wasn't sure he would like it.

"Get around behind him, Lurvy," said Mr. Zuckerman, "and drive him toward the barn! And take it

506

easy — don't rush him! I'll go and get a bucket of slops."

The news of Wilbur's escape spread rapidly among the animals on the place. Whenever any creature broke loose on Zuckerman's farm, the event was of great interest to the others. The goose shouted to the nearest cow that Wilbur was free, and soon all the cows knew. Then one of the cows told one of the sheep, and soon all the sheep knew. The lambs learned about it from their mothers. The horses, in their stalls in the barn, pricked up their ears when they heard the goose hollering; and soon the horses had caught on to what was happening. "Wilbur's out," they said. Every animal stirred and lifted its head and became excited to know that one of his friends had got free and was no longer penned up or tied fast.

Wilbur didn't know what to do or which way to run. It seemed as though everybody was after him. "If this is what it's like to be free," he thought, "I believe I'd rather be penned up in my own yard."

The cocker spaniel was sneaking up on him from one side, Lurvy the hired man was sneaking up on him from the other side. Mrs. Zuckerman stood ready to head him off if he started for the garden, and now Mr. Zuckerman was coming down toward him carrying a pail. "This is really awful," thought Wilbur. "Why doesn't Fern come?" He began to cry.

The goose took command and began to give orders.

"Don't just stand there, Wilbur! Dodge about, dodge about!" cried the goose. "Skip around, run toward me, slip in and out, in and out, in and out! Make for the woods! Twist and turn!"

The cocker spaniel sprang for Wilbur's hind leg. Wilbur jumped and ran. Lurvy reached out and grabbed. Mrs. Zuckerman screamed at Lurvy. The goose cheered for Wilbur. Wilbur dodged between Lurvy's legs. Lurvy missed Wilbur and grabbed the spaniel instead. "Nicely done, nicely done!" cried the goose. "Try it again, try it again!"

"Run downhill!" suggested the cows.

"Run toward me!" yelled the gander.

"Run uphill!" cried the sheep.

"Turn and twist!" honked the goose.

"Jump and dance!" said the rooster.

508

"Look out for Lurvy!" called the cows.

"Look out for Zuckerman!" yelled the gander.

"Watch out for the dog!" cried the sheep.

"Listen to me, listen to me!" screamed the goose.

Poor Wilbur was dazed and frightened by this hullabaloo. He didn't like being the center of all this fuss. He tried to follow the instructions his friends were giving him, but he couldn't run downhill and uphill at the same time, and he couldn't turn and twist when he was jumping and dancing, and he was crying so hard he could barely see anything that was happening. After all, Wilbur was a very young pig —

509

not much more than a baby, really. He wished Fern
were there to take him in her arms and comfort him.
When he looked up and saw Mr. Zuckerman standing
quite close to him, holding a pail of warm slops, he
felt relieved. He lifted his nose and sniffed. The smell
was delicious — warm milk, potato skins, wheat
middlings, corn flakes, and a popover left from the
Zuckermans' breakfast.

"Come, pig!" said Mr. Zuckerman, tapping the
pail. "Come, pig!"

Wilbur took a step toward the pail.

"No-no-no!" said the goose. "It's the old pail trick,
Wilbur. Don't fall for it, don't fall for it! He's trying
to lure you back into captivity-ivity. He's appealing
to your stomach."

Wilbur didn't care. The food smelled appetizing.
He took another step toward the pail.

"Pig, pig!" said Mr. Zuckerman in a kind voice,
and began walking slowly toward the barnyard, looking all about him innocently, as if he didn't know
that a little white pig was following along behind
him.

"You'll be sorry-sorry-sorry," called the goose.

Wilbur didn't care. He kept walking toward the
pail of slops.

"You'll miss your freedom," honked the goose.
"An hour of freedom is worth a barrel of slops."

510

Wilbur didn't care.

When Mr. Zuckerman reached the pigpen, he climbed over the fence and poured the slops into the trough. Then he pulled the loose board away from the fence, so that there was a wide hole for Wilbur to walk through.

"Reconsider, reconsider!" cried the goose.

Wilbur paid no attention. He stepped through the fence into his yard. He walked to the trough and took a long drink of slops, sucking in the milk hungrily and chewing the popover. It was good to be home again.

While Wilbur ate, Lurvy fetched a hammer and some 8-penny nails and nailed the board in place. Then he and Mr. Zuckerman leaned lazily on the fence, and Mr. Zuckerman scratched Wilbur's back with a stick.

"He's quite a pig," said Lurvy.

"Yes, he'll make a good pig," said Mr. Zuckerman.

Wilbur heard the words of praise. He felt the warm milk inside his stomach. He felt the pleasant rubbing of the stick along his itchy back. He felt peaceful and happy and sleepy. This had been a tiring afternoon. It was still only about four o'clock, but Wilbur was ready for bed.

"I'm really too young to go out into the world alone," he thought as he lay down.

Comprehension Questions

1. What happened because Wilbur felt lonely and bored?
2. Why did the animals trust Fern?
3. How did Wilbur feel when all the animals shouted directions at him at once?
4. How did Mr. Zuckerman get Wilbur to come back in the pigpen?

Author

For over fifty years, E. B. White, the author of many books, was an editor and writer for *The New Yorker,* a well-known magazine. *Charlotte's Web,* from which "Wilbur's Escape" was taken, is the best known of his three stories for children. Mr. White lived on a farm in Maine for many years. He said, "My barn was always a pleasant place to be, and I tried to bring it to life in a story for young people." *Charlotte's Web* was a Newbery Honor Book and won a Lewis Carroll Shelf Award. Mr. White also received the Laura Ingalls Wilder Award, May 25, 1984.

Illustrator

Garth Williams spent his childhood in New Jersey with frequent visits to Europe. He studied at London's Royal College of Art and then began a career in magazine illustration. You can see his first major work as a book illustrator in E. B. White's *Stuart Little.* He went on to illustrate a number of children's books, including the Little House on the Prairie series, *Robin Hood,* and *Flossie and Bossie.*

Glossary

Some of the words in this book may have pronunciations or meanings you do not know. This glossary can help you by telling you how to pronounce those words and by telling you their meanings.

You can find out the correct pronunciation of any glossary word by using the special spelling after the word and the pronunciation key at the bottom of each left-hand page.

The full pronunciation key below shows how to pronounce each consonant and vowel in a special spelling. The pronunciation key at the bottom of each left-hand page is a shortened form of the full key.

Full Pronunciation Key

Consonant Sounds

b	**b**i**b**	p	**p**o**p**
ch	**ch**ur**ch**	r	**r**oa**r**
d	**d**ee**d**	s	mi**ss**, **s**au**c**e, **s**ee
f	**f**ast, **f**i**f**e, o**ff**, **ph**ase, rou**gh**	sh	di**sh**, **sh**ip
		t	**t**igh**t**
g	**g**a**g**	th	pa**th**, **th**in
h	**h**at	*th*	ba**th**e, **th**is
hw	**wh**ich	v	ca**v**e, **v**al**v**e, **v**ine
j	**j**u**dg**e	w	**w**ith
k	**c**at, **k**i**ck**, pi**que**	y	**y**es
l	**l**id, need**l**e	z	ro**s**e, si**z**e, **x**ylophone, **z**ebra
m	a**m**, **m**an, **m**u**m**	zh	gara**g**e, plea**s**ure, vi**s**ion
n	**n**o, sudde**n**		
ng	thi**ng**		

Adapted and reprinted by permission from the *Beginning Dictionary,* copyright © 1979, and *The American Heritage School Dictionary,* copyright © 1977, by Houghton Mifflin Company.

Vowel Sounds

ă	pat	ô	alter, caught, for, paw
ā	aid, they, pay	oi	boy, noise, oil
â	air, care, wear	o͝o	book
ä	father	o͞o	boot, fruit
ĕ	pet, pleasure	ou	cow, out
ē	be, bee, easy, seize	ŭ	cut, rough
ĭ	pit	û	firm, heard, term, turn, word
ī	by, guy, pie	yo͞o	abuse, use
î	dear, deer, fierce, mere	ə	about, silent, pencil, lemon, circus
ŏ	pot, horrible	ər	butter
ō	go, row, toe		

Stress Marks

Primary Stress ′
bi·ol′o·gy (bī ŏl′ə jē)

Secondary Stress ′
bi′o·log′i·cal (bī′ə lŏj′i kəl)

a·breast (ə **brĕst′**) *adv. & adj.* **1.** Standing or moving side by side: *The soldiers marched four abreast.* **2.** Up to date with: *abreast of the new fashions.*

a·brupt·ly (ə **brŭpt′**lē) *adv.* In a sudden, unexpected way: *We were all surprised when the band stopped abruptly.*

ac·cus·tomed to (ə **kŭs′**təmd too) *adj.* Used to; familiar with; in the habit of: *My cousins, who live in the country, are not accustomed to city noises.*

ac·quaint·ed (ə **kwān′**tĭd) *adj.* **1.** Familiar; informed: *I am well acquainted with the neighborhood.* **2.** Known to each other: *They became acquainted at school.*

ac·ro·pho·bi·a (ăk′rə **fō′** bē ə) *n.* A very strong fear of high places.

aisle (īl) *n.* A narrow passage through which one may walk, as between rows of seats in a church or theater or between counters in a store.

a·larm (ə **lärm′**) *n.* Sudden fear caused by a feeling of danger.

am·a·teur (**ăm′**ə choor′) *or* (**ăm′**ə chər) *or* (**ăm′**ə tyoor′) *n.* **1.** A person who does something just for pleasure and does not get paid; someone who is not a professional. **2.** A person who does something without much skill.

am·ble (**ăm′**bəl) *v.* **am·bled, am·bling.** To walk or move along at a slow, leisurely pace: *The horses were ambling down the path.*

a·mid (ə **mĭd′**) *prep.* In the middle of; among.

a·muse (ə **myooz′**) *v.* **a·mused, a·mus·ing.** To cause enjoyment; entertain.

an·chor (**ăng′**kər) *v.* To hold in place by means of a heavy weight, usually of metal.

an·ten·na (ăn **tĕn′**ə) *n.* **1.** *pl.* **an·ten·nae** (ăn **tĕn′** ē). One of the pair of long, slender feelers growing on the head of some insects. **2.** *pl.* **an·ten·nas.** An aerial for sending or receiving radio, television, or other signals.

ant·ler (**ănt′**lər) *n.* One of the bony growths on the head of a deer or related animal. Antlers grow in pairs and are often branched. Usually only males have antlers.

antler

ap·pe·tiz·ing (**ăp′** ĭ tī′zĭng) *adj.* Appealing to the taste: *The food at the picnic looked appetizing.*

ar·mor (**är′**mər) *n.* A covering or suit for the body, usually made of metal.

au·to·graph (**ô′**tə grăf′) *or* (**ô′**tə grăf′) *n.* A written name or signature of a famous person. Auto-

---

ă pat / ā pay / â care / ä father / ĕ pet / ē be / ĭ pit / ī pie / î fierce / ŏ pot / ō go / ô paw, for / oi oil / oo book / oo boot / ou out / ŭ cut / û fur / *th* the / th thin / hw which / zh vision / ə ago, item, pencil, atom, circus

graphs are saved by collectors or fans.

autumn (ô′təm) *n.* The season between summer and winter; fall.

awe (ô) *n.* A feeling of wonder, fear, or respect about something.

awe·some (ô′səm) *adj.* Causing wonder, fear, or respect: *the awesome sight of a tidal wave.*

ax·le grease (ăk′səl grēs) *n.* An oil or similar material used to clean the bar on which one or more wheels turn.

back·stage (băk′stāj′) *adv.* In or toward the area behind the performing area in a theater.

bac·te·ri·a (băk tîr′ē ə) *n., pl.* Tiny one-celled plants that can be seen only with a microscope. Some bacteria cause diseases.

bail (bāl) *v.* To empty water from a boat by repeatedly filling a container with water and emptying it.

barge (bärj) *n.* A large, flat-bottomed boat used to carry loads on rivers and canals.

bass (bās) *adj.* Of or related to the lowest musical notes.

bay¹ (bā) *n.* A broad part of a sea or lake partly surrounded by land.

bay² (bā) *n.* A part of a room or building that juts out beyond the main outside wall. It often has windows on three sides.

beech (bēch) *n.* **1.** A tree with smooth, light-gray bark and strong, heavy wood. **2.** The wood of this tree.

birch (bûrch) *n.* A tree with smooth bark that peels off easily.

bit·ten (bĭt′n) A past participle of the verb **bite:** *Have you been bitten by the bugs?*

black·smith (blăk′smĭth′) *n.* A person who makes things out of iron. A blacksmith heats the iron and shapes and hammers it into horseshoes, tools, and other iron objects.

blank·et (blăng′kĭt) *n.* A warm thick cloth used as a cover or anything resembling this.—*v.* To cover with a blanket.

bliz·zard (blĭz′ərd) *n.* A very heavy snowstorm with strong winds.

blurt (blûrt) *v.* To say something suddenly and without thinking.

bob (bŏb) *n.* A quick up-and-down movement.

bold·ly (bōld′lē) *adv.* In an impolite and rude way.

braid (brād) *v.* To weave three or more strips of something together to form a rope.— *n.* A strip of material such as cloth, cord, yarn, or straw used for trimming clothes, making mats, etc.

bri·ar (brī′ər) *n.* A plant with a woody stem or thorns.

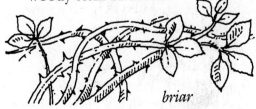
briar

brick·work (brĭk′wûrk′) *n.* A structure made of baked blocks of clay called bricks.

bri·dle (brī′dl) *n.* The straps, bit, and reins that fit over a horse's head and are used to control the animal.

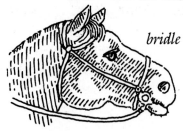

bridle

brin·dle (brĭn′dl) *adj.* Tan, gray, or brown with darker streaks or spots.

brisk·ly (brĭsk′lē) *adv.* In a quick, lively way; energetically: *I walked briskly to the beach.*

bunk (bŭngk) *n.* A narrow bed, often built against the wall.

buoy (boo′ē) *or* (boi) *v.* To keep afloat.

bur·dock (bûr′dŏk′) *n.* A coarse, weedy plant with large, heart-shaped leaves and purplish flowers.

bu·reau (byoor′ō) *n.* A chest of drawers.

bur·ro (bûr′ō) *or* (boor′ō) *or* (bŭr′ō) *n.* A small donkey, usually used for riding or carrying loads.

ca·ble (kā′bəl) *n.* A thick, strong rope made of twisted wire or fiber.

cal·i·co (kăl′ĭ kō) *n., pl.* **cal·i·coes** or **cal·i·cos.** A cotton cloth with a tiny figured pattern printed on it.

cal·o·rie (kăl′ə rē) *n.* An amount of energy supplied by food.

can·yon (kăn′yən) *n.* A deep valley with steep cliffs on both sides and often a stream running through it.

cau·tious·ly (kô′shəs lē) *adv.* In a careful way: *I cautiously climbed the tree to the very top.*

cel·e·brate (sĕl′ə brāt′) *v.* **celebrated, celebrating. 1.** To have a party or other festivity in honor of a special occasion: *We always celebrate my birthday.* **2.** To praise or honor: *The book celebrates several famous women.*

cel·e·bra·tion (sĕl′ə brā′shən) *n.* The act of celebrating: *the celebration of their anniversary.*

chan·nel (chăn′əl) *n.* A body of water that connects two larger bodies of water.

check·ers (chĕk′ərz) *pl.n.* **1.** A game played on a board that has black and red squares. **2.** The pieces used to play the game.

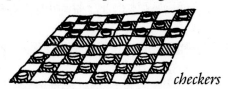

checkers

chest (chĕst) *n.* A piece of furniture usually having several drawers.

churn (chûrn) *v.* To move or swirl violently: *Our boat was rocking in the churning water.*

ă pat / ā pay / â care / ä father / ĕ pet / ē be / ĭ pit / ī pie / î fierce / ŏ pot / ō go / ô paw, for / oi oil / oo book / oo boot / ou out / ŭ cut / û fur / *th* the / th thin / hw which / zh vision / ə ago, item, pencil, atom, circus

clus·ter (klŭs′tər) *n.* A group of similar things growing or grouped close together: *a cluster of flowers.*

cod·fish (kŏd′fĭsh) *n., pl.* **cod·fish** or **cod·fish·es.** A fish found in northern ocean waters, used for food.

con·duc·tor (kən dŭk′tər) *n.* **1.** A person who leads: *the conductor of the orchestra.* **2.** The person in charge of a bus or train: *The conductor told me when it was time for me to get off the train.*

con·sole (kən sōl′) *v.* **con·soled, con·sol·ing.** To comfort during a time of disappointment or sorrow.

con·tent·ment (kən tĕnt′mənt) *n.* Satisfaction: *The director had a look of contentment at the end of the play.*

cor·al reef (kôr′əl *or* kŏr′- rēf) *n.* A strip or ridge of a hard, stony substance that is formed by the skeletons of tiny sea animals massed together. It is often white, pink, or reddish.

cor·ral (kə răl′) *n.* A pen or a place with a fence for keeping cattle or horses.

cot·ton·mouth (kŏt′n mouth′) *n., pl.* **-mouths** (-mouths′) *or* (-mou*thz*′). A snake, the **water moccasin.**

cottonmouth

cross (krôs) *or* (krŏs) *adj.* Irritable or annoyed; angry.

curl·i·cue (kûr′lĭ kyōō′) *n.* A fancy twist or curl, usually made with a pen.

curt·sy (kûrt′sē) *n., pl.* **curt·sies.** A way of showing respect to a person by bending one's knees and lowering the body while keeping one foot forward.

daugh·ter-in-law (dô′tər ĭn lô′) *n., pl.* **daughters-in-law.** The wife of a person's son.

daze (dāz) *v.* **dazed, daz·ing.** To confuse or stun: *The loud explosion dazed us.*

de·cay (dĭ kā′) *v.* To rot or cause to become rotten: *The wood decayed because of the dampness.*

den (dĕn) *n.* The home or shelter of a wild animal.

des·pair (dĭ spâr′) *n.* Lack of all hope: *They gave up in despair of ever winning the game.*

dig·ni·fied (dĭg′nə fīd′) *adj.* Elegant or grand in manner.

dis·card (dĭs kärd′) *v.* To throw away: *We cleaned the cellar and discarded all our old magazines.*

dis·qual·i·fy (dĭs kwŏl′ə fī′) *v.* **dis·qual·i·fied, dis·qual·i·fy·ing, dis·qual·i·fies.** To declare to be unsuitable or unfit to hold a position or win a contest.

doi·ly (doi′lē) *n., pl.* **doi·lies.** A small, fancy mat of lace, paper, or other material placed under a dish or vase, used to protect or decorate furniture.

519

dor·sal (dôr′səl) *adj.* Of, toward, on, in, or near the back of an animal.

drain·pipe (drān′pīp′) *n.* A pipe for carrying off water.

drape (drāp) *v.* **draped, drap·ing.** To cover or hang with cloth in loose folds.

ea·sel (ē′zəl) *n.* A stand for holding a painting or displaying a sign or picture.

easel

edge (ĕj) *n.* **1.** The line or place where an object or area ends; side: *The pencil rolled off the edge of the table.* **2.** The sharpened side of a blade or any other tool that cuts.

em·bar·rass (ĕm băr′əs) *v.* To feel or cause to feel ill at ease: *I was embarrassed when the teacher called on me and I didn't know the answer.* **—em·bar′rass·ing** *adj.*

em·broi·dered (ĕm broi′dərd) *adj.* Having designs done with needle and thread.

em·i·grate (ĕm′ĭ grāt′) *v.* **em·i·grat·ed, em·i·grat·ing.** To leave one's own country and settle in another: *My grandparents emigrated from Italy in 1908.*

en·gage·ment (ĕn gāj′mənt) *n.* **1.** A pledge to marry. **2.** The period during which one is so pledged.

ep·i·logue, also **ep·i·log** (ĕp′ə lôg′) *or* (-lŏg′) *n.* A short section at the end of a story, which often deals with the characters' future.

e·rupt (ĭ′rŭpt′) *v.* To burst out: *The volcano erupted and covered the ground with lava.*

ex·traor·di·nar·y (ĭk strôr′dn ĕr′ē) *or* (ĕk′strə ôr′dn ĕr′ē) *adj.* Very unusual; remarkable.

fan·cy (făn′sē) *v.* **fan·cied, fan·cy·ing, fan·cies.** **1.** To picture in the mind; imagine. **2.** To think; guess.

fierce (fîrs) *adj.* **fierc·er, fierc·est.** Wild or intense: *The dog had a fierce look when it got scared.*

fig·u·rine (fĭg′yə rēn′) *n.* A small decorative figure made of wood, glass, or other material; a small statue.

fil·ter (fĭl′tər) *n.* Something that a liquid or air is passed through in order to clean out any dirt or other matter that is not wanted.

fin (fĭn) *n.* One of the thin, flat parts that stick out from the body of a fish. Fish and other water animals use their fins for swimming and for keeping their balance.

firm·ly (fûrm′lē) *adv.* In a strong way: *He firmly refused.*

ă pat / ā pay / â care / ä father / ĕ pet / ē be / ĭ pit / ī pie / î fierce / ŏ pot / ō go / ô paw, for / oi oil / o͞o book /
o͞o boot / ou out / ŭ cut / û fur / *th* the / th thin / hw which / zh vision / ə ago, item, pencil, atom, circus

fleet (flēt) *n.* **1.** A group of warships. **2.** A large group of ships, cars, or other vehicles traveling or working together: *a fishing fleet; a fleet of taxicabs.*

flut·ter (flŭt′ər) *n.* A quick flapping movement.

fog (fôg) *or* (fŏg) *n.* **1.** A mass of tiny drops of water that looks like a cloud and is on or near the ground. **2.** A confused condition: *The head cold put my mind in a fog all day.*

fog·horn (fôg′hôrn′) *or* (fŏg′-) *n.* A horn, usually having a deep tone, blown to warn ships of danger in foggy weather.

for·est (fôr′ĭst) *or* (fŏr′ĭst) *n.* **1.** A large area with many trees. **2.** Something that resembles a forest: *a forest of tall buildings.*

forge (fôrj) *or* (fōrj) *v.* **forged, forg·ing.** To move ahead in a slow and steady way or with a final burst of speed: *The runner forged ahead with great speed.*

frail (frāl) *adj.* **frail·er, frail·est.** **1.** Thin and weak in body. **2.** Easily broken.

fringe (frĭnj) *n.* An edge made of hanging threads, cords, or strips. Fringes are often used on bedspreads and curtains.

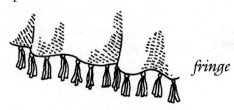
fringe

frus·tra·tion (frŭ strā′shən) *n.* A feeling of helplessness.

fun (fŭn) *v.* **funned, fun·ning.** To behave playfully; joke: *The children were funning while waiting for the school bus.*

gal·lop (găl′əp) *n.* The fastest running pace of a four-footed animal.

gan·der (găn′dər) *n.* A male goose.

gas·light (găs′līt′) *n.* Also **gas light.** **1.** Light made by burning gas in a lamp. **2.** A lamp that uses gas as fuel.

glee·ful (glē′fəl) *adj.* Full of joy; merry.

glid·er (glī′dər) *n.* A special airplane without an engine.

glint (glĭnt) *v.* To gleam or flash; sparkle.

glo·ri·ous·ly (glôr′ē əs lē) *or* (glōr′-) *adv.* In a magnificent manner.

golf club (gŏlf *or* gôlf klŭb) *n.* One of a set of long, thin club-headed sticks used in the game of golf to hit the ball.

grand·stand (grănd′stănd′) *or* (grăn′stănd′) *n.* A seating area at a playing field or other large open building where special events are held.

gran·ite (grăn′ĭt) *n.* **1.** A hard rock used in buildings or monuments. **2.** Something having the appearance of hard rock.

grave·ly (grāv′lē) *adv.* In an extremely serious way.

grind·stone (grīnd′stōn′) *n.* A flat, stone wheel that spins on a rod set in a frame. It is used to shape, polish, and sharpen tools.

grum·ble (**grŭm′**bəl) *v.* **grum·bled, grum·bling.** To complain in a low, discontented voice: *The team grumbled about the rainy weather.*

hand·some (**hăn′**səm) *adj.* **hand·som·er, hand·som·est.** Pleasing in appearance; good-looking.

hard·wood (**härd′**wŏŏd′) *n.* The wood of a tree that has leaves and flowers rather than needles and cones. This kind of wood is often hard and strong. Oak, maple, and mahogany are hardwoods.

har·ness dress·ing (**här′**nĭs **drĕs′**ĭng) *n.* A polish used to clean and protect the straps and metal pieces by which a horse or other animal is attached to a vehicle or plow.

haunt·ing (**hônt′**ĭng *or* **hänt′**-) *adj.* Lingering in the mind: *a haunting tune.*

hay·loft (**hā′**lôft′) *or* (-lŏft′) *n.* An open space in a barn or stable for storing hay.

hearth (härth) *n.* The floor of a fireplace and the area around it.

her·ald (**hĕr′**əld) *n.* A person in past times whose duty it was to take messages or make announcements, as for a king or queen.

hide (hīd) *n.* The skin of an animal: *Leather is made from hides.*

hin·drance (**hĭn′**drəns) *n.* Something that gets in the way of or makes very difficult: *Strong winds may be a hindrance to small boats.*

hob·by (**hŏb′**ē) *n., pl.* **hob·bies.** Something that a person does or studies for fun.

hold (hōld) *n.* A space inside a ship or airplane where things are carried.

hud·dle (**hŭd′**l) *v.* **hud·dled, hud·dling. 1.** To crowd together. **2.** To curl up.

hull (hŭl) *n.* The body of a ship including its sides and bottom.

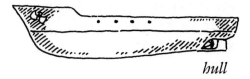

hull

hul·la·ba·loo (**hŭl′**ə bə lōō′) *n.* Great noise or excitement; an uproar.

hu·mus (**hyōō′**məs) *n.* Dark soil formed from dead leaves and other plant parts that have become rotten. Humus may be used to help plants grow.

ich·thy·ol·o·gist (ĭk′thē **ŏl′**ə jĭst) *n.* A scientist who specializes in the study of fishes.

im·pa·tient·ly (ĭm **pā′**shənt lē) *adv.* In a way that shows unwillingness to wait calmly.

ă pat / ā pay / â care / ä father / ĕ pet / ē be / ĭ pit / ī pie / î fierce / ŏ pot / ō go / ô paw, for / oi oil / ŏŏ book / ōō boot / ou out / ŭ cut / û fur / *th* the / th thin / hw which / zh vision / ə ago, item, pencil, atom, circus

in·cred·i·ble (ĭn **krĕd′**ə bəl) *adj.*
1. Hard to believe: *an incredible excuse.* **2.** Astonishing; amazing: *The bird flew to an incredible height.*

in·dig·nant·ly (ĭn **dĭg′**nənt lē) *adv.* In an angry, disapproving way.

in·te·grate (**ĭn′**tĭ grāt′) *v.* **in·te·grat·ed, in·te·grat·ing.** To bring together different racial or ethnic groups.

in·vis·i·ble (ĭn **vĭz′**ə bəl) *adj.* **1.** Not capable of being seen. **2.** Not noticed by others.

ir·reg·u·lar (ĭ **rĕg′**yə lər) *adj.* **1.** Not following a standard shape, size, or arrangement. **2.** Unusual or improper: *You have made a highly irregular decision.*

jeer (jîr) *v.* To shout or shout at in a mocking way.

jer·sey (**jûr′**zē) *n.* **1.** A soft, knitted fabric or cloth. **2.** Clothing made of this material, especially a sweater or shirt made to be pulled down over the head.

king·fish·er (**kĭng′**fĭsh′ər) *n.* A large-billed bird that feeds on fish.

kingfisher

la·goon (lə **gōōn′**) *n.* A shallow body of water, usually connected to a larger body of water, such as an ocean.

lap (lăp) *n.* A single length or turn over or around something, as a racecourse: *Each day I swim another lap of the pool.*

las·so (**lăs′**ō) *or* (lă **sōō′**) *n., pl.* **las·sos** *or* **las·soes.** A long rope with a sliding loop at one end, used especially for catching horses and cattle.

lasso

leg·end (**lĕj′**ənd) *n.* A story that is often connected with a national hero or historical event and that may be based in truth.

less·en (**lĕs′**ən) *v.* To make smaller in amount or quantity.

let·ter (**lĕt′**ər) *v.* To mark or write with signs of the alphabet: *The artist lettered the title of the book by hand.*

life·boat (**līf′**bōt′) *n.* An open boat carried on a large ship and used for saving lives at sea.

light·house (**līt′**hous′) *n., pl.* — **hous·es** (-hou′zĭz). A tower with a powerful light at the top for guiding ships.

loft (lôft) *or* (lŏft) *n.* A large open space under a roof, usually used for storage: *a loft full of old furniture.*

log·ging (**lô′**gĭng) *or* (**lŏg′**ĭng) *n.* The work of cutting down trees and moving logs to a mill.

lug·gage (lŭg′ĭj) *n.* The suitcases, bags, and boxes taken on a trip; baggage.

lu·mi·nous (lōō′mə nəs) *adj.* Giving off light; shining.

lunge (lŭnj) *v.* **lunged; lung·ing.** To make a sudden forceful movement forward: *The cat lunged at the mouse and caught it.*

mag·nif·i·cent (măg nĭf′ĭ sənt) *adj.* Very grand and fine; large and beautiful.

ma·rine (mə rēn′) *adj.* Of or living in the sea.

mar·ma·lade (mär′mə lād′) *n.* A jam made from sugar and the inside and the tough outer covering of fruits.

mar·vel (mär′vəl) *v.* **mar·veled** or **mar·velled, mar·vel·ing** or **mar·vel·ling.** To be filled with surprise or wonder: *We marveled at the beauty of the sunset.*

mas·sive (măs′ĭv) *adj.* Very large and heavy; huge.

mast (măst) *n.* A tall pole for the sails, rigging, etc., of a ship or boat.

maze (māz) *n.* A complicated, winding arrangement of paths through which it is hard to find one's way.

mer·chant (mûr′chənt) *n.* **1.** A person who makes money by buying and selling goods: *The tea mer-* chant buys tea from Asia and sells it in America. **2.** A storekeeper.

mid·dlings (mĭd′lĭngz) *pl. n.* Coarsely ground wheat mixed with bran.

milk·weed (mĭlk′wēd′) *n.* A wild plant with milky juice and large seed pods.

milkweed

mill·er (mĭl′ər) *n.* A person who works in, operates, or owns a building for grinding grain.

min·i·a·ture (mĭn′ē ə chər) *or* (mĭn′ə chər) *n.* Something that is much smaller than the usual size.

mind (mīnd) *v.* To attend to; be careful about.

miz·zen·mast (mĭz′ən məst) *or* (-măst′) *n.* The third mast to the rear on sailing ships carrying three or more masts.

mole[1] (mōl) *n.* A small brown growth or spot on the skin.

mole[2] (mōl) *n.* A small animal that digs burrows under the ground. Moles have very small eyes and short, silky fur.

mole

ă pat / ā pay / â care / ä father / ĕ pet / ē be / ĭ pit / ī pie / î fierce / ŏ pot / ō go / ô paw, for / oi oil / ŏŏ book / ōō boot / ou out / ŭ cut / û fur / *th* the / th thin / hw which / zh vision / ə ago, item, pencil, atom, circus

mo·men·tum (mō **měn′**təm) *n*. The force or speed that an object has when it moves: *The sled gained momentum as it raced down the hill.*

mon·key wrench (**mŭng′**kē rěnch) *n*. A tool with a jaw that adjusts to fit different sizes of nuts and bolts.

monkey wrench

mon·o·logue (**mŏn′**ə lôg′) *or* (-lŏg′) *n*. A long speech given by one person.

moss (môs) *or* (mŏs) *n*. One of a group of small green plants that do not have flowers. Moss often forms a covering on damp ground, rocks, or tree trunks.

mount (mount) *n*. A horse or other animal for riding.

move·ment (**mōōv′**mənt) *n*. One of the large sections of a musical piece having its own beginning and end.

mu·se·um (myōō **zē′**əm) *n*. A building for keeping and showing interesting and valuable things.

mus·tache (**mŭs′**tăsh′) *or* (mə**stăsh′**) *n*. The hair growing on the upper lip.

net (nět) *n*. A strong fabric that has holes that are evenly spaced, used to catch fish.

noose (nōōs) *n*. A loop in a rope with a knot that lets the loop tighten as the rope is pulled.

numb (nŭm) *adj*. Without the ability to feel or move normally: *I stood in the cold water for so long that my feet were numb.*

off·shore (ôf′shôr′) *or* (ôf′shōr′) *or* (ŏf′shôr′) *or* (ŏf′shōr′) *adj*. Moving away from shore: *The offshore wind blew us out to sea.*

or·phan (ôr′fən) *n*. A child whose parents are dead.

or·phan·age (ôr′fə nĭj) *n*. A home for the care of children whose parents are dead.

pad (păd) *n*. A number of sheets of paper glued together at one end.

par·cel (**pär′**səl) *n*. Something wrapped up in a bundle; a package.

par·ka (**pär′**kə) *n*. A warm jacket with a hood. Parkas are often lined with fur.

parka

pass (păs) *or* (päs) *n*. A narrow road or path: *We drove over three mountain passes to get to the river.*

peg (pěg) *n*. A piece of wood or metal that is used to fasten things together, to plug a hole, or to hang things on.

pen[1] (pĕn) *n.* An instrument for writing with ink, formerly made from a large quill, now having a metal point and often a supply of ink in the holder. — *v.* **penned, penning.** To write or compose with a pen.

pen[2] (pĕn) *n.* A small, fenced-in area, especially one in which animals are kept. — *v.* **penned** or **pent** (pĕnt), **penning.** To confine in or as if in a pen.

pen·man·ship (pĕn'mən shĭp') *n.* The art, skill, style, or manner of handwriting.

perch[1] (pûrch) *n.* **1.** A branch or rod that a bird grasps with its claws while at rest. **2.** Any resting place.

perch[2] (pûrch) *n., pl.* **perch** or **perch·es** Any of several mostly freshwater fishes often used for food.

pheas·ant (fĕz'ənt) *n.* A large, brightly colored bird with a long tail.

pheasant

pin·na·cle (pĭn'ə kəl) *n.* **1.** A tall, pointed formation, as a mountain peak. **2.** The highest point.

pin·to (pĭn'tō) *n.* A horse or pony with spots or other markings that are not regular.

pi·o·neer (pī'ə nîr') *n.* **1.** A person who is the first to enter and settle a region. **2.** A plant or animal that is the first kind to grow or live in a place where there have been no living things.

pitch·fork (pĭch'fôrk') *n.* A large fork with sharp prongs that are far apart. A pitchfork is used to move hay or straw.

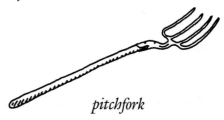

pitchfork

plank (plăngk) *n.* A thick, wide, long piece of wood that has been sawed.

pneu·mo·nia (nŏŏ mōn'yə) *or* (nyŏŏ mōn'yə) *n.* A serious disease of the lungs.

pod (pŏd) *n.* A plant part in which seeds grow. The pod splits open when the seeds are ripe. Peas and beans have pods.

pom·pom (pŏm'pŏm') *n.* **1.** A ball of wool, feathers, ribbons, etc., used as a decoration. **2.** A small buttonlike flower.

pop·o·ver (pŏp'ō'vər) *n.* A light, puffy, hollow muffin. While baking, it expands and pops up over the rim of the pan.

por·cu·pine (pôr'kyə pīn') *n.* An animal covered with long, sharp spines called quills.

ă pat / ā pay / â care / ä father / ĕ pet / ē be / ĭ pit / ī pie / î fierce / ŏ pot / ō go / ô paw, for / oi oil / ŏŏ book /
ŏŏ boot / ou out / ŭ cut / û fur / *th* the / th thin / hw which / zh vision / ə ago, item, pencil, atom, circus

por·ter (pôr′tər) *or* (pōr′tər) *n.* A person hired to carry or move luggage at a station, airport, or hotel.

port·fo·li·o (pôrt fō′lē ō′) *or* (pōrt-) *n., pl.* **port·fo·li·os.** A carrying case for holding loose papers, drawings, etc.

pre·cious (prĕsh′əs) *adj.* Of high price or value.

prick·ly (prĭk′lē) *adj.* **prick·li·er, prick·li·est.** Having small sharp thorns, or points called prickles: *a prickly cactus.*

pro·vi·sions (prə vĭzh′ənz) *pl. n.* Supplies of food and other necessary items: *The guide packed the provisions for the river trip.*

pu·ny (pyoo′nē) *adj.* **pu·ni·er, pu·ni·est.** Small or unimportant in size, strength, or value; weak: *That puny horse is not fast enough to run in the race.*

quail (kwāl) *n., pl.* **quail** or **quails.** A rather small, plump bird with a short tail and brownish feathers.

quail

quea·sy (kwē′zē) *adj.* **queas·i·er, queas·i·est. 1.** Sick to one's stomach. **2.** Easily troubled; squeamish.

quilt (kwĭlt) *n.* A covering for a bed. A quilt is made of two layers of cloth sewn together with a padding of cotton, feathers, or other material in between.

rack·et[1] (răk′ĭt) *n.* A form of the word **racquet.**

rack·et[2] (răk′ĭt) *n.* A loud, continuous, unpleasant noise.

rac·quet (răk′ĭt) *n.* A form of the word **racket** (the term in sports). A device used in some sports to hit a ball, consisting of a frame with tightly laced strings and a handle.

re·flect (rĭ flĕkt′) *v.* To give back an image or likeness, as does a mirror or clear water.

re·flec·tion (rĭ flĕk′shən) *n.* **1.** An image or a likeness. **2.** A thought; idea.

re·fresh·ment (rĭ frĕsh′mənt) *n.* Food and drink; a light meal or snack.

re·main (rĭ mān′) *v.* To be left: *Only three peas remained on my plate.*

re·mains (rĭ mānz′) *pl.n.,* Something that is left.

re·pel·lent (rĭ pĕl′ənt) *n.* A substance used to drive off a pest or pests: *The bug repellent will keep the flies away.*

res·er·va·tion (rĕz′ər vā′shən) *n.* An area set aside by the government for a certain purpose.

re·spon·si·bil·i·ty (rĭ spŏn′sə bĭl′ĭ tē) *n.* Something that one must do; a duty.

re·sume (rĭ zōōm′) *v.* **re·sumed, re·sum·ing.** To begin again after a break; continue: *The play resumed when the laughter died down.*

rhap·so·dy (răp′sə dē) *n.,pl.* **rhap·so·dies.** A musical piece with a free or irregular form: *I learned to play two new piano rhapsodies.*

rheu·ma·tism (rōō′mə tĭz′əm) *n.* A disease that causes swelling of the muscles, tendons, bones, or joints. It also makes them stiff and causes pain.

rig·ging (rĭg′ĭng) *n.* The system of ropes, chains, and tackle used to support and control the masts, sails, and yards of a sailing vessel.

right·eous (rī′chəs) *adj.* Morally right; just: *a righteous cause; a righteous person.*

ro·de·o (rō′dē ō′) *or* (rō dā′ō) *n., pl.* **ro·de·os.** A public show in which cowhands display their skills in horseback riding and compete in riding broncos or steers, roping cattle, and similar events.

roll (rōl) *n.* A rise and fall in a surface: *the roll of the hills of the countryside.*

romp (rŏmp) *v.* To race about playfully: *The dogs romped around the yard.*

rud·der (rŭd′ər) *n.* A movable flat piece of metal or wood at the rear of a boat, used for steering.

rung (rŭng) *n.* A rod or bar that forms a step of a ladder.

run·ner (rŭn′ər) *n.* **1.** Someone or something that runs: *Only two runners finished the race.* **2.** One of the blades on which a sled, sleigh, or ice skate moves.

sack (săk) *n.* A bag made of strong, coarse material.

salm·on (săm′ən) *n., pl.* **salm·on.** A large fish that lives in northern waters, having pinkish-colored flesh and used for food.

sash[1] (săsh) *n.* A wide ribbon or piece of cloth that is worn around the waist or over the shoulder.

sash[2] (săsh) *n.* A frame for the glass in a window or door.

sa·vor (sā′vər) *v.* To taste or enjoy with great pleasure: *I ate the meal slowly, savoring every bite.*

scaf·fold (skăf′əld) *or* (skăf′ōld) *n.* A platform that is used to support people who are constructing or repairing a building.

scat·ter (skăt′ər) *v.* To spread or throw about: *The children are always scattering their toys around the room.*

scav·enge (skăv′ĭnj) *v.* **scav·enged, scav·eng·ing.** To search in rubbish or garbage to find something useful or something to eat.

scor·pi·on (skôr′pē ən) *n.* An animal related to spiders. A scorpion has a narrow body and a long tail with a stinger that carries poison.

ă pat / ā pay / â care / ä father / ĕ pet / ē be / ĭ pit / ī pie / î fierce / ŏ pot / ō go / ô paw, for / oi oil / ŏŏ book / ōō boot / ou out / ŭ cut / û fur / *th* the / *th* thin / hw which / zh vision / ə ago, item, pencil, atom, circus

scu·ba gear (**skōō′**bə gîr) *n.* Special equipment used by divers, which allows them to breathe underwater.

scythe (sī*th*) *n.* A tool with a long, curved blade attached to a long, bent handle. It is used for mowing and for gathering crops.

seed·ling (**sēd′**lĭng) *n.* A young plant that has grown from a seed.

shield (shēld) *v.* **1.** To protect or defend; to guard.

shim·mer (**shĭm′**ər) *v.* To shine with a flickering or faint light: *The stars were shimmering in the pale moonlight.*

ship·yard (**shĭp′**yärd′) *n.* A place where ships are built, repaired, and made ready for sailing.

shot (shŏt) *n.* **1.** The firing of a weapon. **2. a.** A bullet or other object fired from a weapon. **b.** A group of tiny balls or pellets of lead fired from a shotgun.

shrew (shrōō) *n.* Any of several small, mouselike animals with a narrow, pointed snout.

shrew

shrewd·ly (**shrōōd′**lē) *adv.* In a clever and sharp manner: *The lawyer spoke to the jury shrewdly.*

shriek (shrēk) *v.* To make a loud shrill sound: *I shrieked above the noise of the crowd to get attention.*

sleigh (slā) *n.* A light vehicle or carriage with runners, usually pulled by a horse and used for traveling on ice or snow.

slith·er (**slĭth′**ər) *v.* To move along by gliding, as a snake does.

slops (slŏps) *n.* Waste food fed to animals.

smudge (smŭj) *v.* **smudged, smudg·ing.** To smear or blur.

snor·kel (**snôr′**kəl) *n.* A plastic tube and mouthpiece used to breathe underwater.

snout (snout) *n.* The long nose, jaws, or front part of the head of an animal.

sole[1] (sōl) *n.* **1.** The bottom surface of the foot. **2.** The bottom surface of a shoe or boot. — *v.* **soled, sol·ing.** To put a sole on a shoe or boot.

sole[2] (sōl) *adj.* **1.** Being the only one; single; only: *her sole purpose in life.* **2.** Belonging only to one person or group: *He was the dog's sole master.*

sole[3] (sōl) *n.,pl.* **sole** or **soles.** A flat fish that is related to the flounder: *Sole are good to eat.*

so·na·ta (sə **nä′**tə) *n.* A musical piece having a specific form, usually for one or two instruments.

splin·ter (**splĭn′**tər) *n.* A sharp, thin piece of such things as wood or glass split or broken off from a larger piece or object.

sprawl (sprôl) *v.* To sit or lie with the body, arms, and legs spread out: *We were so tired from the hike we sprawled out on the grass and took a nap.*

spring (sprĭng) *n.* **1.** The act of leaping or jumping. **2.** The season of the year between winter and summer. **3.** A natural fountain or flow of water.

square (skwâr) *n.* **1.** An open space surrounded by streets on all sides. **2.** A figure having four sides that are the same length.

squash (skwŏsh) *or* (skwôsh) *v.* To be or become crushed or flattened: *The tomato squashed on the floor.*

stam·pede (stăm pēd′) *n.* **1.** A sudden violent rush of startled or scared animals, such as horses, cattle, or buffalo. **2.** A similar sudden or headlong rush of people.

state (stāt) *n.* **1.** An emotional condition; a mood. **2.** A group of people living within a specified area under a single, independent government.

state·ly (stāt′lē) *adj.* **state·li·er, state·li·est.** Elegant or grand in manner or appearance; majestic: *a stately home; a stately oak tree.*

sta·tus (stā′təs) *or* (stăt′əs) *n.* **1.** The condition of a person or thing. **2.** A position or rank in a group.

steep·le (stē′pəl) *n.* A tall tower rising from the roof of a building.

steeple

stern (stûrn) *adj.* **1.** Serious and severe: *a stern talk on manners.* **2.** Strict; firm: *stern discipline.*

stow·a·way (stō′ə wā′) *n.* A person who hides on a ship, plane, train, etc., to get a free ride.

stub·ble (stŭb′əl) *n.* **1.** Short, stiff stems of grain or other plants that are left after a crop has been cut. **2.** Something that looks like this, especially a short, stiff growth of beard or hair.

stun (stŭn) **stunned, stun·ning.** *v.* To shock or confuse: *Our three home runs stunned the other team.*

sulk·y (sŭl′kē) *adj.* **sulk·i·er, sulk·i·est.** Quiet because of one's ill temper or bad mood.

surf (sûrf) *n.* The waves of the sea as they break upon the shore or the white foam that is on the top of breaking waves.

sur·round·ings (sə roun′dĭngz) *pl. n.* The things, circumstances, and conditions that surround a person: *The surroundings in the country are peaceful and quiet.*

swab (swŏb) *v.* **swabbed, swab·bing.** To clean or dry decks, floors, etc., with a mop: *We found the sailors swabbing the deck.*

swal·low (swŏl′ō) *n.* A bird that has narrow, pointed wings and a forked tail. Swallows chase and catch insects in the air.

swerve (swûrv) *v.* **swerved, swerv·ing.** To turn or cause to turn

ă pat / ā pay / â care / ä father / ĕ pet / ē be / ĭ pit / ī pie / î fierce / ŏ pot / ō go / ô paw, for / oi oil / ŏŏ book / ōō boot / ou out / ŭ cut / û fur / *th* the / th thin / hw which / zh vision / ə ago, item, pencil, atom, circus

530

quickly or sharply: *The car swerved off the road and onto the sidewalk.*

tap·i·o·ca (tăp′ē ō′kə) *n.* A food that comes from the root of a cassava plant, used to make puddings.

ten·e·ment (tĕn′ə mənt) *n.* A cheap apartment building that is found in the poorer sections of a city.

ter·race (tĕr′əs) *n.* A paved, open area next to a house; patio.

till (tĭl) *v.* To prepare land for growing crops by plowing and fertilizing.

tin·gly (tĭng′lē) *adj.* Having a prickly or stinging feeling.

tow (tō) *v.* To pull along behind with a chain, rope, or cable.

track (trăk) *v.* To follow the footprints or trail of.

trail (trāl) *v.* **1.** To follow behind. **2.** To lag behind.

treach·er·ous (trĕch′ər əs) *adj.* Not to be trusted; deceptive; dangerous.

tre·ble (trĕb′əl) *adj.* Of or related to the highest musical notes.

tri·ath·lon (trī ăth′lən) *or* (-lŏn′) *n.* A three-part sporting event including swimming, biking, and running.

trough (trôf) *or* (trŏf) *n.* A long, narrow box or other container. It is used for holding water or feed for animals.

trudge (trŭj) *v.* **trudged, trudg·ing.** To walk in a heavy-footed way. — *n.* A long difficult walk.

trum·pet (trŭm′pĭt) *n.* A loud, high-pitched sound like that of a trumpet (musical instrument): *The trumpet of the elephant was heard throughout the jungle.*

trun·dle bed (trŭn′dl bĕd) *n.* A low bed that can be rolled under another bed when not in use.

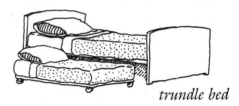

trundle bed

tuft (tŭft) *n.* A cluster of hair, feathers, grass, yarn, etc., growing or held close together.

tur·bu·lent (tûr′byə lənt) *adj.* Violently agitated or disturbed; stormy: *The turbulent waters made the boat sway back and forth.*

turn·stile (tûrn′stīl′) *n.* A device used to control or count the number of persons coming into a public area by admitting them one at a time between horizontal bars that revolve on a central vertical post.

tusk (tŭsk) *n.* A long, pointed tooth, usually one of a pair. It projects outside of the mouth of certain animals. The elephant, walrus, and wild boar have tusks.

un·furl (ŭn fûrl′) *v.* To spread or open out; unroll: *unfurl a flag.*

ven·i·son (vĕn′ĭ sən) *or* (-zən) *n.* The meat of a deer, used as food.

vest (věst) *n.* A short jacket without sleeves or collar, worn over a shirt or a blouse.

vic·to·ri·ous (vĭk tôr′ē əs) *or* (vĭk-tôr′ē əs) *adj.* Of or resulting in winning: *a victorious cheer.*

wedge (wěj) *n.* A block of wood, metal, or other material that is wide at one end and comes to a point at the other.

wedge

whale shark (hwāl shärk) *n.* A large shark of warm waters.

what·so·ev·er (hwŏt′sō ěv′ər) *or* (hwŭt′-) *or* (wŏt′-) *or* (wŭt′-) *adj.* Of any kind at all.

whine (hwīn) *or* (wīn) *v.* **whined, whin·ing. 1.** To make a high-pitched sound. **2.** To complain in a childish, annoying way.

whiz, also **whizz** (hwĭz) *or* (wĭz) *n.* One who has remarkable skill.

wick·ed (wĭk′ĭd) *adj.* Very mean; vicious.

wind re·sis·tance (wĭnd rĭ zĭs′təns) *n.* Wind that pushes against an object and slows it down.

wood·chuck (wŏŏd′chŭk′) *n.* A North American animal with brownish fur and short legs. Also called a ground hog.

woodchuck

wood·shed (wŏŏd′shěd′) *n.* A small, simple building for storing firewood.

ă pat / ā pay / â care / ä father / ě pet / ē be / ĭ pit / ī pie / î fierce / ŏ pot / ō go / ô paw, for / oi oil / ŏŏ book / ŏŏ boot / ou out / ŭ cut / û fur / *th* the / th thin / hw which / zh vision / ə ago, item, pencil, atom, circus

Reading and Writing Aids

Reading Aids

Use these aids to help you read words you have not seen before.

1. Use the letter sounds and the context, the sense of nearby words, phrases, and sentences.

   - Sometimes the general sense of the passage may be the best context clue.

     "If you **heed** my advice," said Mr. Phelps, "you will surely succeed." (follow)

   - A synonym, a word with nearly the same meaning, can be a context clue.

     In fairy tales, foxes are often sly. Are real foxes that **cunning**? (sly, clever)

2. Look for a base word with a prefix, a suffix, or both. Use the context and the meanings of the base word and its prefix, suffix, or both to figure out the meaning of a word.

If you **mislabel** these packages, they will be sent to the wrong place.

Prefix	Base Word	Meaning
mis-	label	"label wrongly"

The speaker became **famous** for her wise sayings.

Base Word	Suffix	Meaning
fame	-ous	"having fame"

When the friends shook hands, we could see that their **disagreement** was over.

Prefix	Base Word
dis-	agree

Suffix	Meaning
-ment	"action of not agreeing"

3. If you cannot figure out the meaning, use a glossary or a dictionary.

Study Aid

Use the SQRRR method to learn and remember information.

Step One: Survey. Look over the main headings and summary statements.

Step Two: Question. Turn the headings into questions you expect the material to answer.

Step Three: Read. Read the material under the headings to answer your questions.

Step Four: Recite. Answer your questions in your own words.

Step Five: Review. Look again at each heading, and recite the answers to your questions.

Writing Aids

Step One: Choose a topic. Think about a topic. Choose a topic about which you already know something or about which you can easily find information.

Step Two: Write your first draft. Just get your ideas down on paper; you will have a chance to make changes later.

Step Three: Revise your first draft. Revise means to make changes. Use these questions to help you revise:

- Did you stick to your topic?
- Did you include all important information?
- Did you present information in the correct order?
- Did you include necessary details and descriptions?

- Did you include necessary dialogue?

Step Four: Proofread your first draft. Proofread means to read over and correct mistakes. Use these questions to help you proofread:

- Did you indent all paragraphs?
- Did you use capital letters correctly?
- Did you include all necessary punctuation marks?
- Did you spell all words correctly?
- Did you write each sentence to express a complete thought?

Step Five: Make a final copy. Make a final copy to share with someone. Prepare a neat, clean copy that shows all revisions and corrections. Then proofread your final copy.

Bibliographical Note
The study method described in the lesson "SQRRR" and in "Reading and Writing Aids" is based on the widely used SQ3R system developed by Francis P. Robinson in *Effective Study*, 4th ed. (New York: Harper & Row, Publishers, Inc., 1961, 1970).

Credits

Cover and title page illustrated by D. J. Simison Magazine openers illustrated by Judy Anne Griffith

Illustrators: 8–9 Judy Anne Griffith **10** (left) Nancy Edwards Calder **10** (right) Chris Conover **12–28** Nancy Edwards Calder **38–43** Juliana Lea **46** Lane Yerkes **69** Lorinda Cauley **73–74** James Teason **76** Lane Yerkes **78–96** Collete Slade **99** Cecilia von Rabenau **107–130** (illustrations) Chris Conover (borders) © Mitchell & Malik **134–135** Judy Anne Griffith **136** (left, top) Christa Kieffer **136** (left, bottom) Higgins Bond **136** (right) Lane Yerkes **137–158** Jane Chambless-Rigie **166–178** Christa Kieffer **182–198** Eileen McKeating **208–216** Chuck Eckart **220–236** Higgins Bond **238–251** John Holder **253** Lark Carrier **254–268** Lane Yerkes **272–273** Judy Anne Griffith **274** (left) Marc Tetrault **274** (right) Troy Howell **276–286** Marc Tetrault **288**

Lane Yerkes **290–303** Dee de Rosa **323** Sue Thompson **324–336** Mai Vo-Dinh **353** Pam Levy **354–358** John Dawson **363–366** Dee de Rosa **369–384** Troy Howell **390–391** Judy Anne Griffith **392** (left) Jan Wills **392** (right, bottom) Garth Williams **392** (right, top) James Watling **394–410** Mai Vo-Dinh **426–436** Jan Wills **441–442** Lane Yerkes **444–464** J. Brian Pinkney **467** Kim Howard **470–493** James Watling **495** Laura Cornell **497** Jan Wills **499–512** Garth Williams **514–532** George M. Ulrich

Photographers: 11 Grant Heilman Photography **30** © Brown Brothers **48–49** © Cheesbord/Focus on Sports **51–53** © Brian Payne/Black Star **54** (left) © Christopher Morrow **54** (right) © Dan McCoy/Rainbow **56–67** James L. Ballard/Ligature, Inc. **73** © Joy Spurr/Bruce Coleman Inc. **75** Grant Heilman Photography **100** © Bob and Carol Calhoun/Bruce Coleman Inc. **133** James L. Ballard/Ligature, Inc. **160–163** Michal Heron **181** © Bill Binzen **206** © Mary Stouffer/ Animals Animals **218** (left, top) © John Troh/ Animals Animals **218** (left, bottom) © Robert Maier/Animals Animals **218** (right) © John Shaw/ Bruce Coleman Inc. **275** Suen-o Lindblad/Photo Researchers, Inc. **307** Lou Jones **310** © Mickey Gibson/Animals Animals **312** © Bruce Coleman, Inc. **313** George H. Harrison/Grant Heilman Photography **314** © Luis Castanada/ The Image Bank **315** © Peter Davey/Bruce Coleman Inc. **316** © David Huges/Bruce Coleman Inc. **317** © M. P. Kahl/Bruce Coleman Inc. **318** © Carol Huges/Bruce Coleman Inc. **319** (top) © Adrienne T. Gibson/ Animals Animals **319** (bottom) R. S. Virbee/ Grant Heilman Photography **320** © Peter Davey/Bruce Coleman Inc. **321** Suen-o Lindblad/Photo Researchers, Inc. **340** (left) © Dr. E. R. Degginger **340** (right) © B. Smith/ Bruce Coleman Inc. **342–343** © David Doubilet **345** © Douglas Faulkner **347–351, 388** © David Doubilet **393** Cradoc Bagshaw/Rodale Press **413** © Hhiroyuki Matsumoto/Black Star **414** © James Balog/Black Star **416** © Bruce Coleman Inc. **416** (bottom right: inset) © Charles Moore/Black Star **420** © Laurie Riley/Stock Boston **421** © Fine Homebuilding Magazine **422** © David Summer/West Stock **423** Cradoc Bagshaw/Rodale Press **429** © Carl E. Krupp **468** Michal Heron